PENGUIN HANDBOOKS

THE JOY OF CAMPING

Richard W. Langer is the author of *The After-Dinner Gardening Book* and *Grow It! The Beginner's Complete In-Harmony-with-Nature Small Farm Guide—From Vegetable and Grain Growing to Livestock Care.*

"This year, *The Joy of Camping* has entered our life (and, in due time, our rucksack), with specific, articulate, even joyful advice."
—*New York Magazine*

"Backed by years of camping experience throughout the world, Langer has written one of the most comprehensive and informative camping guides yet. . . . Useful for both beginners and experienced campers, this book is definitely recommended."—*Library Journal*

THE JOY OF CAMPING

The Complete Four-Seasons, Five-Senses
Practical Guide to Enjoying
the Great Outdoors
(Without Destroying It)

RICHARD W. LANGER

ILLUSTRATIONS BY SUSAN MCNEILL

PENGUIN BOOKS INC • BALTIMORE • MARYLAND

Penguin Books Inc
7110 Ambassador Road
Baltimore, Maryland 21207, U.S.A.

First published by Saturday Review Press, New York, 1973
Published by Penguin Books Inc, 1974

Printed in the United States of America

To

Mac and Lois

who, during forty years of
dedicated service and hard
work in the jungles and
along the beaches of West
Africa, have done more
roughing it than I ever will

CONTENTS

Getting About in the Wilderness

Discovering the Way of the Wilderness

INTRODUCTION

Stowing away to nature, if sometimes only for a weekend, restores the spirit as little else can. Exploring the woods, or a mountain meadow, or the bends of a lazy river, sleeping under the open, snuggled deep into a warm sleeping bag, or in less clement weather, in a small and homey tent just big enough to be comfortable—these things take us back to a calmer life that is too easily forgotten in our overly scheduled urban and suburban existence. Once in a while we should treat ourselves to counting falling stars between the branches of a sheltering tree above our heads or just beyond the misty gauze of our netted tent entrance, while other folks are home watching late-night movie reruns.

Nature is still a wild and beautiful thing, hard though that may be to remember when we meet it only as an inconvenient snowstorm tying up traffic or a hot midday sending us diving back into an air-conditioned office. And there is wilderness enough left for all of us. Where once it surrounded man, however, now we must seek it out. Most of us needn't go so very far to find a small unspoiled piece of it if we but step off the well-traveled trails. It's as close as a weekend's backpacking jaunt, traveling light and free through the nearest forest preserve or state park, from the trail head to trail's end and back, or round in a circle for a different view of the terrain. A canoeing or kayaking weekend can take us even deeper into the wilderness if the river is easy and the portages few. And in winter—that's when skis or snowshoes can carry us far from the trampled slush of city streets to hills where our own tracks make the first human imprint on the fallen snow.

Too many of us, enveloped in today's technological cocoon, have come to think of the year as a single entity, forgetting about the individual seasons. The wilderness has something different to offer at each time of the year, something, too, to suggest about a mode of travel for each. Spring, for instance, is perhaps the most perfect time for canoeing or kayaking. The waters are high, running swift in river and seasonal stream alike. Many a small brook that would have to be detoured with a portage at other times of year is made passable with pole or paddle by the spring melt from the distant mountains.

When the warmth of summer settles over the land, it's a good time to relax and enjoy nature in quieter, cooler ways. Pitch your tent in some uncrowded spot under the shade of the forest and stay awhile, making it your base camp. Choose an area you've always wanted to get to know better. Then on days you feel like exploring, set out with a lunch, or a light rucksack packed for an overnight stopover away from your home camp—secure in the knowledge that you have a small, quiet place, not too far away, ready and waiting for you on your return. Or climb the cool mountains, for spring comes late there, and the flowers will be in bloom.

Then there's autumn, when the trees and the mountain brush are in radiant fall color. The weather is cool enough so you won't become drenched with perspiration carrying fairly substantial provisions and gear. Head for the far hills with your pack, crossing alpine meadows and keeping your eyes open for animals preparing to meet winter.

Winter—nature is in many ways at its finest then, blanketed in snow and ice, refreshing itself for yet another spring rebirth. It's a time when many campers curl up inside with their catalogs, which is all right. But it's also a time for the joys of snow camping, making the slender cross-country ski or the quiet-stepping snowshoe your transport on long tours or day jaunts from a sturdy base camp.

If you're just starting out camping, consider renting the equipment you need for your first few outings rather than buying right away. Many of the larger camping and mountaineering shops have rental plans, some of them even rental-purchase plans. Since there is a wide variety of choice in modern-day camping gear, trying it out first will give you a chance to discover personally and by actual use what type of skis, or canoe, or pack, or tent is right for you. Even if you own your gear, renting sometimes has advantages. Say you've been thinking about a canoe route that looks really great, but it's a long one, and you don't want to have to paddle all the way back. Often you'll find a rental with pickup available at the other end of the route. Or say you've chosen a general-purpose tent as the most practical one for you, and then some fine January weekend you decide you'd like to do a bit of winter camping; renting will supply a fully equipped alpine tent for the occasion.

Things have changed a lot from the days of rough-and-tumble, ax-and-gun survival camping. Today's quality equipment is lightweight, streamlined for efficiency, sturdily constructed—and unique in the long history of camping. Tents have floors and insect netting, sleeping bags filled with layers of down verge on the luxurious, and those devilish blackened pots of the old-time outdoors kitchen have been relegated to antiquity by efficient little stoves that make cooking out in the wilds as simple as using the range at home—all this without lessening your pleasures and enjoyment of nature. Quite to the contrary, in fact, where once a camper's time was almost fully taken up by the sheer number of tasks involved in setting up camp—gathering and chopping wood, starting a fire, often with wet tinder, cooking a meal from salted and dried foods, cutting stakes for an unwieldy tent, and trying to keep warm at night in a bulky but inadequate bag—now those tasks that haven't been eliminated altogether have become quick and painless. That leaves today's camper many more hours free to enjoy his surroundings, to roam and explore, to swim, to fish in the cool waters, to hunt for berries for a trail pie, to photograph flowers, to look for meteors in the night sky. The camper today has time to use and sharpen his senses for the sheer joy of it—breathing in the fragrance of a meadow in bloom, listening to the pines in the wind, the rain falling softly on the moss, and the songs of the birds, time even for quiet log-sitting, one of the greatest old-time ways of "hunting" the shy wild animals in whose habitat you are only a visitor.

And, for all this, modern camping equipment is not expensive, though it may seem so at first glance. Think of the fact that it lasts and lasts; to measure its true cost, you would have to spread the sum of your investment over several years. To equip the whole family with the best gear available will cost no more than, say, two weeks at a seashore or mountain resort. So at most the first camping venture with your own, rather than rented, equipment, will cost you about the same as any other vacation would. The following years your vacation in the wilds is almost free. You'll need food, and if you've gotten hooked on a new angle of camping you might be adding an extra item or two, but your basic expenses are all prepaid—and you have the added benefit of free escape weekends. A whole new world opens up when you find that you have a place to go whenever you want a change of pace or scenery—the great outdoors, man's heritage, yours. Why not discover for yourself its bountiful pleasures?

Living in the Wilderness

HOME IS A TENT

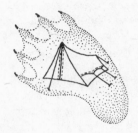

There are few experienced campers who set out to meet the wilderness without taking a shelter of some sort along. And if it's your first time camping, even for only an overnight introduction, with beautiful weather guaranteed by all the forecasts, a tent adds warmth, comfort, and security. You don't have to sleep in it. You may even set it up, trim and taut and tidy, and then decide you'd like to slumber under the stars after all. But it's still nice to have around, in case the wind rises or the rain comes or you get—just a wee bit, you understand—jittery about those odd rustlings in the underbrush. Canvas or nylon walls certainly seem flimsy compared to those of a house. Yet creatures of the woods respect their shadowy impregnability (unless you have food inside the shelter with you, and after reading the chapter on provisioning, you will, of course, know better than to do that).

Many forest preserves and parks offer log lean-tos, or even cabins for the weary camper. But before you plan on skipping a tent and slipping somnambulantly into one of these rustic shelters at the end of the day's trail, consider the facts. Everybody and his dog head for

them. Chances are the one you arrive at as dusk falls will be filled
to capacity—with campers often not of the strong, silent type. Even
during the mythical out-of-season period you're apt to find the shelter
sadly overflowing—this time with discarded cans, wrappers, and
rotted leftover food scraps. Rumors of ecology are only now beginning to filter down to the layman camper. Most certainly, whatever
else is or isn't there, you will find an unsoft carpet of that most foul
of modern discards, the snap-top can tab. (I fervently hope the
eternal fires of hell are built on these, so their inventor may pace over
them barefoot forever.) Then too, animals have learned to dine regally
on man's droppings around these carelessly housekept shelters. And
although part of the joy of camping is wildlife, in your food and gear
it can be a costly nuisance. Reconsider a tent, and the freedom to
pitch it in a quiet, welcome spot.

Which tent is right for you? Well, that depends on what kind of
camping you have in mind. The tents available today are a fantastic
improvement over those from only a few years ago. Many are of the
multiple-use variety. Still, multiple-use tents are, by definition, hybrids, and hybrids can't have everything. Their differences should be
considered in terms of function. Summer canoeing is a far cry from
winter ski touring, for instance, and some of the gear you need for
one won't do for the other.

In all likelihood you will start out summer camping. Pick a tent
basically with this in mind. Later you may buy a second, or even a
third, tent, depending on what particular times and places of the great
outdoors you get really hooked on. But by then you'll know a lot more
about tents.

THREE LITTLE TENTS ALL IN A ROW

Rarely should you consider anything bigger than the two-man
tents. You're not trying to take a seven-room house to the woods when
you go camping. You're looking for compactness, easy portability,
warmth, and coziness in cold weather. In warm weather you'll want
to be outside the tent. Rain? Well, even a huge pole tent won't keep
you from feeling somewhat cooped up if you want out. Buy a couple
of good ponchos—rain is one of the elements of the natural world you
set out to find when you left the city or suburbs. Listen to it pattering
on the rain fly of the tent. It's a soft sound.

Even more rare are the circumstances where you'll need anything bigger than a three-man tent. So rare, indeed, I can't think of any. This goes for families of three, four, five, or what have you. Five or six people in a tent may not be the Black Hole of Calcutta, then again. . . . Yes, but what about the kids?

Kids go for tents like bees for basswood. Think back to your own childhood, when you were forever busy crawling into little houses (my favorite was the kitchen woodbox) or making a brand new one by hanging a blanket over the table or a set of chairs. Kids like tents so much they'll even camp out in the backyard at home. So why not a tent of their very own for the trail? Besides the privacy and comfort of sleeping only two in a tent, children will usually accommodate parents by playing house with their own tent, sometimes even permitting their elders a well-deserved late snooze in the morning.

The backyard play camp, incidentally, is an excellent way to break children in on sleeping in their tent. If you have the opportunity to let your kids practice before you set out towards the wilds, by all means avail yourself of it.

How young can you start a child out in his or her own tent? Reasons of parental convenience, such as responding to calls for milk or a less soggy diaper in the middle of the night, may dictate three in a tent, but our daughter Genevieve, presented with the opportunity of sacking out in one by herself when fourteen months old, seemed to view it as a cozy little nursery, apparently with much more interesting walls, doors, and furnishings than the one at home. Needless to say, when camping with young children, separate tents should be within easy reach and hearing distance of each other—no matter how tempted you may be to pitch yours at the other end of the lake.

THE TARP

The most elementary tent is the tarp. This is simply a waterproof square of material usually somewhere between nine by nine feet and fourteen by fourteen feet in size. It has reinforced grommets at the four corners, the midpoints, and quarter points of each edge, as well as five tie tapes distributed along the top surface, to permit creation of a wide variety of roofs. It can be slung between two trees, wrapped over a canoe, pitched triangularly from a midpoint grommet, suspended in turn from a suitably high branch, and so on.

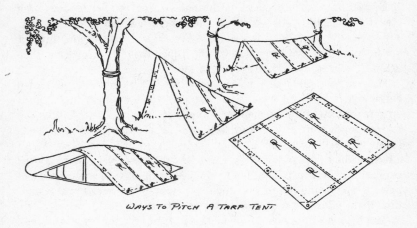

WAYS TO PITCH A TARP TENT

Even in tarps modern tent technology has made advances. The first tarp tent I had was a water-resistant ten-by-ten-foot cotton one that weighed all of a ton—actually closer to seven or eight pounds. My present one is a nine-by-nine-foot model weighing a fraction over one pound and fitting into a small outside pocket of my pack. The difference is nylon—through which water goes like a sieve—double-coated with polyurethane—through which water goes not at all.

If you use a tarp, you'll also need a ground cloth, which will add a bit more bulk and weight to your gear, although not much if it's simply a sheet of plastic. You can get away with skipping the ground cloth if you use Ensolite padding and a bivouac cover with your sleeping bag (these are discussed more fully in the chapter "Snuggling Down"). Or, if you carry a poncho, it will double as a ground cloth on smooth ground.

Compactness is not the only consideration in a tent. The tarp's use is quite restricted except for the hardiest of woodsmen. I never use mine in mosquito country. Nor is it sufficient in areas of frequently inclement weather. A tarp tent will give you shade, keep the dew off your sleeping bag, add some warmth to your nights, and cut down a considerable amount of wind. It will also protect you and your belongings from vertical precipitation. Notice the word vertical. A good storm will blow the rain in on the most expertly rigged tarp tent.

Take, for instance, the night we spent at Schroon Lake in the Adi-

rondacks some years back. It rained, and rained, and rained. Nice
and vertical the whole time. But there's such a thing as ground water.
We were on a slight slope, and although I had dug trenches around
the tarp tent, by three o'clock in the morning rivulets were running
past our sleeping bags with such force I expected us to float down
the hill like Hans Christian Andersen's one-legged tin soldier on his
bar of soap. The next day was sunny and bright. The wet corners of
our bags dried out by noon. The world was wonderful once more. And
I still use a tarp tent on occasion.

You should consider the tarp tent for weekend trips in areas of
infrequent rainfall. You should also seriously consider taking a tarp
along on day hikes in rough country where there is an odd chance of
being stuck overnight unexpectedly. A third reason for having one is
to use it as an extra fly, shading and protecting the area between two
or more tents when family camping.

If you do get a tarp, make sure it's double-coated with polyurethane, for best results. There is also one indispensable accouterment,
namely, fifty feet or more of lightweight but strong nylon line. The
tarp, except when rigged over a canoe—one of its most effective
setups, incidentally—needs plenty of line to suspend it from appropriately located trees. Trees have a fickle way of being just two feet
further apart than you have rope to reach. A second item, not indispensable but very handy, particularly if your tarp lacks sufficient ties
and grommets, is the tarp garter, or Visklamp. It looks like a combination jacks' ball and shower curtain ring and works on the same
principle a garter does. You put the ring flat against the tarp wherever
you wish to attach a line, then you push the tarp through the large end
of the ring with the ball and slide the whole thing up to the slim end.
Then just tie your line on to the large ring, lead it to the rigging point
you've picked out, and you're set.

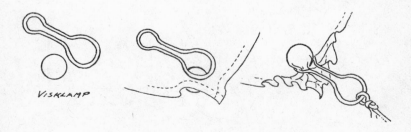

VISKLAMP

A last word: The key to pitching a tarp tent is to have a minimum of sag on your roof. To this end, if you are using nylon line, which tends to stretch, tighten things up before hitting the sack at night.

THE TUBE

At last a disposable tent, weighing just over a pound, good for two weeks in the wilds, and costing no more than a pizza pie back home. It will probably not be with us long, however. Like so many other good things, it is too easy to abuse. Careless campers, who seem to feel it's just too much work to carry home a few ounces of disposable plastic after they are through with it, leave shreds of this tent scattered all over the countryside. Because of this, many of the better camping suppliers no longer carry tube tents.

One could wish modern woodsmen would universally honor the new ethic, "pack it in, pack it out again," for the tube tent is a handy emergency shelter, far more easily rigged by the novice than the tarp. All it requires is one line threaded through the tube and tied at each end to a tree. Since it is a tube, no ground cloth is necessary. Remember, however, it is primarily a one-trip tent, although, used with care, it will last a summer of weekends.

The usual tube tent is nine to nine and a half feet long, with an eight-foot circumference for the one-man model, a twelve-foot circumference for the two-man version. Get one made of four-mill or thicker

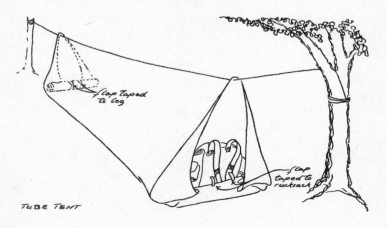

TUBE TENT

plastic. Get an opaque-colored one rather than clear. You won't walk into it at night as readily. The tint will also reflect solar radiation, keeping the inside cooler in warm weather.

There are two things to remember besides never leaving your torn tent behind in the wilds. *Never never* close off the ends of the tube. Plastic cannot breathe. If it is sealed off, neither can you. Secondly, during heavy rain, water will tend to splatter in at the base. To minimize the effects of this, stand your rucksack up at one end about ten inches inside the edge, place a log or similar object the same distance from the other end, then lift the plastic up like a doorsill against them. A couple of doubled-over pieces of cloth adhesive tape or even Scotch tape, which clings like a demon to polyethylene, attached as loops to the ends of the tent before you set out on your trip will permit you to anchor the sill easily after you've climbed into the tent.

A more permanent version of the tube tent is the Trailwise fabric model made by Ski Hut. It's made of urethane-coated nylon and has the added benefit of a stronger floor. Tapered towards the rear, it has hooded eaves at both ends, making it more of a tent than a tube. Still, if it's your first time out and you're not planning to rough it, you should probably consider something more substantial than even a modified tube tent.

SECURITY IS A REAL TENT

Snakes don't really like best of all to search out a warm sleeping bag for a snooze, honestly they don't. Nevertheless, on rare occasions they have been known to do so. And no matter how remote this possibility is on your camping trip, knowing it couldn't happen in a fully enclosed tent adds a comfortable degree of security to your own snoozing. Particularly if it's early on in your camping career.

Let's face it, a bit of nervousness in approaching the wilderness, away from so-called civilization, is natural today. When a society features a way of life in which its members feel they control nature—getting dark? turn on the lights; cold? turn on the heat; need help? reach for the telephone—how could it be otherwise?

There's really little to fear in the wilds for the careful camper. I know I'm safer canoeing down a river in no-man's-land than crossing a street in New York. But the fear lingers on subconsciously. Rare is the camper who hasn't been spooked at least once in a while. And when it happens, being able to close yourself off completely in a real tent is a reassurance.

I still vividly remember one moonlit night on the shores of Bora Bora. Susan and I were comfortably stretched out between some bushes far enough from the coconut palms so no milky missiles could drop on us during the night, yet close enough to them for a quick breakfast. Shortly after we bedded down, there began a general rustling accompanied by the castanets of snapping claws—coconut crabs, measuring over a foot from claw to claw, were doing a dance macabre with their mandibles all about us. Now coconut crabs are vegetarians. We *knew* they were vegetarians. Nevertheless, it was a restless night in paradise without a tent. The silver lining, of course, was crab claws sweeter than the best Maine lobster for breakfast.

A TUB FOR A FLOOR

The floor of a real tent should be of the tub, or wraparound, variety and preferably seamless to eliminate the possibility of ground leaks. A tub floor comes up and around to form the lower six to twelve inches of the tent sides. This waterproof sill prevents seepage if your gear or sleeping bags happen to touch the lower walls. It also keeps raindrops splattering off the ground from saturating the tent itself, which is not and *should not be* waterproof. A waterproof tent—and there are some being made—will raise a small rainstorm inside the tent while you sleep. Moisture from your breath and body rises to the roof, can't go through, condenses, and drops back over your sleeping body, turning your abode into a miniature cloud chamber. The moisture involved is not just a few drops, incidentally, but up to a full quart per person per day.

A RAIN FLY FOR THE ROOF

But if a tent isn't waterproof, how is it going to keep you dry? Simple. You cover the tent with a second roof, one that is waterproof and appropriately named a rain fly. This is suspended anywhere from three to six inches above your tent. Water bounces off this top layer, while inside moisture passes through the tent itself into the space between and then out at the sides. The double layer also keeps a tent considerably cooler during the day and warmer at night.

TENT FABRICS

Although backpacking tents are all made of synthetics, to save on weight, tents for other camping endeavors are often constructed of high-quality cotton. Unlike synthetics, pima cloth is woven so tightly that when the rains come, the minute swelling of the fibers reduces the size of the weave pores to such an extent the water will not penetrate the fabric. However, you can't brush up against it or capillary flows will be initiated. Also in its favor, the tight weave of pima cotton is less wind-permeable than the synthetics. Then too, because of its porous structure, it accepts water repellents (as opposed to waterproof coatings) readily.

On the negative side, cotton requires more care than synthetics, mainly in that it must be dry before being packed, and it tears more easily than, say, ripstop nylon. This doesn't mean it's going to rip automatically. Most quality cotton tents are of six-ounce-per-yard fabric. A good deal of abuse is needed to rip that.

All in all, old-fashioned tried-and-true cotton is an excellent tent material except for the weight factor. As a purely personal esthetic aside, cotton just feels good to the touch, as compared with the slipperiness of nylon.

Nylon has one undisputed advantage: its light weight. The material for any good canvas tent will weigh from two to four times as much as its nylon counterpart. Nylon's big disadvantage used to be that it ripped when you looked at it. However, by running reinforcement threads closely throughout the fabric, you get ripstop nylon, which—true to its name—stops rips. Another advantage, though not much of one for campers who normally take good care of their tents, is that nylon is almost mildewproof, so you don't have to worry about drying it out thoroughly before packing it up and moving on.

THE CATENARY CUT

A floppy tent may look sloppy from a distance. From inside it can drive you wild. When the winds are high, it's not exactly like listening to a soft military roll on kettledrums but it's close enough. Besides, a wrinkled roof catches snow and rain, and is a strain on the tent in general.

To eliminate sag and looseness, particularly along the roof line, good tents are catenary cut. In this process the fabric is cut on the bias to compensate for the known curvature of sag between the end support points of the ridge. This means a concavity, slight, of course, is built right into the tent ridge line, and no further slack should develop when you set it up. Hence no loose fabric and no flapping. It also makes the tent fractionally lower, by the way. Never mind, you won't be spending that much time striving for uprightness in a tent.

FOREST TENTS

Forest tents, as you might guess from the name, are intended for use primarily below the tree line and are popular multipurpose tents. They need not be as aerodynamically stable as alpine tents, designed for higher altitudes or winter camping.

There are floorless forest tents, but you're far better off with a tub-floor model. You'll have to lug along a ground cloth of some sort otherwise, so there is no real weight saving. Besides, with a floor, and screened doors and windows, or vents, also standard, you can seal yourself off for a good night's rest from mosquitoes and slugs and other crawly things.

There are several one-man forest tents available. They are rarely used, however, since even most loners will lug the minimal extra weight of the two-man model just to have the additional space.

Most two- and three-man forest tents use the A-frame construction recently popularized in inexpensive vacation homes. Double poles at each end add a bit more weight to the overall package than the old single-pole arrangement. However, they do away with the entrance blockage of the center pole and add stability, as well as keeping the tent walls trim and taut, free from flapping.

Looking more specifically at tents in the forest category, any list of good ones would include Ski Hut's Trailwise Mountain tent, which despite the name is really a forest tent. The double-urethane-coated ripstop nylon floor measures four feet, eight inches by seven feet, five inches and wraps up the sides of the tent, also of ripstop nylon, for nineteen inches. Overall tent height is forty-eight inches. Weight, com-

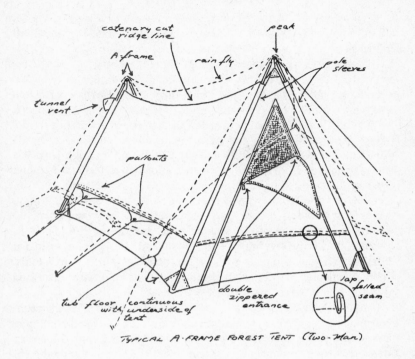

catenary cut
ridge line

peak

A-frame

rain fly

pole
sleeves

tunnel
vent

pullouts

tub floor / continuous
with underside of
tent

double
zippered
entrance

lap
felled
seam

TYPICAL A-FRAME FOREST TENT (Two-Man)

plete with poles, stakes, and fly: seven pounds, four ounces. The front opens completely with zippers and has a zippered screen behind it. There's nothing-more delightful, incidentally, than parking your tent overlooking quiet, moonlit waters somewhere on a summer's night, and being able to open the tent doors wide to the sounds and the scenery of gently lapping waves or a rushing stream. The only thing more pleasurable, perhaps, is not putting up the tent at all. But back to the Trailwise.

At the rear is a tunnel entrance, which comes in very handy during snow season, both because zippers can freeze up and because it gives you a sheltered space outside the tent itself in which to remove and brush off your boots. However, I would still categorize the tent as a forest model, since some of the other features of an alpine tent (more on that later) are missing.

Aside from its being a plus in snow, I find little to recommend the tunnel entrance. For the most part such appendages are bulky, hard to keep as neat as all the pictures show them, and basically a pain to crawl in and out of. But the zippered screening behind the tunnel entrance as well as on the ventilation tunnel above it afford excellent air circulation even in the most bug-infested country.

I'm told there are people who develop an immunity to bug bites after long years of camping. My immunity used to consist of Susan, who drew all the bugs. Now they go for Genevieve. There's bound to be someone in the family interested in the screening a tent has.

For the really weight-conscious camper who desires a sturdy, breathing nylon tent with fly, there's the Eddie Bauer High Lite. The two-man model is seven feet, two inches long; five feet, three inches wide at the front; four feet, three inches wide at the rear; and four feet high at the front, with a rear height of only two feet. Mighty cramped for some, yet you'll see plenty of these and similar models around at the far end of the walking trails and on the summits come summertime. Polyvinyl-impregnated floor and fly. Insect screen over entrance. Weight, complete with stakes, poles, guy lines, and fly: five pounds and nine ounces. Can be used in light rain without the fly; then it's four pounds, nine ounces.

One tent I haven't tried but have heard a lot about is Stephenson's Warmlite. Stephenson is somewhat the odd man out in the camping supply business. His catalog photographs are peopled with nude playmates cavorting through the tents and sleeping bags. Designwise, his equipment tends to be equally unorthodox. The floor of the Model #6 two-man tent is eleven feet long by five feet wide at the front and four feet at the back. The highest point measures forty inches from the ground. The overall design uses aluminum hoops instead of poles, giving it a covered-wagon look and better wind stability than flat-sided tents. What makes the Warmlite seem definitely worth trying is that for all its room, the two-man model complete with frame, insect screening, and condensation liners, which absorb the moisture from your breath and thus supposedly compensate for the fabric's water impermeability, weighs an incredible two pounds, nine ounces. Not included are the stakes. Again incredibly, there are only three of them used instead of the usual half dozen or so. One of these days I'm going to try a Warmlite.

Fine, you say, but the thought of one of these three- or four-foot-high roofs above your head is already giving you claustrophobia, not to mention a backache when you think about getting dressed in the morning. There are two solutions to this dilemma. First, if you haven't done any camping before, it may all be imaginary. Small tents become very cozy after you've used them a couple of times. We switched from a two- to a three-man tent on one recent extended trip to give Genevieve, then a little over a year old, a bit more maneuvering space. But we did miss the snug womblike warmth of our two-man model.

If you're going camping for the first time, why not rent a tent, to try it out for size? This is a good idea anyhow, considering that your tent will probably be your biggest single camping investment. Most of the larger mountain and camping supply stores today have a rental program. In many cases part of your rental fee can be applied to eventual purchase if you so decide. And if you don't happen to immediately fall in love with one tent, renting gives you a chance to try out several different kinds.

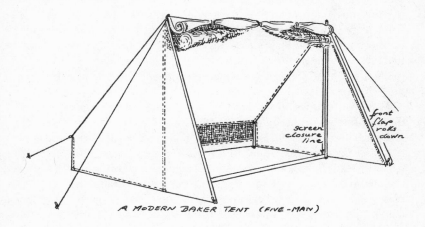

A MODERN BAKER TENT (FIVE-MAN)

A second option is to get an altogether different type of tent. There are three specific forest models I have in mind, each with its own special plus. The first is Moor and Mountain's revival and transformation of the classic Baker tent. In the old days the Baker tent was the epitome of a superior wilderness shelter, featuring roominess, quick access, flexibility, and, being essentially a giant canvas reflector oven, easy heating. For the modern camper, however, its problems outweigh its advantages, and the Baker tent vanished into obscurity, kept alive by only a few trappers and rangers.

It had no floor, much less insect protection, and the process of erecting it usually called for cutting down five to seven saplings in

Living in the Wilderness

the eight-year-old bracket, making it not only a tedious setup but a destructive one as well. As an extreme example, consider that in 1972 well over four million people passed through Grand Teton National Park, not exactly one of America's largest. Assuming everyone used an old Baker tent or other pioneer rigged model, even if the poles were reused by different parties all summer, at five poles per tent the park would have lost four to six million trees. Which is probably more saplings of that size than are to be found in the whole park. Obviously, cutting tent poles from trees is out, except in the most remote regions. Even there it's a questionable practice.

So on to Moor and Mountain's solution. It's called the Norfell Forrester, and weighs under nine pounds complete with pegs and poles. It sleeps five, being nine feet wide by seven and a half feet deep, on a urethane-coated ripstop nylon floor. The back has a foot-high insect-net-covered window running the whole length for ventilation. At the front there is a three-inch splash and dust sill that helps to keep the floor clean. A storm flap closes around the entire six-and-a-half-foot-high front by means of a nylon zipper. The storm flap may also be pitched out as a dining fly, giving you a roofed-over area exceeding nine by twelve feet.

Manufactured for Moor and Mountain by Hood Sailmakers, one of the best known in the industry, the Norfell Forrester is worth serious consideration if you feel you need a big tent, particularly if you're planning on canoe camping or setting up a base camp, in both of which cases weight is not a primary consideration. In heavily forested regions, the lightness of the nylon, as opposed to traditional canvas, permits the tent to be field-hung from trees and bushes, using the ample number of tie points and grommets provided. Without stakes and poles the weight drops to only six pounds, ten ounces.

Another tent that will give you six-foot headroom and modern tent construction besides is North Face's Cathedral tent, catchily named after the peak in Yosemite. It's a very stable hexagonal three-man tent with a striking appearance. The floor is four feet, two inches on a side and eight feet across. Using a ridgepole-modified triple-A-frame construction, it has no interior poles, a space-saving convenience that becomes almost essential when camping with young children. A tunnel entrance on one side, a double-zippered door on the other, and three screened vents assure that ventilation is excellent and access easy. Made of 1.9-ounce ripstop, with polymer-coated tub floor and nylon zippers. Shock-cord-loaded poles that spring into place make for speedy erection. Packed into two separate stuff bags to equalize the weight, the tent complete with poles, fly, guy lines, and pegs weighs ten pounds.

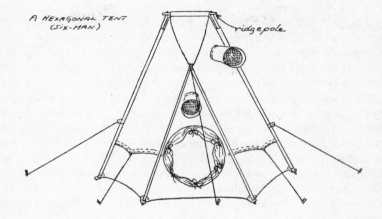

A HEXAGONAL TENT
(SIX-MAN)

ridgepole

When I take the family canoe camping, we can carry considerably more weight with us than when backpacking. Weight is even less of a problem for those who want to set up a base camp somewhere in the wilderness, moving out each fine day to explore a portion of the surrounding area and returning to their homey campsite for the evening. In both cases there is one tent that is not yet perfect but sure comes close. It's the Draw-Tite, developed back in the 1930s by outdoorsman Robert Blanchard. Working with lightweight heat-treated aircraft aluminum tubing, he designed a self-tensioned tent frame from which the tent itself was tightly suspended by means of hooks and shock cords. The exterior frame literally pulls the tent out in all directions, eliminating sagging and flapping completely. In addition to always giving you a smooth tent surface, it minimizes wear, since stress is evenly distributed. And it provides an entranceway and interior entirely free of clutter.

Modern tent designs have come a long way since the thirties, and the A-frames give you pole-free entrances and interiors as well. But what no other tent has besides the Draw-Tite, manufactured primarily by Eureka, is freedom from stays, guy lines, and in most cases even tent pegs. It's a truly self-supporting tent. Once you've set it up, if you decide you don't like the location, all you do is pick the tent up and move it. As is. You probably won't do this often. Still, it's a nice feature, as we discovered one dark night after finding we had set the tent up right next to an ant hill. The large wood ants couldn't get into the tent, but they were a royal nuisance when we stepped out, particularly since it was beautiful summer barefoot weather.

For years we used a two-man Eureka Draw-Tite. With each trip we became more enamored of it. The modern backpacker may cringe at thirteen and a quarter pounds, which is what the two-man model weighs. But for any other form of camping it's unbeatable. The same exterior frame that keeps the tent walls free of ropes and stakes also permits you to set up the tent on sand or solid rock, where other tents are difficult, if not impossible, to erect. And pitching a Draw-Tite is simplicity itself. Identical aluminum sections slip together to make the frame from which the tent is suspended. There are no lines to set or adjust. The whole thing can literally be done blindfolded. We usually have the tent up and ready by the time it would take to figure out where the stakes should go best for a regular tent. Mighty handy when you get caught in a downpour and want to make camp as quickly as possible.

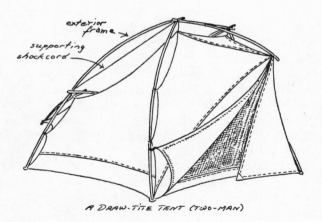

A DRAW-TITE TENT (TWO-MAN)

The body of the tent is made of 6.5-ounce-per-square-yard combed poplin with a tight 200-thread-per-inch weave. The newer models have a heavy-duty coated tub floor, seven feet, nine inches long by five feet wide, in the two-man size, which wraps up well on the sides. Our three-man model, eight feet, ten inches by seven feet, has an unfortunate seam across the middle of the floor. However, after sealing it off, we had no trouble with it even during two-month stretches of solid camping.

A rain fly for the small flat roof, forty-eight inches and sixty-four inches at the highest point for the two- and three-man models, respectively, is recommended for snow camping or in areas where continuous rain can be expected. We never had to bother putting one on our old two-man Eureka even during three- or four-day storms.

Storms, while we're on the subject, are where this tent again proves its worth. It's so stable I sometimes think the third little pig should have eased off the job and used a Draw-Tite Alpine rather than expending all that energy building a brick house. No matter how hard he huffed and he puffed, the wolf would never have blown it down. If really high winds are expected, however, it is recommended that you tap in a peg or two along the bottom edge.

Ventilation is excellent in the Draw-Tite, with a screened rear window beneath a canvas eave so it can be left open in the severest storms, and three-way zippering screen and storm front flaps set at a lovely rakish angle that shelters the entranceway by its overhang. The zippers, unfortunately, are metal, but hopefully it won't be long before Eureka switches to the self-repairing, snagproof nylon ones.

And since no one is ever totally happy with his tent, there's one more improvement I've always wanted. I'd like the option of fiberglass poles, which would save considerable weight. Also the aluminum occasionally needs straightening out, and it gets mighty cold to handle when temperatures drop down below zero. I'd pay a small fortune for fiberglass poles to fit a Draw-Tite.

Another option I always wanted was a nylon model, again to save weight. And there are in fact three nylon Draw-Tites on the market now.

Eureka's two-man model comes in orange and blue ripstop, with nylon zippers and aluminum frame. Weighs in at nine pounds, two ounces. Same design as the traditional poplin one—but three inches shorter.

Bishop's Ultimate Outdoor Equipment and Eddie Bauer have also come out with Blanchard-design tents manufactured by Eureka. Both are half a foot shorter in the two-man model than the original Eureka canvas version, though slightly wider along the back of the roof line. They are also about 10 to 20 percent lower overall than Eureka's tent, giving an interior appearance of less room.

The Eddie Bauer model uses 1.5-ounce ripstop nylon. The tub floor and the fly are urethane-coated. Comes in two stuff bags, with a total weight of eight pounds, thirteen ounces. Split between two backpackers, it would definitely be worth having even with the extra avoirdupois over the usual hiker's tents.

Bishop's version of the Draw-Tite is essentially the same, except it doesn't have the front and back eaves of the Bauer model. This streamlining adds some additional aerodynamic stability for high-altitude expedition use.

"Expedition model," incidentally, is a term you'll see bandied about frequently in camping shops. Often it's just "in" terminology and public relations work. The Draw-Tite design, however, has been used by expeditions from the Antarctic, withstanding $-102°$F. temperatures and 135-degree winds, to Mount Everest.

The Bishop tent is slightly heavier than Eddie Bauer's (nine pounds, three ounces for the two-man model) because it uses 1.9-ounce nylon for walls and floor. Extras available with the Bishop model include connecting and storage vestibules with sleeve entrances (eight ounces for the connecting vestibule, one pound and three ounces for the storage vestibule in the two-man size) and a frost liner for winter camping (one pound, ten ounces cut to fit the same model).

Now all Eureka, Bishop, or Bauer has to do is switch to fiberglass poles, add a tunnel entrance to the rear, and a winter cook hole with vent, and we'll be set with a single tent to fit all the seasons.

WHAT MAKES AN ALPINE TENT

True mountain tents, designed not only for windy high altitudes but snowstorms as well, have several features not usually found in forest tents. Although they are important under gusty blizzard conditions, these modifications add a not inconsequential amount of weight, plus expense, to a tent. Equipment fanatics will want them all, no matter what they cost. The more easygoing camper is apt to stick with a forest or multipurpose tent, which will serve him admirably under most winter conditions. However, if you are planning on plenty of high-altitude snow camping, you're in luck, for some of the finest tents are made with you in mind.

There are five essential modifications that distinguish the alpine tent from others: cook hole, exhaust vent, frost liner, tunnel entrance, and snow frock valance. Some of these may be found on the hybrid, or multiple-use tent, of course, but the true mountain tent will have them all.

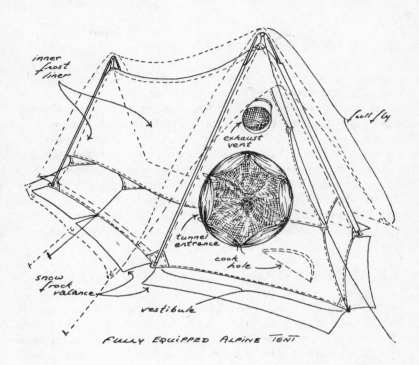

FULLY EQUIPPED ALPINE TENT

THE COOK HOLE AND EXHAUST VENT

A zippered opening in the tent floor, set well away from the wall, for fire safety and convenience, permits access to the ground below an alpine tent. If you must cook in the tent, this is where you will set up your stove. It will also be your garbage pit, either by accident or design. The idea is that when you spill the stew, it falls to the ground rather than sliding slowly and inexorably across the tent floor, past your rucksack, underneath your sleeping bag. Cooking in your tent is a practice not recommended except in really extenuating circumstances until you're comfortably familiar with your equipment. Better to munch on cold gorp.

Any extensive inside cooking will cause moisture condensation in the best of tents. To minimize it, alpine tents have a small hooded closable tunnel vent half a foot or more in diameter at or near the cook hole to permit an updraft exhaust of the moisture-laden air.

THE FROST LINER

In weather below 20°F. frost lining becomes an essential part of a tent. The removable frost liner is cut from light cotton fabric and attached as an inner wall. In some cases nylon is used; although lighter, it is far inferior for this purpose since it holds comparatively little moisture. Ice crystals forming from tent moisture condense on the surface of the liner during the more extreme temperature conditions rather than falling—especially at night—on your sleeping bag. At a convenient moment you take down the frost liner and shake it off outside the tent. If you don't get a chance to do this before the tent warms up, the ice crystals will melt. But the frost liner will then absorb the moisture rather than letting it drip down your back.

THE TUNNEL ENTRANCE

Tunnel entrances are another essential in the winter camping conditions the alpine tent is designed to meet. Zippers are prone to freezing, jamming, or breaking in extremely cold weather, rendering the usual tent flaps worthless. Also a flat vertical entranceway is more readily blocked by snow than a tunnel.

As a rule, a tent tunnel entrance is roughly three feet in diameter, with a three- to four-foot sleeve that can be pulled out and suspended to a guy line or attached to the tunnel entrance of a second tent to make a cozy set of twins during long heavy rains or severe storms. It certainly makes for easy tent-keeping. With the tunnel extended it's not difficult at all to enter a tent unaccompanied by blowing snow even in a determined blizzard.

THE SNOW FROCK VALANCE

A last modification found in the alpine tent is the exterior snow frock valance or flaps. Pieces of coated fabric of the same material as the floor extend out from the base of the tent to lie flat on the ground. Usually about a foot wide, the flaps can be covered with a thick layer of snow and then stomped down thoroughly to keep the wind from slipping under the tent floor. Not only do they add warmth, but in the case of a severe gale they prevent your tent from breaking its mooring and drifting off like the *Hindenburg*.

MAYBE A VESTIBULE

An additional plus you may want to look for in an alpine tent is a vestibule or two. One or both ends of the tent, instead of being made flat, are curved out to give you extra cooking and maneuvering room when you're tent-bound. Avoid tents with unfloored vestibules unless they have sills to keep the dirt from being tracked into the main part of the tent. If a sill is provided, the bare-ground vestibule makes an excellent cook hole.

DO YOU REALLY WANT ALL THAT?

There are several good alpine tents. Among the best are Gerry's Himalayan, Sierra Design's Glacier, and North Face's St. Elias. Gerry's Himalayan, weighing thirteen pounds, eight ounces with the works, has a seven-by-five-foot floor space with an additional two-foot vestibule at each end. Fiberglass wands curve the main walls out, making the interior even roomier.

The Sierra Design Glacier is less to tote at nine pounds, eight ounces complete. It has a floor space four and a half by seven and a half feet, including an alcove with sleeve door set rakishly off to one side.

Lightest of the lot, at six pounds and twelve ounces, is North Face's St. Elias, identical to their forest tent except for six inches extra width and the addition of a frost liner and snow flaps.

The choice among these and other alpine tents should be made carefully, since they represent a considerable investment. Perhaps the first question you should ask is whether you'll really do enough extreme winter and high-altitude camping to justify the expenditure. For an occasional frolic in the snow your Eureka Draw-Tite, North Face Cathedral, or other quality forest tent will do fine. Also, for an occasional winter outing, renting is a good option. But assuming you need a winter tent, what you should look for besides the alpine features is, the same as with any tent, quality of craftsmanship.

CHECKING OUT A TENT

The thread used to stitch a tent together should match the material: nylon thread with nylon, cotton thread with cotton. Cotton is really the best of all threads because it swells when wet, sealing the stitch holes. However, when it is used on nylon tents, owners tend to treat the whole tent as if it were synthetic and do not take the time to let it dry out as well as if it were a cotton tent. This induces premature rot in the cotton thread, materially lessening the seam life of the tent.

Seams preferably should be lap-felled and double-stitched for maximum strength, particularly with lightweight fabrics. Horizontal seams should lie so that the folded-over part dips towards the ground on the outside. Otherwise the seam will tend to hold water like a rain gutter. The stitching should be evenly spaced and neat. Remember, neatness does count.

Nylon, even ripstop, is susceptible to unraveling. All nylon edges should be heat-sealed. Most tent makers hot-cut their fabrics, effectively binding off the edge as they snip, all in one process.

Peaks, corners, pole sleeves, and particularly pullouts and grommets should be reinforced. Any part of the tent to which a line is going to be tied should be strengthened with a patch to spread the stress. Set the tent up and check all stress points while it's raised. That's the way you'll be using it.

Zippers are best made of nylon, the coil variety being the most desirable of all, with nylon teeth in second place. Following these are the old brass zippers. Aluminum teeth come in a far distant fourth. Check out not only the quality of the zippers, but their arrangement as well—always with these questions in mind: How convenient would this particular setup be for me and my party when we're inside? Is the door easy to work? Can the window be closed if the gear is at the back under it? And so on.

MAKING YOUR OWN

If you're handy with a sewing machine, consider making your own tent during those dark days when you're by the homeside hearth. Not from scratch, unless you're both a fanatic and equipped with the necessary, fairly technical engineering know-how, but with a kit from Frostline or Carikit. Several styles come with precut, prelabeled parts to be put together in a stitch-by-number fashion. Instructions are clear and easy to follow, so if you've sewn at all you don't need to acquire any additional skills. Neither do you need an industrial sewing machine. A home model will do fine. And you save about 50 percent over equivalent models of finished tents. That's true of Frostline's and Carikit's other camping gear, too.

The Frostline Sun-Lite two-man, in nylon, is a cozy little forest tent with a ridge height of three and a half feet, a urethane-coated floor seven feet, one inch by four feet, three inches, and mosquito netting at each end. The front and back ends close from the bottom using Velcrotape, a product I personally haven't gotten used to yet. Snow tends to pack into the hairs so they close poorly. (Speaking of hair, watch yours if it snags in Velcro. Chewing gum it's not, but Susan has had some unkind words to say about it when her long locks tangle in the Velcro snaps on our sleeping bags.) The completed tent, including a waterproof urethane-coated fly and poles, but not stakes, weighs five pounds and four ounces.

TENT ACCESSORIES

There are all kinds of tent accessories available, from the absolutely useless pole shelf to the—and may the great woodsman Nessmuk forgive me—absolutely essential whisk broom. I'm not a tidy creature by habit, as Susan would demonstrate simply by leading you to my study. Yet on one canoe trip we paddled back, at my insistence, a whole day's journey through the rain rather than go on without the small whisk broom left behind at the starting point. Since that occasion I have adopted the practice of packing it right into the tent bag. Woe be to anyone who removes it therefrom.

The whisk broom is not a fetish. What makes it so important is the nature of modern fabrics and the almost universal acceptance of floored tents. Ripstop nylon does not tear readily. But the shell of a tent is sensitive to small punctures. Pine sap turns it into cotton candy. It doesn't accept water repellents readily, but it greets dirt with open arms. And rolling up pine needles, burrs, and sand in your tent when breaking camp will reduce the life of the tent by half.

There will always be some litter stuck to the outside bottom of the tent floor when you start rolling it up. Just whisk it away as you roll. Wait. Before you take down the tent and start rolling, whisk out the inside too. No matter how careful you've been about removing your shoes before crawling into the tent—or hadn't you even thought of doing that?—some of the outdoors always follows you in. In Europe it's quite common to switch from street shoes to house shoes when entering a home. The custom has a rightful place in the great outdoors too, if home happens to be a tent. Here, however, teetering on one foot while you unlace the other shoe, or backing rather ungracefully into a sitting position inside the tent, the shod feet still sticking out, it's harder to extricate yourself from the footgear without tracking in a little something or other.

So get a small whisk broom, pack it in your tent bag, and by all means use it. It's little enough work when you consider that's all the housekeeping you have to do. For winter camping a small sponge comes in handy for the times you don't manage to sweep out tracked-in snow before it turns to slush.

MENDING A TENT

Speaking of water, any tent can and may develop a small seam leak, particularly along the edge of the floor and in corners. A little squeeze bottle of Neoprene sealer complete with pointed nozzle should be kept in your tent bag to remedy the situation quickly and painlessly. Make a mental note of any spot that leaks—when it leaks. Otherwise you may not find it till the next rain. Seal it before you leave the tent for the day, first making certain all possible vents are open. Sealer sure doesn't smell like pine boughs, and it can give you a nasty headache as well. But after two or three hours the smell will be gone along with your leak.

Besides sealer, a small repair kit put together with your particular tent in mind is handy, indeed almost essential. Canvas tents will rip on occasion. The new nylon tents are very susceptible to fire damage. They won't burn. They simply melt, a fact of which one tent salesman up around Hudson Bay has quite graphic proof. He'd been trying to sell the Crees, who live in the traditional canvas wall tents, on the new nylon tents. Sales resistance was running so strong he literally couldn't give one away. Finally, after much bargaining, he talked Jim Went-out-spring-goose-hunting-and-got-stuck-in-the-mud (I'll always remember the English translation of his name if nothing else) into trying one out. Jim promptly cut a two-foot-square hole in the roof, led a stovepipe through, and finished it off with the usual flashing holding the tent in place. As dinner was cooking the tent roof melted and oozed into the stew. So much for nylon tents up around Hudson Bay.

Now obviously you're not going to lead a flue up your nomadic tent. And your fire, if you have one, should not be close enough to permit sparks to land on your tent. Still, accidents of various kinds do happen. Remedy? For a nylon tent, a few inches of two-inch-wide adhesive ripstop nylon. The same kind of tape, but waterproofed, should be used for the floor and fly.

If you have a canvas tent, a couple of elbow-sized patches, sturdy thread, and as fine a needle as two thicknesses of the material will allow can do the job. As always, it's a good idea to apply sealer to the seams.

STAKES

Pegs or stakes are often not included in the complete tent package because terrains vary vastly and so do the suitable stakes. Luckily stakes are cheap. The curved aluminum models nest together (use a rubber band to keep them that way). Medium-length ones (eight and a half inches) are a good all-around compromise in that they will hold well either in forest or meadow land or driven into sand, where shorter ones would give way. High-impact plastic stakes, usually in nine-inch or twelve-inch lengths, are very durable and do not bend as aluminum sometimes does. Their primary use is in sand, and there the somewhat large holes they leave behind are easily filled in. Skewer pegs of chrome-moly steel ten to twelve inches long are favorites for pebbly ground.

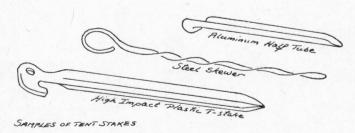

Aluminum Half Tube

Steel Skewer

High Impact Plastic T-stake

SAMPLES OF TENT STAKES

Mother Nature is accommodating. Most of the time you should be able to lead at least some of your guy lines to trees or bushes, which offer strong, problem-free moorings. Happiest of all, of course, is the camper who has a self-supporting tent and thus can pass up the pounding, line-tightening ritual altogether. He'll be studying the stars or lazily answering the coyote pups practicing their yipping just that much sooner.

SNUGGLING DOWN

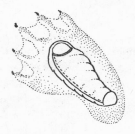

It was a cold and stormy night, oh, quite a number of years ago, with the wind blowing a kaleidoscope of snow relentlessly across the Lake of Lucerne. As was my custom on that lengthy trip through Europe, I had abandoned my battered, lumpy, kapok-filled, hundred-pound (at least) sleeping bag for a biweekly rejuvenation at a hotel. After a skin-shrivelingly long hot bath, I threw open the window and curled up beneath linen-covered eiderdown bolsters lofting four or five feet towards the ceiling. Drifting luxuriously off to sleep with visions of Ludwig the Second's Neuschwanstein in my head, I slept the sleep of a thousand and one nights.

In the morning the chambermaid brought me hot buns and a huge, steaming cup of cocoa. I snuggled down in sheer joy, dunking the buns, studiously ignoring my impending evening's return to that drafty, shivering kapok bag.

The memory lingers on today. The bag does not. Down-filled sleeping bags, once a rarity, swept the country in the sixties. Sleeping in the wild can now be every bit as comfortable as that luxurious night —except that, in my case, I'm the one who gets up to make the morning coffee.

IN THE BAG

There are still some kapok and similarly filled sleeping bags on the market. As a rule they're considered good enough for children. Rather unfortunate. I don't see any particular reason why the youngsters should freeze. Avoid synthetic-filled bags as well, including Dacron, Fortrel, Kodel, unless you plan to do only occasional summer camping, don't mind carrying twice the weight and bulk of a down bag, and really want to cut corners financially. Better to think of a good down sleeping bag as a ten- or fifteen-year investment. Which it is, with good care.

If you must buy a synthetic—in some cases feather allergies are the deciding factor—get a bag filled with Dacron Fiberfill II. It's much softer, more resilient, and less prone to lumping than the old polyesters. Although its compressibility is not as good as that of down, it's considerably better than in the past. Insulation quality has also improved greatly. But make sure you eat breakfast before stuffing the bag. You'll need the extra strength.

With down prices reaching for the path of the wild goose and the quality of synthetics improving, the time will no doubt come when the down sleeping bag will lose a large segment of its loyal following. But for now and the conceivable future it's king.

There's down and there's down. Eiderdown is passing into extinction along with the eider duck from whose breast and nest it is plucked. It's been replaced by the by-product down of commercial goose and duck factories. The best-quality down from these birds is that of fowl raised in northern countries such as Canada, Finland, and Poland. Although they breed an awful lot of ducks in Taiwan, the warmer climate inhibits the development of first-class down: the ducks don't need to keep warm there.

When a reputable manufacturer specifies that his bags are filled with Northern goose down, you know you have the best possible filling. The difference in thermal efficiency, if any, between white and gray down has never been established. The purists prefer white. Since I can't see the gray goose freezing his tail feather off alongside a white one, I'll settle for either.

Duck down is about 10 to 15 percent less efficient than goose down from a thermal and compression point of view. However, it is more than adequate for most purposes, and increasingly manufacturers are switching to the smaller fowl's feathers in an attempt to keep bag prices a little bit lower.

Waterfowl down is a mixture of the two. But there are no specifications on how much is honk and how much is quack. In general you'll find the big-name quality suppliers' bags do not lay eggs. By sticking to these or to bags recommended by friends, you should stay on the right track.

LOFTLEIDER

When you set out to buy a bag, you'll hear a lot about loft. Loft is nothing more, nothing less than the thickness of the bag when it's all fluffed up. The thicker, the warmer; and loft usually ranges from six to twelve inches. Our Sierra Design 200s, for instance, loft up to over eight inches. Our battered old summer Camp & Trail Atomwates struggle for an Olympian height of four inches.

Before you get carried away with figures, incidentally, those for loft aren't quite true. When you're inside the bag, you compress the down beneath you to almost zero. So to be accurate about it you'd have to cut the manufacturer's figures in half.

To get the most mileage out of the loft your bag has, lay it out early in camp, even if sacking out is the last thing on your mind. With sleeping bags as with bread, long, slow rising is the key to lightness. Your prelofted bag will be warmer when you crawl in than one freshly uncoiled from its stuff sack.

APPROXIMATE LOFT/MINIMUM TEMPERATURE CHART
FOR DOWN-STUFFED MODIFIED MUMMY BAGS

Minimum Temperature	Total Loft (inches)	Down (ounces)
+40	4	22–24
+25	5	24–26
+10	6	26–28
+5	7	28–32
0	8	32–36
−5	9	36–40
−25	10–11	44–50

THE SLEEPING BAG SHELL

The quality of sleeping bags supplied by reputable camp gear manufacturers is so high overall that a discussion of types, construction methods, and materials is important primarily to differentiate them from the bags being pandered by mass-market retailers taking advantage of the camping boom. A second reason to look closely at the bags is to find some small feature that may have particular appeal to you.

Most sleeping bags today use downproof ripstop nylon for at least the outside shell. The downproof factor becomes more significant as the years pass. After a decade of use our old Camp & Trail Atomwates, made of the then traditional balloon cloth, leave behind a couple of small white fluffy souvenirs at every campsite. The more tightly woven downproof nylon technically obliterates this problem, although the thinner-quality fabric, 1.8 ounce or less, will lose its calender after some years and leak as well.

The ripstop feature keeps that accidental puncture you get from turning into a hole big enough for you to stuff the feathers back in one by one. The color of the nylon shell is a matter of personal taste. I happen to prefer the dark greens and blues to the screaming violets and international orange. Never mind that. Choose what you'd like to live with for the next decade.

The inside shell of a sleeping bag is quite often made of nylon taffeta, because some people find it softer and less icky-feeling than the ripstop nylon (more on that later). In any case, the inside color of the sleeping bag is equally often a nice dark color like chocolate or nutmeg that won't show dirt much.

SLEEPING BAG SHAPES

Sleeping bags come in three general shapes: mummy, barrel, and rectangular. You may also run across a few abbreviated bags known as foot sacks, but they'll be in the mountain climber's section of your store.

The roomiest of the lot is the rectangular bag. That also makes it the bulkiest. However, if you toss and turn a lot, and plan to enjoy the wilderness leisurely with a base camp, it's fairly practical. To save

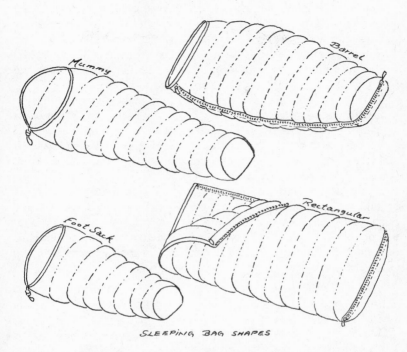

SLEEPING BAG SHAPES

weight, a large majority of rectangular bags are made without a hood, which means they'll be less than efficient in keeping out the cold. On the plus side, they often can be unzipped along both the side and the bottom to open out into a large quilted down comforter for guests at your vacation cottage.

Barrel bags are for those who lie on their backs with their knees to the sky and those who sleep in the fetal position. Square at the top, almost mummy at the bottom, they bulge in the middle like a barrel, leaving plenty of knee- and elbowroom for chasing rabbits as you dream. Again, the majority are made without hoods.

Mummy bags aren't what they used to be—you can move in the new ones. In fact they're downright comfortable compared with the old Army-surplus iron maidens. This is not to denigrate the Army bags if you can sleep in them. I shift around too much in my sleep to use them. But they are probably one of the last great surplus buys. A bit heavier than the camper-designed models, they're as warm as a toaster set on "dark."

Our latest bags are the Sierra Design 200s, a joy to sleep in. Like other quality bags, they have a circular flat bottom so your feet can stick up and wriggle. For some reason, till the last couple of decades sleeping bag manufacturers assumed all campers had hinged ankles so that at night the feet could be made to lie flat, parallel with the legs. Consequently they put flat envelope bottoms on their bags.

Surprisingly enough, another factor that makes current bags so snoozable, besides their somewhat more generous cut, is the same slippery nylon whose feel I instinctively dislike. Nylon, like satin, is so slippery that when you turn over, the bag doesn't chase you. If you've ever slept in a bag that seemed to have a mind of its own, you'll appreciate this feature instantly.

Standard with mummy bags is a hood that can be drawn closed around the head and shoulders. Some 20 percent of your blood and body heat go to your head to keep the brains from addling. Without a hood, this busy circulation can mean severe heat loss on cold nights. Additionally, if there is a draft, it somehow invariably manages to slip in around you where the hood should have been.

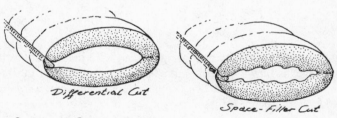

Differential Cut

Space-Filler Cut

CROSS SECTION OF SLEEPING BAGS

DIFFERENTIAL VERSUS SPACE-FILLER CUT

The advent of differentially cut sleeping bags caused a mass conversion to this form. The inner shell is shaped to be smaller than the outer one. As a result, it's impossible to poke your elbow, foot, or knee deep enough into the down to touch the outer shell and cause cold spots. On the other hand, it means the inner shell can't fall loosely along the contours of your body. Stretched more tautly, it leaves some air pockets.

At the moment some manufacturers are considering going back to the space-filler cut, where the inner and outer shells measure the same in diameter. Others, like Holubar, never went for the differential cut in the first place. So which do you get?

Although you'll hear a lot of pros and cons for both, it seems to me a tempest in a teapot. Most manufacturers follow each other back and forth on trends the way Detroit did with car fins. Select your bag for its other qualities.

KEEPING THE DOWN IN PLACE

Don't be baffled by baffles. All they are is pieces of cloth or netting —at their most effective when compatible with the shell for consistent life, nylon with nylon, for instance—that keep the down from collecting all in one spot in the bag. Essentially they form tubes running either around the circumference or in a chevron pattern. I don't think there's a down bag made anymore with longitudinal, or top-to-bottom, compartments. If you find one, avoid it. Chances are all the down will settle by your feet. Nice for the feet. But the rest of you will freeze.

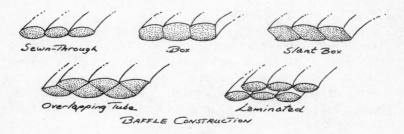

Sewn-Through   Box   Slant Box

Overlapping Tube   Laminated

BAFFLE CONSTRUCTION

The five standard baffle systems, in increasing order of complexity of construction, are: sewn-through, box, slant box, overlapping, and laminated. Sewn-through leaves you with cold bars equivalent to the sear marks on a charcoal steak, so forget it. Box is good, slant box is better. Overlapping is excellent, particularly for subzero bags. However, at this stage of the game the sheer weight and mass of the baffling begins to affect the bag considerably. Laminated tubes begin to reach the more-cloth-than-down stage. For winter bags only.

FOR THOSE WHO DON'T LIKE SATIN

Some bags, such as those made by Pinnacle and Holubar, still come with liner attachments so you can use bag-fitted cotton or muslin sheets, both to help keep the bags clean and to eliminate the slippery, satiny, cold feeling of nylon. The liners also add a degree of warmth. Unfortunately they do tangle if you toss and turn. Most manufacturers no longer incorporate ties or other sheet fasteners in their bags. But at the risk of sounding too fastidious, after sleeping out three months in a bag without being near anyplace where it can be cleaned, I find myself wishing the designers would apply some of their imagination to a tangle-free fastening system for liners rather than abandoning the whole idea.

When you're out for only a week or two at a time, daily airings will keep your sleeping bag fresh. For longer trips, if you can't get a bag with sheets and decent fasteners, consider making your own. Sheets can be washed and dried in a few hours in the sun. Sleeping bags can be washed too, of course, by hand if necessary, but the less the better.

ZIP ZIP ZIP ZIP ZIP ZIP

Each night camping, as we snuggle down to sleep, there can be heard breaking the silence of the woods *zip zip zip zip zip* and *zip*. That's the zipper on the the storm door followed by the three on the screen door. At which point, if it's been a light-hearted day, we start giggling. Next there's *zip* as Susan closes her bag, *zip* as I close mine. There's no *zip* for Genevieve; hers is a crawl-in bag. We would not be so happy, however, if the zippers failed to work; neither would you. The zipper is the weakest part of your bag, and one of the most important.

Metal zippers are definitely out for either sleeping bag or tent; they jam, freeze, and break too easily. Nylon-toothed zippers are good, particularly if the teeth are large—although there can also be too much of a good thing, and some of the monster zippers are getting out of hand.

Not many manufacturers besides North Face presently use nylon coil zippers, but I hope they will soon. These zippers, while more expensive, are almost completely jamproof, don't snag, and are self-repairing.

Zippers should work from the bottom as well as the top. Although down bags have a wide comfort range, as much as fifty degrees' difference in temperature depending on your metabolism, there are times when they get too warm. If you end up camping year-round—and even a three-day winter weekend will do more to wash the hectic pace of today's urban life out of your system than three weeks at a resort hotel—you'll also end up getting two sleeping bags, a lightweight and a heavy-duty model. For three-season camping, spring, summer, and fall, one bag will suffice. As long as you can unzipper it from the bottom. When things get too warm, you do just that. With the hood open too, air will flow through the bag from top to bottom, ideally keeping you at just the right temperature.

To keep you warm instead of cool, all zippers should be lined lengthwise on the inside with a down-filled baffle which, again ideally, drops when you're zippered in to cover what would otherwise be a long drafty slit. The baffle should not be merely attached directly to the zipper edge, where it would create a sewn-through cold line. Rather it should be suspended from the inside shell of the bag itself as well. A question I just toss out without an answer: Why do most manufacturers stitch the baffle on a right-hand-zippered bag from the top so it hangs down, and left-hand ones from the bottom so the flap doesn't always really cover the zipper?

I've got one last thought on zippers. The longer, the better. Mummy bags for some strange reason do not come with zippers extending all the way around the bottom. This means you can't open them up completely to use as comforters. However, at least get one that zippers all the way to the foot, again because you'll have better ventilation when it gets hot, also because it permits you to air the bag without turning it inside out. Then too, if you're getting pair bags, one with left- and one with right-hand zipper, the full-length opening means you can zip them together more comfortably when you feel like it. Actually two people in zipped-together bags are a bit like two cats. There tends to be a lot of kicking and hogging the covers. Also there's a lot more air space in the double to cool you down. Nevertheless, we always get mating bags. It's a nice thought even if you don't use them very often.

IS IT YOUR BAG?

Looking over a sleeping bag with a critical eye isn't enough to base a choice on. The only way to find out if it's really the bag for you is to crawl in and try it. Most camping gear can be bought by mail, and so for that matter can a sleeping bag. *If* you've tried one like it before. This is a custom-made bed that you're going to use for a long time to come. You'd better feel comfortable in it.

There are some shops, rarer than those renting tents, from which you can get the use of a bag for a weekend. By all means avail yourself of this service if you find it. You may be positive you can't sleep in a mummy. You may find out you can after all once you try it. If you can't rent a bag first, at least take off your shoes and crawl into the one you're eyeing, right on the store floor.

Remember that a sleeping bag has to be long enough so you can really stretch your toes comfortably and turn over besides. Something else to take into account if you plan on doing any winter camping is your boots. You just may want to take those boots to bed with you— leather has a tendency to feel like cold steel if left outside in a zero-degree night. When choosing a sleeping bag allow enough extra room for them at the bottom, wrapped in a piece of plastic to keep things clean.

BAGGING YOUR KIDS

Children's sleeping bags are frequently filled with synthetics. Besides economy and an occasional allergy, the usual reason is apt to be bed-wetting. Polyester absorbs next to no moisture, retains most of its insulating qualities while wet, and is easy to clean. However, these factors still haven't sold me on letting Genevieve shiver when we winter camp, and she has her own down bag.

Alpine Design makes two children's duck-down bags, good to 20°F. But their Tundra Sleeper has a center zipper, which I abhor because it's right on top where you want maximum loft; and their Meadow Sleeper has no hood. Also, since Genevieve was only a year old when we bought hers, we didn't want a bag quite as long as Alpine's, in case she crawled down too far for her own good.

Why not zip the two adult bags together and put the baby in the middle between you? Well, some families do. Then again, some people don't need much sleep.

Our solution was a Sierra Design foot sack. North Face makes a similar model appropriately named the Elephant's Foot. These half-bags are designed for use by mountain climbers in combination with a down parka. They are ideal for sleeping in those cliff-hanging, contorted positions in which only dedicated rock climbers find themselves. They also work beautifully as full-length sleeping bags for kids from three months to five or six years, since the top is shaped higher on the ground side than on the covering side and equipped with a drawstring, intended as a belt but forming a nice semihood for a child. Genevieve took to hers like a duck. We tied it off halfway so she couldn't burrow too deeply—probably a typical parental over-precaution since a down bag can breathe. And as things turned out, even when the temperature hovered between 10° and 20°F. all night, she was warm enough to sleep halfway out.

MAKING YOUR OWN

Probably the best idea in children's bags, although again for some strange reason it features a center top zipper, is the Frostline Child-Add-On Bag kit. Not only can you make this bag yourself, from Frostline's easy-to-assemble kit, but as the child grows you can add on sections, increasing the length one foot at a time.

Both Frostline and Carikit make several adult-sized sleeping bag kits as well. They will save you almost 50 percent over the ready-made equivalent. Require some sewing skill, but nothing fancy. If you're used to a sewing machine you're all set. The down comes in individual packets, labeled so you'll get the right amount in the right compartment. Once you've put together the bag from the kit, which includes everything, even thread, you squeeze the premeasured down into the matching baffled compartment, stitch up the last seam, and head for the woods.

THE NO-BAG SLEEPING BAG

If you're going camping for the first time and don't want to spend the money for a sleeping bag just yet, a blanket roll is a workable substitute on a summer trip. All you need is two warm blankets. Fold each one in half. Then slip one inside the other so the two folds are on opposite sides. Then tuck the bottom under itself and crawl in for a good night's sleep.

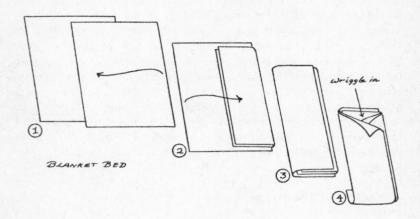

BLANKET BED

UPHOLSTERING

All right, go ahead and laugh. I've never been able to sleep without something under my head. An air pillow doesn't work because it's like fighting a large Ping-Pong ball all night. On the other hand, I'm certainly not going to lug a real pillow from home along. For years I simply rolled up my jacket or sweater. That works fine. Then I went one step further. I started stuffing them in the sleeping bag stuff sack. Works even better.

MATTRESSES

Now maybe I'm getting soft, the joints setting a bit more firmly, the back not as supple as before. But that's not the reason I've started using a pad under my sleeping bag—it's those new improvements in camping equipment again. Before, you could take an air mattress with you. It probably not only tended to leak, but, at any appreciable altitude, made you black out while huffing and puffing to inflate it.

Of course you could take a pump too, but there went that old demon weight again. Besides, sleeping on one was like trying to lie still on a surfboard riding the big crest. It is possible to stay on but. . . .

Then there was foam rubber. Its insulation quality was poor, because cold ground air circulated freely through the pores. Water anywhere around? It lapped it up. And the bulk was just about twice that of a sleeping bag.

So I kept happily sleeping on the tent floor or ground cloth. Then along came closed cell pads, usually called by one of their trade names, Ensolite or Thermobar. Ensolite can't absorb water. If a tent floor seam leaks, your bag still stays dry. It's an excellent insulator, bringing the cold-weather efficiency of your sleeping bag up several notches.

Ensolite is usually sold in three-eighth- or half-inch thickness and in various lengths, to accommodate you whether you want just enough to reach from head to hip or enough to stretch all the way to your heels. Closed cell pads are firm, and although they will smooth out lumpy ground, they are not exactly cuddly. They do roll up into a comparatively small volume and are the best mattress for anyone camping light.

As a last note, I would hesitate to even mention pine boughs, the traditional old-timer's bed, except I have a point to make about them. By whacking off thirty or forty lower branches from the pine and spruce trees around camp, then laying them down fish-scale fashion between four logs, the woodsman of yore made his fragrant bed. Even back in the good old days, however, this practice was reserved for the semipermanent camp remaining occupied for a week or two. Today such behavior would be completely inexcusable. With a number of people out looking for the wilds the same as yourself, a whole national park could be turned into an eyesore in one season by this kind of he-man woodsmanship. It had its time. That time is gone.

UNDER AND OVER THE BAG

There comes a night when you can't resist sleeping under the stars instead of in your tent. The old rubberized bottom of the kapok bags certainly was better for that. Uncoated nylon, even ripstop, is too sensitive to be slept upon directly on the ground. Also dew will collect on top, and the bag isn't really—should not be, in fact—water-repellent. But don't let all that deter you. Either filled (for added warmth) or bivouac covers, with tough waterproof nylon bottoms and water-resistant tops, are available for the bags.

MAKING IT LAST

Something to remember, especially if you're sleeping under the sky: Never lay out a nylon bag close to the fire. It won't flame up on you when the sparks land. But one spark can melt a hole the size of a silver dollar. Then just try catching the down. Needless to say, also avoid drying it by the fire in case of an accidental soaking.

Then there's the to-clean-or-not-to-clean debate. I'm on the clean side, because I like to be able to bunk down without having to chase my bed around the tent first. Although nylon is not attractive to moths, the salt and oil you leave behind interest all sorts of small intriguing insects.

You'll be airing out your bag regularly as you go, of course. Sunshine and fresh air are the most natural detergents there are, and a busy campground on a fine day more and more resembles a kaleidoscope as the bright colors of modern sleeping gear adorn bushes and ground. But occasionally—not too often, mind you—a bag needs a bath.

Dry cleaning works, or so they say. A number of campers aren't around to testify on the matter. They're the ones who used their bags directly after dry cleaning and died in their sleep from the fumes still pent up in the bags. If you do have your gear dry cleaned, make sure the cleaner uses Stoddard's Fluid, which is much easier on the down than the other solvents. And make absolutely sure you air the bag out for at least *two weeks* in a well-ventilated space.

The best solution for us—and as I say, there's more than a little debate among the various partisans—is to spot clean the shell as it needs it and wash the bag as a whole after two months' or so use. Sheets or liners can stretch this period indefinitely (another reason I hope they make a comeback).

Washing can be done in the tub or in a machine, but only in the front-loading tumbler type. Never use the top-loading agitator model; the strain on the baffles is tremendous, and the bag can snag on the agitator. The same goes for picking up a bag that is filled with water. Squeeze it out gently first, or all the interior baffles will rip. Use warm

water and Ivory soap or Woolite only. It's best to run a whole second
cycle without any soap to make sure every last bit is rinsed out of the
down.

Using a warm rather than hot setting, the washed bag can be
tumble-dried. Toss in a clean sneaker with it to help break up the
down clumps. The static electricity produced by rubber rubbing on
nylon will help the process along. Even three or four cycles in a drier
is not really enough. Open-air sun drying, several days of it, is the
best final touch.

Before you stow your bags away, check them over for any needed
mending. Better then than along the trail next time out. This is a good
point to remember for all your gear, incidentally. It's harder to take
time out from the great outdoors to do such chores than to take it
from a rainy, housebound day at home.

If possible, don't store sleeping bags in their stuff sacks for extended
periods. At home they can be dumped loosely into a large storage box
so the down can remain decompressed. Supersized storage stuff sacks
available from Holubar serve the same function. A bag should never
be neatly rolled, however much this offends the tidy, since it tends to
clump the down. Best of all is to hang it full-length in a dry attic or
basement if you have the space.

COVERING UP

A tent and a sleeping bag come to a bit of an investment, you decide, so what about all the specialized camping clothes? Well, there really aren't any to speak of, except comfortable shoes or boots and rain gear. Even the rich wear old clothes in the country, and there's no reason you shouldn't—unless you've been swept into the downhill skier's fashion race, which seems to be overflowing a bit to back-packers these days.

What you do have to watch and be prepared for is sudden changes of temperature. You can't go home for an extra sweater. An extreme example of what can happen on even a short trip occurred when Susan and I decided to climb Mount Kinabalu in Borneo. It was 80°F. at sunrise over the lush tropical valley, and the humidity fairly glistened on the tulip trees and undergrowth as we started the ascent from the trail head at 6,000 feet. Our pipe-puffing guide wasn't much for rest periods, tapping his foot impatiently and staring up at the cloud-covered peaks whenever we stopped for a few minutes. So by late after-noon we were at the 11,500-foot-elevation trail hut. Only the smallest alpine shrubs still clung to the mountain face. The wind howled. By the time supper was ready, frost and a light snow left hardly a memory of the morning's mugginess.

Never underestimate the effect of altitude on the temperature. Nor the effect of the sun's withdrawal. Desert regions over 100°F. during the day can drop close to or even below freezing in some spots at night. Take these factors into account when planning your wilderness venture. This doesn't mean you should overload on clothes, but know something about the region into which you're heading, consider your own susceptibility, or lack thereof, to cold and sun, and pack accordingly.

The minimum for even a weekend outing is one complete change of clothes. For such a short time chances are you won't need them. On the other hand, for many people nothing will turn a wonderful tramp through the woods into unadulterated misery more quickly than having to spend a day in clinging wet clothes after an accidental dunking or sudden squall.

When hiking with children, who take to water even more readily than ducks, have along two complete changes. The first dunking in the stream is apt to be followed almost immediately by a second dip to prove to everyone that the water really is wet. Lugging the extra clothes is a small burden when you think of the incalculable value to the child of his outdoor experiences. I remember one city-born-and-bred seven-year-old's utter astonishment at spending the better part of a day tracing a stream to its small, trickling source, only to find out there was no faucet or fire hydrant. No matter how much children might read or be told about nature, there's nothing like actually being there.

THE SECOND SKIN

Starting with underwear, the word is cotton for everybody. When you're moving about a lot, perspiration builds up and nylon gets clammy. Cotton absorbs the moisture. A small point, but important for comfort. The various mesh and net fashions available today work fine, but are really no great advantage unless you perspire profusely or like walking around a summer camp with a hairy chest bristling through them for appearance' sake. Speaking of appearances, Susan always picks her underthings for a canoe trip in prints and colors, with an eye to their doubling as bathing suits.

For winter camping, long johns, either cotton knit or the thermal variety, are used with some frequency and are surprisingly comfortable. Red ones are cheerful on a gray day. Wool next to the skin in severe weather is warmest of all, of course, but I never could stand the itching.

In the vast majority of cases, you can just take along what you'd normally wear and find most comfortable.

ONE SHIRT, TWO SHIRTS, THREE SHIRTS, FOUR

There's nothing like an old shirt. Shirts somehow just manage to get soft and really wearable when the fraying starts. Yet turning collars is hardly worth the effort anymore. So shirts are usually disposed of far before their useful life is over.

All my old dress shirts end up camping sooner or later, except for cuff-linked models and those pure synthetic ones that absorb no moisture and charge themselves with static electricity like a Van de Graaff generator. Cotton flannel shirts need no breaking in, and Susan swears by a couple of incredibly faded cotton knit pullovers that never seem to wear out.

No one will look at a frayed and faded collar when you're camping. Be comfortable. That's the main thing.

In the cool of a summer evening you may well need something warmer than a thin shirt. One of those soft, good-quality, 100-percent-cotton chamois woodsmen's shirts is an ideal solution. Not fashionably tapered or cut, they are the height of luxury and softness. Make sure to get one with full-length tails. Many are jacket-cut, extending only an inch or two below the waist; designed to be worn outside the pants, they will ride up your back when you're carrying a pack. Tails not only keep the shirt in, but tuck down deep to give a highly desirable extra layer of clothes over your lower torso.

Layering is the basic principle of dressing for the outdoors. A cotton shirt, a chamois shirt, and a wool shirt or sweater, one on top of the other, is as warm in winter as a heavy wool lumberman's jacket. Though one jacket sounds preferable to three shirts, in point of fact it's not. You'll be amazed how warm you get carrying a pack, or even just plain moving about. Wearing layers of clothes, you have a readily controlled thermostat at your fingertips. You start out dressed comfortably for the cool of the morning. As your activity builds up and the day warms towards noon, all you do is remove one layer at a time, tucking it under a strap of your pack. Then when evening falls and you make camp, you bundle up bit by bit once more.

How many layers you wear and when you don and doff them depends strictly on your own metabolism. I rarely get beyond the chamois shirt layer unless it's winter and we're sitting about camp being very lazy indeed. Susan, on the other hand, won't crawl out of the sleeping bag without her wool sweater, even in fall. And on a cold winter morning all the layers she can get hold of disappear into the bag with her, emerging some time later as a solitary bundle about her still dubiously shivering form.

The best outer layer (not counting rain gear) is 100-percent wool. The shirt often sold under the name "Alaskan" has the advantage of being quite tightly woven and thus more resistant to wind than a sweater. It also has button-down flap pockets for keeping sundry small things, like a pipe and tobacco, an extra bandana, the flashlight, or the waterproof matches, handy. Kept away from moths and sparks, an Alaskan lasts forever—or at least twenty to twenty-five years, which is good enough. My wool layer is usually a battered V-neck sweater I've had for fifteen years and am sort of attached to. The best of all sweaters, if you don't mind the bulk and really want to keep warm, are those made from raw wool. Not having the lanolin processed out, they shed water and will keep you as dry as a sheep during drizzles.

The preference for wool is no sheepshearer's public relations plug. Wool simply is the best material for warmth, resilience, and durability. Even when damp or wet, wool retains its bulk, and thus a large part of its warmth. Down, on the other hand, will clump up when even slightly moist, losing all its insulating quality.

FEATHERS ON YOUR BACK

Every fall back in Sweden my uncle would restuff his fishing jacket with fresh straw for the winter. I used to call it his scarecrow, even though once the double-walled coat had been filled and stitched up, no straw stuck out around the cuffs.

Straw is good, down is much better. For winter camping, down sweaters, vests, and parkas are great—if you can stand the heat. My metabolism can't take it. But there's many a snow camper who wouldn't set foot out of his tent without one.

Down parkas work on the same principle as down sleeping bags, and have two distinct advantages over wool. First, they compress fantastically in your pack, taking about a fourth the space of equivalent wool warmth. Hand in hand with this space-saving factor goes the weight-saving one. Ducks and geese fly, sheep don't. Secondly, the tightly woven nylon shell of down clothing, while it can't be made waterproof lest you find yourself in a Turkish steam bath, is considerably more wind-resistant than wool.

On the negative side, however, are some equally practical considerations. Wearing a down parka tends to be like wearing a balloon, which does make one feel awfully clumsy. Then too, if it gets wet, the insulating qualities of down are less than poor. It mats up and you can't do a thing with it. Also it can't be layered with other clothes unless your metabolism operates on a par with that of a salamander. Good for subzero camping, but rarely worth the expense otherwise.

MY KINGDOM FOR A PAIR OF PANTS

Fashion for years has raised havoc with casual pants to take camping. The tapered slacks you see in cigarette ads depicting the smoker in sylvan settings will shave the hair off your calves in two miles and scrape the epidermis off in two more. Wearing them for five miles or more I'm convinced could cripple you for life. Bell bottoms snag on underbrush and flap in the wind. In true winter weather they're just plain cold.

Work clothes and jeans used to be a natural alternative. Today, alas, even most of these are fashionably cut one way or the other. Susan did manage to unearth a pair of unmodishly straight-legged khakis somewhere just in time to replace her threadbare out-of-style jeans.

Whenever I'm lucky enough to get a baggy pair of dress or suit pants in a nonsynthetic fabric, I hoard them for camping once they're past their prime. But I remove any cuffs, since they snag easily when I'm walking through the brush. Except for some of the heavy tweeds, these pants aren't as durable as denim when it comes to sliding down rocks. In every other respect they are superior. By preference I get wool pants, and as I've said before, wool simply is the best material for outdoor wear. Army-surplus wool pants are a great bargain, when you can find them, as are leftover wool suit pants from your local thrift shop or charity bazaar. Malone makes heavy, twisted-yarn 100-percent-wool slacks that are excellent on windy winter days. For an additional plus, the pockets, where my penknife usually wears holes, are extra strong.

Another solution to the pants problem, at least in summertime, is shorts. The Little Lord Fauntleroy image that embarrassed some potential male shorts wearers has all but disappeared. They are now common among campers all over the country. A word of warning: they too must be loose. Lederhosen are great—after a couple of years' breaking in. Bermuda shorts are rarely satisfactory, binding and rubbing too much above the knee for comfortable walking. And watch the sun. If you don't, the top of your kneecaps and the back of the calves, kept under wraps ordinarily, will give you a restless night after a day in shorts.

Halfway between the long and the short are knicks. For those who grew up after the traumatic generation of boys who spent their youth waiting to graduate to "real" pants, they are ideal walking wear. I've become so fond of mine I wear them around New York on occasion —even though it means somebody inevitably approaches me to try to sell their set of used golf clubs. Knicks are not as hard to find as one might expect. Most climbers prefer knickers, so a steady, if small, market has remained for them over the years, both in wool and, for summer, corduroy. And now, with cross-country skiing beginning to boom, the *de rigueur* knicks are making a comeback. They fade in and out of women's fashions every few years, too, so if you girls grab a couple of pairs from the rack on their next reappearance, you'll be set.

Climbing knicks sometimes suffer from a shortage of pockets, but, as compensation, the ones they do have are knee-deep. They usually have a double seat, sometimes square-cut, ideal for those who spend a lot of time sitting around camp. If possible, get a pair without Velcro cuff closures. With the button-style cuff, it's easy to leave them open and roll down the knee socks when you want to cool off a bit. Velcro cuffs when left open have a tendency to catch and snag.

RAIN GEAR

All right, I admit it, I don't have a rain parka. In fact I don't have any rain gear at all. Now on occasion I've gotten wet—and I mean soaked. Like the time the skies opened up when we were hiking along a beach in the New Hebrides on our way to a village on the other side of Santos. Fourteen inches of rain in four hours wrinkled the skin like an old prune. But so would a waterproof parka have done, since it was over 80°F. Rather drown in fresh rain than my own sweat, that's all.

Then there was the time we were paddling down the interminable beginnings of Long Lake during a typical Adirondacks rainstorm. Most of the land on the southern end of Long Lake is privately owned, so we had to keep going. It rained. And rained. A ways up the lake, where its waist nips into an hourglass figure, there is a bridge. We headed for it, planning to pull under till the worst of the rain was over. When at last we reached the shelter, it turned out to be a steel grating bridge that let the rain through like a sieve. The gear was packed to stay dry, as is canoeing custom. We weren't. Fortunately, the paddling kept us warm.

There are campers like myself who don't mind getting soaked occasionally in order to save lugging around a parka that doesn't really work anyhow. Therein lies the rub. If I ever found any rain gear that kept me dry like an old yellow sou'wester I had when I was working on the cod trawlers, and if, unlike a sou'wester, it didn't weigh more than half a pound, I'd get it. But lightweight nylon shells, excellent for wind protection, barely stop a light dew; and coated nylon drenches you from the inside. Treated cotton breathes better, but in a real downpour it also leaks. Besides, it will add two to three pounds of rarely used weight to your cargo.

Still, the majority of campers prefer at least to attempt to stay dry during those hopefully rare rains. If you're one of them, a poncho may well be better than a parka.

The poncho is essentially a tent with a hole in the center and a hood to cover your head when it's in the hole. Most good ponchos are big enough to wear over your pack or rucksack, although they can't be made long enough to keep you dry below the knees, or you'd constantly trip on the corners. A good poncho will also have grommets along the edge to permit using it as a tarp. If the ground is reasonably free from sharp objects, it can be used equally well as a groundsheet. This flexibility extends the service of the poncho to the point where it may be worthwhile to have along. A rain parka, on the other hand, is limited strictly to its original function.

Ponchos range from thin plastic, good for half a trip, to urethane-coated nylon, which will last years with care. Rubber-coated cotton—remember the old Army parkas?—is heavy, not to say bulky, but it's the most waterproof of the lot.

Nylon or rubber-coated ponchos should be carefully hung up when stored. Since they tend to look crumpled even while you're wearing them, the temptation is to stuff them away in your rucksack or a bottom drawer reserved for a jumble of camp gear. However, this will cause the coating to crack, sometimes eliminating their usefulness in as short a period as a year.

FROM SEVEN-LEAGUE BOOTS TO BARE FEET

A good pair of hiking boots has its place in camping equipment. But it's by no means an exclusive place. Too many times I have seen hikers set out on well-defined, easy trails, a pair of extra-heavy trail boots weighing them down like twin ball and chains. Anything on your feet is heavy, a lot heavier than it would be in your hands. When you start looking for footgear, keep saying to yourself, "An ounce on my foot is like a pound on my back." At all times you should keep your footgear as light as the terrain will allow. Even when wearing boots—and the two activities for which they are essential are mountain climbing and skiing—stick with the lightweight models.

The Indians were the great woodsmen of North America. Many still are. And traditional Indian footwear consists almost exclusively of lightweight moccasins. Those who can walk the forest without snapping a twig know also the value of not burdening the feet unnecessarily.

Now the average urban dweller would not be able to walk any distance at all in a pair of mocs. Moccasins are thin-soled, give no support whatsoever, and become as slippery as ice to walk on when wet even from dew. The Indians' practiced feet did not feel the thinness of the soles and their lighter loads did not demand the support of boots. If you start young and use them for several years, you too can trek in moccasins. For those who don't have time for the initiation period, there are alternatives. Meanwhile moccasins are the ideal shoe to wear around camp while your hiking footwear cools off.

One of the best light walking shoes I have found is the Clark Wallabee. Available in both men's and women's sizes, it is made of soft calfskin, with a generous, shock-absorbing crepe rubber sole. It does not come up to support the ankle; however, unless this portion of your anatomy is very weak, wearing Wallabees and watching where you walk—a commonly overlooked but really quite handy habit to get into—will get you through 90 percent of the North American wilderness in comfort.

When it comes to canoeing, I would no more wear boots than

anchors on my feet. Usually I choose a pair of regulation-blue canvas boat shoes with a liberal amount of lacing, shock-absorbing crepe soles, and arch supports. They are airy and light, easy to cast off when in the boat, dry out quickly when tossed overboard by the baby, and give me adequate support when portaging an eighty-pound canoe over relatively rough terrain.

The propensity for drying out quickly is a factor not to be underrated in a shoe traveling by water, and one on which leather scores very poorly. Many's the time we've had to drag our canoe through marsh and swamp. Sinking down three feet into gook as you walk is really not an uncomfortable feeling as long as you don't have Humphrey Bogart and *The African Queen* on your mind. In fact, provided you have a pair of shoes that will protect your feet and not take a week to dry out afterwards, you may even learn to enjoy it. It's such a totally different physical experience from anything stepped on in the ordinary course of the urban or suburban day. Sneakers do just as well as boat shoes, I'm sure. I've just never liked them. Probably because I was always inept at basketball.

There will be times when you want a true walking boot: you're going to backpack over rough, trailless terrain, or heavily snowed-in country, for instance. When you do, you'll find your local camping supplier or a mountaineering shop has numerous models to choose from, and sometimes sound advice on fitting. If at all possible, avoid ordering by mail. This implies no reflection on the quality of boots stocked by mail-order houses, for they are mostly supplied by excellent manufacturers. It's merely that it is almost impossible to get a good fitting through the mailbox.

When you're trying on boots—and work shoes from Army and Navy stores—fit them while wearing the type and number of socks you expect to use. This means taking extra socks with you when you go shoe-shopping.

Most boots have heavy lugged soles, rubber or synthetic, that provide cushioning as well as good traction. The current "in" material goes under the trade name Vibram (which, as an aside, will leave large black scuff marks on your floors at home).

Uppers should be of quality leather, either suede or smooth. For years suede was sidelined because of its supposedly poor waterproofing capacity. Now it has been discovered, or rather rediscovered, that waterproofing carefully applied to the napped leather is actually held better by it than by the smooth. What you have to remember is that, quantitatively, the rougher surface takes more waterproofing. By the same token suede is the more abrasion-resistant of the two.

The fewer seams there are in your uppers, the better the boot. Uppers stitched to the midsole from the inside are rare except on quality climbing boots. However, the inside stitching makes for better waterproofing and a longer-lasting shoe. It also often trims a couple of ounces off the heavy soles, since they can then be cut closer to the shoe. Well worth the extra money if you can get a comfortable pair.

For the most part, hiking boots are cut on European lasts, and the bottom curvature of the uppers is such that you often need a half-size larger shoe than normal.

Avoid high boots that tend to cramp your calf muscles. Ankle boots are the most versatile.

Once you do select a comfortable pair of boots, break them in before you set off—or they will break you. Take short strolls around the block, mow the lawn in them, do anything that requires walking. Depending on the weight of the boots and the stiffness of the leather, it will take at least a hundred hours of use before your feet call them partner.

For that matter, never wear a new pair of any kind of shoes camping. That goes for surplus U.S. Army Tropical boots and Reichle climbers right on down to sandals and moccasins. Now I'll be the first to admit that on occasion, when I didn't have the time to break in new footwear, I've broken this rule—and I've gotten the blisters to prove it. Shoes need breaking in. The trail is no place to do it.

One for the road: Never dry shoes by a fire, or you may well be walking out on a pair of sweaters wrapped around your feet.

SOCKS THE HEIGHT OF LUXURY

The standard saying is that shoes will make or break your walking. I certainly would not minimize the importance of comfortable, well-broken-in shoes, but without good socks too, you'd probably be better off walking barefoot. Again wool comes out on top, although with knickers you may have to settle for a blend—I've found it very difficult to get all-wool knee socks. Many hikers wear a light pair of cotton or silk socks underneath their wool ones, both because they find them less scratchy against their skin and because they help reduce friction. Try it sometime, see how it feels, adopt it if it works for you.

For the most part, deserting my layering principle, I prefer one heavy ribbed pair without elastic tops. I'd rather have the sock slide down than cut off circulation.

Whatever you choose, take plenty, especially in wintertime, when you may want to sneak a pair on inside your sleeping bag for really warm cozy feet, or to double as emergency mittens when you've soaked through all the gloves you brought along. Cut your toenails before you go. And take some moleskin with you just in case. . . .

MITTENS AND GLOVES

I always carry a pair of wool driving gloves with leather palms and fingers. For winter camping, mittens will keep your hands warmer, but they turn them into two sets of thumbs and make clumsy work of almost any manual operation. The wool-and-leather gloves keep me reasonably warm; the leather fingers perform tasks wool-covered ones couldn't, especially the wintry ones like wood chopping with a slippery ax. For added warmth, blow into your gloves before putting them on.

THE OMNIBUS BANDANA

If you think the old Western bandana disappeared as Tom Mix rode over the sunset, you have another think coming. It weighs next to nothing and is as versatile as a sky hook. We usually take three apiece, using them for anything from havelocks to potholders, napkins, wash-cloths, handkerchiefs, and towels. In mosquito country, a really great way to keep the bugs away without soaking your face in insect repellent is to douse your bandana liberally with it and then wrap it around your neck. Easy to wash and literally dry in minutes on a windy or sunny day.

TOPPING IT ALL OFF

Hats aren't hitting the fashion pages much these days, but on the trail everyone has them as a protective measure against rain, sun, glare, insects, and other minor annoyances. In winter or the cool of night there's also the warmth factor. Warm feet and warm head are essential comforts; cold feet and head, pure misery. The two best trail caps are the wool stocking model for winter—Navy watch caps are great—and the crushable felt hat for summer wear. To make the felt one cooler, snip some vent holes just above the brim. You can use your imagination on what wild patterns to create with them.

WASH

When you're out of range of a Laundromat for a long time, better to rain-rinse items really in need of a cleaning than scrub up a storm of soapsuds. Pick a nice long night's downpour and set the clothes out to scrub themselves on a rock. If you must use soap, make it bio-degradable; and do your soapy wash well away from the edge of a lake or other bodies of water, except for fast-flowing streams. Hang the wash over bushes and branches to sun-dry.

Yourself? Go skinny-dipping.

STOVE YES!
KITCHEN SINK NO!

There's a certain mystique about the campfire, and rightfully so. But it has several drawbacks that should be taken into account.

For one thing, let's be honest, sometimes it's just not practical. It makes a royal mess of your pots, no matter which of the time-honored preventatives you use, including covering the outside with soap. The French Canadian and Indian guides and trappers I have met use Coleman stoves almost exclusively for cooking in the bush. Then too, sitting by a fire will make a cool evening seem very cold indeed when you leave its warm circle.

Secondly, while a campfire in the evening is cozy, warm, secure, romantic, in other words, just plain great, to really get to know the outdoors of darkness you have to give up the fire some nights. Animal life always waits till you've doused the embers to come visiting. And after a fireside muse it will take your eyes more than an hour to get the kind of night vision you would have had if you hadn't been staring into the flames.

Third and most tragic is the fact that in many campsites there's really no wood left to burn. The more popular national parks are turning into just that—parks with manicured lawns. This is no reflection on the parks, merely an indication of their heavy use. A use that in a few short years may mean that campers will have to buy firewood before entering in addition to having their axes and saws sequestered at the entrance to the park for the duration of their stay. When it comes to desert camping or venturing above the tree line, there's no wood to be had anyway. Perhaps that is just as well, for those who do venture there learn early to appreciate some of the other things a dark evening in the wilderness has to show them.

All these things help explain the growing popularity of that dependable, convenient, all-weather marvel of engineering, the camp stove. By all means plan to build a fire when it's possible, when you really need one, when you really, really want one, but take a stove along for most of your cooking.

THE LITTLE STOVES THAT COULD

The Optimus/Svea/Primus brands of stoves, products of the consolidation of Sweden's leading manufacturers in the field, are the closest thing to Aladdin's lamp modern technology has to offer. Our old Primus 71, basically the same thing as the Optimus 80, has had a rough, durable life. Soaked in a canoe spill, flooded with lentils from a tipped pot, banged and dented in packs of bags from Maine to Manitoba, after ten years it endures faithful to beck and call for yet another pot of tea or stew. It seems almost indecent to ask service of it any longer, and recently we purchased a Svea 123. But that was actually because the Svea fits into a Sigg cook kit, which the Primus does not. Camp stoves have indeed come a long way from the cumbersome suitcase models of the past.

WHITE GAS STOVES

The Primus 71, weighing twenty ounces, and the Svea 123, eighteen ounces, are compact little stoves that utilize white, or unleaded, gas and need no priming. They are miracles of efficiency. We usually manage to cook anywhere from four to eight hot meals on one filling of the Primus's half-pint tank, depending on the menu, the altitude, and the temperature. The Svea 123 tank has a slightly smaller capacity, a third of a pint. Both stoves fit in the palm of your hand.

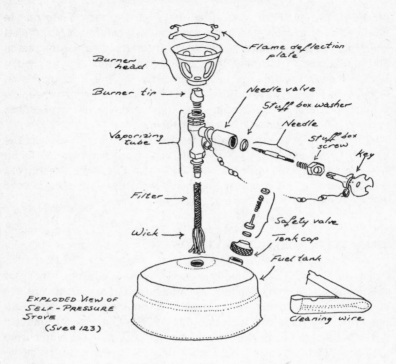

Burner head

Flame deflection plate

Burner tip

Needle valve

Stuff box washer

Needle

Stuff box screw

Key

Vaporizing tube

Filter

Wick

Safety valve

Tank cap

Fuel tank

EXPLODED VIEW OF SELF-PRESSURE STOVE (Svea 123)

Cleaning wire

Even eight hot meals, of course, aren't enough for most camping trips. To carry spare white gas, you'll need one of the slim spun-aluminum bottles usually sold wherever the stoves are. These have gasketed screw tops. Although they may look as if they might leak, they never do—at least not the first half-dozen years. After that I've found it best to replace the gasket.

Additionally, you will need a doll-sized funnel, preferably with a fine mesh filter as an extra precaution against impurities. The funnel enables you to pour gas from the bottle into the stove without spilling. A tiny shielded cleaning wire mounted on a flat aluminum blade comes with each stove. Use it. Just poke it through the flame hole once or twice each time before lighting the stove. That's to make certain nothing has clogged this vital orifice.

Most of the small white gas stoves work on the self-pressure principle. The heat of the flame expands the gas below, forcing it as vapor up through the flame hole. If the hole is clogged, the vaporized gas has to go somewhere else or the stove would explode like a Molotov cocktail. To this end there is a safety valve. However, I've never had any problems with mine, nor do I know anyone who has. There are stories about safety valves blowing, told by friends who had friends who had friends. . . . I've never been able to trace a rumor down to anyone who actually had the stove go up under him. I'm sure if I did I would find it was because he either failed to use his cleaning wire or poured in regular gasoline from his local gas station. Even service stations that do sell white gas, incidentally, do not have it as purified as the white gas especially filtered for camping stoves. Use Coleman gas or another well-known brand. It's more expensive, but worth it. You're not filling up the car, remember. Just a pint bottle or two will do.

To ready the stove, check that the valve is closed, then fill the tank about three-quarters of the way up with gas. Never fill it completely. There has to be room for the fluid to expand into gas vapor. Otherwise the stove won't function well; in fact, a jet of fuel will shoot from the burner as soon as you open the valve, probably scaring the daylights out of you. Put the cap back on as soon as you've filled the tank.

Next, take the cleaning wire and poke it into the burner hole a couple of times to make sure it's clear. Do it even the first time you try out a brand-new stove, just to get into the habit. Another habit to get into is putting the cleaning wire back in the base, lid, or windscreen of the stove—someplace, in other words, where you won't forget it when you go to pack the stove up again.

Now there are several available choices in next steps, depending on whose school you follow. The object is to heat up the fuel tank to initiate vaporization of the gasoline. The original instructions that came with the trusty Primus were to cup the tank firmly in your hands so the 98.6°F. temperature of your body builds up the pressure. Then when you open the valve, gasoline is forced out of the burner hole and into the saucerlike depression surrounding the bottom of the vaporizing tube. It works. However, it takes time. If it's cold out, you may in fact have enough time to whistle Beethoven's Ninth from beginning to end before you get your morning coffee.

The second method is to use an eyedropper to siphon off some gas from the spare fuel bottle or the stove tank, and then squirt a couple of drops on the vaporizing tube and into the depression. Among other things, however, an eyedropper is just one extra item to lose, break, or drop into the tank.

Some campers carry a separate bottle of alcohol to fill the saucer with, on the theory that it leaves no soot and burns better, which it doesn't. It does add an extra bottle.

Then there's my way. I just pick up the stove, unscrew the filler cap on the tank, and huff and puff until I've driven enough fuel out the burner to get some down into the vaporizing depression. Then I screw the filler cap back on. This method requires cocking your head and keeping the stove relatively vertical. Also, drinking gasoline is most unhealthy, so don't let your mind wander and absent-mindedly think you're holding onto a canteen. There is no reason why you should get gasoline in your mouth if you're careful and no one slaps your back heartily while you're huffing. If you should, spit it out. I am what I would call relatively careful and have never had a mouthful of trouble.

Whichever method you choose to get the fuel from the inside to the outside, your next step is to close the needle valve. Then light the gasoline on the outside. It will flare up somewhat melodramatically. (It might be a good idea to try it out a few times at home, in the familiarity of your backyard, to get used to the reaction. For that matter, it's a wise idea to try out any new camping equipment before you leave home with it.) When the flames are just about to go out, open the needle valve about three-quarters of a turn. The stove should leap into action with a lightly roaring blue flame. The first or second time you try it, the flame may be a sputtering yellow. That means you didn't use enough priming gas and the pressure is too low. Close the valve and let the stove cool off a few minutes. Start over again.

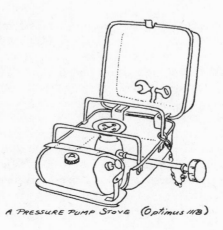

A PRESSURE PUMP STOVE (Optimus 111B)

It's not as much trouble as it might sound. But if it's already too much for you, the ultimate stove—and there's no such thing as the perfect one for everybody—might well be the self-cleaning Optimus 111B. It's larger, weighing three and a half pounds. However, it has a manually operated pump to build up pressure, simplifying the lighting operation, also making the stove more efficient in high altitudes, say over 12,000 feet, and in below-zero weather. It will bring a quart of water to a boil in four minutes, compared to six for the Primus 71L. In addition, the one-pint-capacity tank holds enough fuel for almost two hours.

A last-but-not-least advantage to compensate for the stove's greater weight is steadiness. It sits much lower, making spilling less of a probability than with the tall, quite unstable self-pressured models.

The Optimus 22B is a twin-burner version of the 111B weighing six and three-quarter pounds. Good for extended family camping. However, two 111Bs actually give you more flexibility in the outdoor kitchen when you reach the stage where one burner no longer suffices.

After all that is said, I still stick with my Primus 71 and Svea 123.

"They've never let me down," shrugged the lumberjack, tugging at his suspenders, "so why should I get rid of them?"

KEROSENE BURNERS

Some campers who are a bit leery of gasoline buy kerosene stoves. Since kerosene is less volatile than gas, it's less dangerous. However, the only serious accident I know of involving a camp stove occurred when someone put gasoline in a kerosene stove and ended up with a fireball. He wasn't a complete fool, for you can use gasoline in a roar-burner-equipped kerosene stove. But leave that to the really experienced camper in an emergency. There is no control valve on a kerosene stove; filled with gasoline, it can literally become a bomb.

Fond as I am of them—and that's because the smell of kerosene pervaded my uncle's fishing hut when I was a kid—kerosene stoves are a noxious, smoky mess. There's no earthly reason to take one camping unless you're heading for regions like Afghanistan or the Andes where getting any variety in fuels is a problem. Kerosene is always available, and stoves like the Optimus OO roar burner don't care whether they are dirty or clean. This single factor makes a kerosene stove indispensable in very remote or primitive areas. Anywhere else, stay with the white gas stoves.

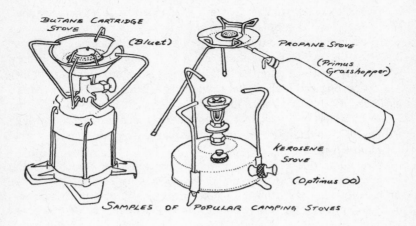

Samples of popular camping stoves

BUTANE CARTRIDGE STOVES

Butane stoves, although on the market for only a decade or so in Europe and considerably less time here, are by far the biggest-selling single-burner stoves for lightweight camping. I just toss that in, before I say I wouldn't use one unless you paid me—fairly well at that—so you can make up your own mind.

Butane is easy to light. Just use a match the way you would on the stove back home when the pilot light isn't on. You don't have to worry about spilling. However, butane is much heavier in relation to the amount of heat you get, is ten times as expensive as gasoline, and takes two to three times as long to heat a given amount of water. Butane stoves are next to worthless below freezing, and at 15°F. the fuel turns to slush so you can forget about it altogether. High-altitude cooking with butane also does not work well.

As far as the safety factor goes, I don't understand why people worry so about gasoline stoves when they've got butane ones to worry about. The butane, being under pressure, will occasionally leak out in your pack. The smallest problem then is its atrocious smell. There is no way to tell how much fuel is left, so a number of times you end up changing cartridges halfway through cooking your meal. And even an empty cartridge has enough vapor left in it to blow an arm off, should someone be crazy enough to change it near a campfire. If a full cartridge happens to get punctured with a spark-producing metal object—well, *c'est la vie*.

PROPANE STOVES

Propane eliminates most of the problems of butane, although its cold-weather and altitude efficiency is not up to that of white gas. The problem here, however, is one of weight. The smallest one-burner propane stove, the Primus 2361 Grasshopper, weighs twelve ounces, which is good. But a cylinder with six hours' burning time weighs almost two pounds, which is very bad.

STOVE COMPARISONS

Stove	Dimensions (inches when packed)	Weight (ounces)	Fuel Capacity (pints)	Burning Time for Fuel Tank at Capacity (minutes at sea level)	Boiling Time (minutes for 1 qt. water at sea level)	Fuel Type
Svea 123	4¾ × 4¾ × 5	18	0.35	45	6.0	Gasoline
Optimus 80	3¾ × 3¾ × 5½	19	0.45	60	8.75	Gasoline
Optimus 111B	4 × 6¾ × 7	54	1.0	90	4.0	Gasoline
Grasshopper	3¾ × 3¾ × 18	42	1.7	360	9.5	Propane
Bluet	3½ × 4½ × 9½	16	0.8	190	12.0	Butane
Optimus 00	3½ × 5½ × 7	37	1.0	90	4.5	Kerosene

ALCOHOL STOVES

A lot of small boats are fitted out with alcohol stoves because if you spill the alcohol and it seeps down into the bilge, you won't have an explosion. Alcohol is nonexplosive, almost nontoxic, and thus used to appeal to campers a bit nervous about their ability to handle gas stoves. Either those campers' nerves have steadied or they've switched to propane or butane. Whatever the case, these stoves, which admittedly take three times as long to cook with as gas, seem to have vanished from the camping market.

STERNO

Ideal for heating cocktail hot dogs to the point of being lukewarm. Use one can per dog.

STOVES AND THE WIND

Most stoves come with a wind screen of one kind or another. Varying from inefficient to barely tolerable, they will permit the use of the stove in gentle zephyrs. However, once the real winds start blowing, you have to place the stove in a well-protected place. This is not the fault of the stove manufacturers. By necessity, stoves must be liberally vented and quite exposed. Otherwise they could not function.

A rocky crevice, the shelter of a log—which in turn makes a handy if not flat-topped cook's table—or even the lee of the tent will usually suffice to block the wind. Find a shielded spot before you start cooking if there's a gale about. Having to shift all your gear and relight a put-out stove is a nuisance.

THE WELL-LIT GALLEY

Lamps are not for cooking on, it's true. But since they're your only other piece of camping equipment that uses fuel, let's include them here. Also the most functional use for a lantern is to cook by its light in a camp that has been set up unavoidably late. Not only that, but food tastes better when you can see it. Daylight is the best lighting for setting up camp and putting dinner on, but if it's already gone, well, you've got to manage without it somehow.

Before I go further, let me add that my experience with camp lanterns is limited. I never take one along on my own trips, seeing little need for anything but a flashlight to flip on momentarily to locate an elusive pair of socks for sleeping in or to check out the terrain when nature calls unexpectedly on a dark moonless night. I simply plan on making camp early, woods-life style. Those few occasions when the elements change my plans for me, I use the flashlight to find the salt shaker too. A bright Coleman will kill your night vision for several hours—a pity if you wish to enjoy the wilds.

As an extreme example of the overuse of lanterns, I remember one evening north of Burwash in the Yukon. It was a cool crisp night with small raggedy clouds drifting occasionally across the sky. We'd set up camp off the road—the Alcan Highway offers well-appointed camping facilities, but unfortunately they are invariably right next to the road. The stars came out with our evening coffee, the millions of them that one never sees with city lights around or even in the distance. What more could one ask for?

A tent trailer pulled in. Up it went. On came the lamps. It glowed like a newly landed flying saucer. But the party had been considerate enough to choose the far end of the campsite, so the glow didn't bother us much. We simply turned our backs and continued looking skyward.

Then, as if on cue, it began. A glimmer of misty light in the north sky, then more, and more. The darkness began to phosphoresce with the colored curtains of the aurora borealis. We watched for hours. It was a night for sleeping out, but when the clouds edging over the sky began shedding flakes of snow, we voted against it and headed reluctantly for the tents. The lights in the tent trailer by then had been extinguished. Its occupants had never come out, never known the heavens were alight. They had missed a great deal inside their lantern-lit cocoon.

There is the argument that long winter nights at least necessitate a lantern, particularly up north. And here I would agree to some extent. When you're down to eight hours of light a day or less, night can seem very long. You may want to read the maps or sew up some rips in your gear. Then you will need a lantern. But for the most part the nights are bright enough to see where you're going and what you're doing. A storm is another matter. But then during a storm you'll probably be snuggled up sleepily in your tent anyhow.

Quiet evenings under the stars, or in a tent lit only by the shadowed tracery of moonlight through the tree branches, talking to your companions, are experiences not to be missed. In an era where "I talk, you listen" has become the norm, where people keep one eye glued to the TV while conversing disjointedly out of the side of the mouth, and ride to work in little glass boxes, with only the one-way blabber of a wake-up-it's-another-miserable-morning disc jockey for companionship—in this era conversation totally unstructured except by the proximity of two or more individuals otherwise isolated in the great outdoors sometimes comes with difficulty. But once you've stepped through the door of silence, you may be surprised at what you find on the other side. So if you do bring a lantern, use it sparingly.

LANTERNS FOR EVERY PURPOSE

The predominant camp lantern today is the Coleman mantle type
burning white gas. A multiple-use convenience if you have a stove
consuming the same fuel. These lanterns produce light equivalent to
a 200- or 300-watt light bulb, depending on the model. They are
clean, efficient, easy to use, hot, and terribly bright. If you want to
curl up by the river bank late Sunday night with that day's edition of
The New York Times, there's no doubt that this is the lantern for
the purpose.

The old-fashioned kerosene lantern, of which there are many
models, turns out a fraction of the wattage a gas model does. It is also
messier, as kerosene always is. Again, however, if you use a kerosene
stove, consider a fuel-compatible lantern. They don't get hot enough
to be a real hazard, burn for twelve to fifteen hours on a filling, and
give a warm, glowing light. Psychologically the difference in light
coloration between gas and kerosene is equivalent to that between
fluorescent and incandescent lighting, only much more so.

There are also propane and butane lamps to match the stoves.
With the butane you really gain nothing by the compatibility, however, since most butane cartridges, like those produced by Bleuet,
cannot be removed from either the stove or the lamp until empty. You
can't switch a half-full cartridge back and forth. Also you again have
the poor efficiency at high altitudes and low temperatures.

Propane cylinders can be switched from stove to lamp and vice
versa. With some foreign makes, like Primus, you may have to
get an adapter in order to use American-made fuel cylinders. However, there is the added plus that, except for the small disposable
bottles, propane tanks can be refilled. Not only does this save you
money, but you won't be lugging back empty cylinders for nothing.
Nor will the temptation to leave them behind in the wilderness be
there. Sad to say, I've already found numerous disposable butane
cartridges discarded in the wilds, and they haven't been with us for
more than a few years yet. Propane is better in high altitudes and low
temperatures than butane, but nowhere near as good as pressurized
white gas.

THE CAMPFIRE

Now the first thing usually discussed when it comes to a campfire is which wood is best. A noble pursuit. However, the best wood for a campfire is the kind you find at your campsite. Hickory is excellent for charcoaling steaks. It gives you great hot coals for any kind of cooking. But if you're in an evergreen forest, this information is of precious little use. The same goes for the other hardwoods. If they aren't around, you can't use them. Conversely, if you are in a primarily leafy forest, most of the trees will be hardwoods, and so you will use them.

About the only practical consideration here is that meat roasted over resinous woods such as pine, spruce, and fir sometimes acquires a sharp resiny taste. If one of these is the only wood available, let it burn down till it's almost reduced to coals. The coals will not be as hot nor last as well as those of the hardwoods, so cooking will take longer. But by giving the resin time to burn away, you avoid an off-flavor.

When you go wood-gathering, remember the old Indian adage: "White man build big fire, stand far away. Indian build small fire, sit close." Keep your fires small. It not only makes them safer, but conserves wood. I know that sounds a bit picky. After all, there you are in the middle of a big forest. A few logs, what can they matter? Well, I've seen campfires that chewed up ten two-foot-long eight-inch-diameter logs in an evening. That's the equivalent of a small tree.

Let's look at what happens. There were probably about fifty million campers in North America last year. Now not all of them built roaring fires every night. But some were out for two or three weeks, so let's just call it fifty million times seven days, which eliminates the pyromaniacs. Seven times fifty million is three hundred and fifty million. Assuming for convenience' sake 3.5 persons to a party, that leaves a hundred million fires, each one representing one small tree. At, say, a hundred trees per acre, this would mean clearing a million acres annually just to keep the fires burning bright on the campfire hearth. "TNSTAAFL," * as they used to say around the old taverns.

So keep your campfires small. Don't chop down a thing, the green

---

* *There's No Such Thing as a Free Lunch.*

wood won't burn anyhow. Limit your wood-gathering strictly to fallen branches and deadwood. Just downed limbs should suffice in almost any location.

WHERE TO BUILD THE FIRE

There's a school of camping today which advocates tearing down your fireplace and putting all the stones back exactly where you found them when you break camp. Although I can appreciate the motivation behind this "leave everything the way it was" concept, when it comes to fireplaces it just isn't wise except in the most remote areas. Camping is by now so widespread, and really good campsites on popular trails and canoe routes so relatively hard to find, that this overneatness is often more destructive than helpful.

Take the La Vérendrye canoeing area in Quebec Province, for instance. You're allowed to camp anywhere along the lakes and rivers. But just try it! The forest, coming right down and sticking its toes in the water's edge, is simply too dense. Invariably one ends up at a semiestablished campsite, frequently one where boulders have been arranged rather sloppily into a fireplace. Where they haven't been, you end up arranging some yourself, but if it's been a long day's paddle, your job is apt to be just as sloppy and hurried. Far better than trying to scatter the blackened stones into a natural setting before departing the next day is improving the fireplace so that parties to come don't try to build yet another one a few feet away. Too often we've arrived at campsites with a whole circle of charcoaled earth and half-burned litter where campers have built multiple fireplaces instead of salvaging the old. And in any campsite used half a dozen times during a summer, the good rocks, having been moved back and forth from natural position to fireplaces half a dozen times, can't possibly be made to look natural again.

Finding a neat fireplace, especially one with enough wood stacked beside it to start a fire, campers following you will be attracted to the same spot, rather than setting up a couple of hundred feet away, scarring the wilderness all over again for no reason. Signs of man's intrusion into the wilds will be minimized rather than multiplied. Granted, it also means that when you arrive at a site with a fireplace already neatly built, you won't feel like you're the first mortal ever to tread that trail. But then again, you knew that anyhow.

A fireplace is most safely built on a rock outcropping. A sandy stretch or hard-packed, stony, or claylike mineral soils are also good. But building on loamy ground with a high content of organic material, particularly in heavily forested country, can mean igniting subterranean roots, which sometimes smolder for weeks before resurfacing, yards away from the original, long since forgotten fire.

A tree will make a million matches, and it only takes one match to destroy a million trees. You can never be too careful. Forest fires are immensely destructive. I'm hesitant to add, except to be factual about it, that they do—rarely—serve a quite useful function. Modern forestry has discovered that once-in-a-blue-moon fires—by razing, say, a stand of old trees ready to die and preparing the earth for another cycle of growth—fulfill a natural purpose. Which shouldn't come as a surprise, since nature's been setting just such fires from time immemorial. But don't you start a forest fire; this is no place to decide to help Mother Nature.

Several factors besides the ground conditions dictate the location of your fire. There should be no overhanging branches lower than ten feet above the flames. Squaw wood, the dead limbs still held fast to a tree—which, incidentally, make good firewood and whose removal does no damage—should be even higher.

Don't, don't build the fire on a promontory or other exposed place. The wind that springs up the moment you've got the fire going will fan the flames, making them burn well. Too well. You'll use much more wood than necessary; it will heat poorly, since cold air will constantly replace the warm; and most important, you'll greatly increase the danger of forest fire. A good gust will not only pick up sparks and send them flying, but sometimes carry off even a two- or three-inch-long twig or splinter, whose weight has been reduced to almost nothing by burning, but whose center is still glowing hot.

A last consideration, one of comfort, is smoke. Here I'm supposed to tell you to make sure the fire is so located in relation to your tent that the smoke stays away. Good luck, Charlie Brown. I don't ever seem to build a fire that sends the smoke where it's supposed to. Still, it's worth a try guessing in which direction the fickle wind is least likely to blow.

I camp with a smoke catcher these days. Sitting by an evening fire or watching the coffee come to a boil, I'm no longer plagued with smarting throat and tearing eyes. Unfortunately, smoke catchers fall in that almost mythical class of camping equipment that also includes sky hooks and left-handed stake adjusters. Mine consists of Susan, who for some inexplicable reason always pulls the smoke with her, no matter which side of the fire she moves to. It's totally senseless, unscientific, even ridiculous. But Susan's the closest thing to a smoke magnet I've ever seen.

THE FIREPLACE

A camp fireplace serves two functions: to contain the fire and to balance your grill or pan if you're cooking over it. Although there are countless designs serving these purposes, you're best off sticking with either the U or the keyhole.

Both are built with rocks. One warning, however: Don't get your rocks from a stream. Porous ones will have enough moisture in them to form steam when heated. They will split with an ear-shattering explosion. Usually the detonation is harmless enough, though not always. And if you had a grill balanced on one of these mini-mines, your supper will be all over the ground.

The U-fireplace is just what its name implies: rocks forming a U, one end open for feeding the wood in, the back closed off to reflect the heat forward. You don't need to be a stone mason, one layer of large rocks will do. No large rocks around? You may have to stack small ones two layers high. If so, don't worry about cracks and holes in the wall. It should be steady, but wind chinks will assure a good supply of air for your fire.

The keyhole fireplace is, again, just what the name implies. Round at one end and tapering to a six- or eight-inch-wide slit at the other, it is very functional. You burn wood in the circle. As coals form, you poke them over into the slot. Your cooking is thus not subjected to the vagrancies of leaping flames, but has an even, constant coal heat.

KEYHOLE FIREPLACE

STARTING A FIRE

It is possible to start a fire with a fire drill or flint and steel. It is also possible to swim the English Channel. Both require skill and training. Primitive fire starting makes fine reading when you're sitting at home in a rocking chair, a hot cup of cocoa by your side. As for actually employing the methods, far better to carry a good supply of waterproof matches squirreled away in three or four different pockets of your gear and clothing. Even the old trick of using a magnifying glass or a pair of eyeglasses to concentrate the sun's rays to ignite tinder falls more under the category of interesting than practical. Who takes a magnifying glass on a weekend outing? And what if you don't wear glasses? And where is the sun? The times when you really need an emergency fire are bound to be the times when it's been raining as if it were going to be forty days and forty nights again rather than the fire next time.

Besides matches, you need three things to start a fire easily and well: tinder, kindling, and fuel. Tinder traditionally ranges from dry moss and lichen to old mouse nests. Having never found any mice, old or otherwise, around my campsites, though I'll admit to a couple of shrews, I look instead for match-sized sticks. Gather a batch of small, dry twigs and make a miniature teepee or pyramid of them. This is your tinder, equivalent to primer for a gas stove.

If it's been raining heavily or you're in a swamp, you may have to tuck some fire starter—another small item to remember to stow away in odd crannies of your gear—inside the kindling. Either fire ribbon or solid tablets like Hexamine and Heatabs work surprisingly well. Leftover candle stubs will do, but they just don't turn out the same BTUs.

Next you need some kindling, because tinder will not generate enough heat to ignite most fuel-sized chunks of wood or logs. Kindling consists of pencil-sized and slightly larger branches. Make a pyramid of these over the tinder.

Leave some air space between the tinder below and the kindling above, some more space between the kindling sticks themselves. If you want a rule of thumb, the distance between two burning pieces of wood, be they twigs or logs, should be about half their diameter. This interval is vital not only to permit circulation of the necessary oxygen, but also to reflect the heat back and forth between the two sticks. It's very difficult to keep one log burning well. The flame from one log burning is about the same as the sound of one hand clapping. Two of them with space in between will burn just fine.

Fallen branches and squaw wood that you've gathered follow the tinder. In a state or national park where logs are available, they can be split into one- or two-inch pieces. Build their teepee so the flat sides do not lie face to the fire, but are wedged so the flames will lick two sides at once. The more surface area there is exposed to the flames, the better the fire will take.

Now just light the tinder and your campfire should soon be burning merrily. As a last word, frying fish is better done over the fire than on a stove; they tend to stick to the pan less. The campfire is also a good place to keep the coffee hot when you don't want to keep your stove lit. A good camper should be able to get all the fire he needs for these purposes from one large fallen branch. Tinder from the twigs at its tips, kindling from the branchlets, and fuel from the main bough broken into six- or seven-inch-long pieces. Give it a try next time.

QUENCHING THE FIRE

At the risk of sounding like Smoky the Bear's cousin, let me add that the fire must be out before you go to sleep or leave camp. Not just the flames gone, but completely out, every vestige of spark. Stir up the ashes and sprinkle water over everything. Sprinkling is much more effective than just throwing a bucketful of water over the remains. Most people are rather nervous about getting burned. Look at the coals of the fire you've extinguished. Seem to be out, right? Would you be willing to stick your finger into what used to be the glowing embers? No? You probably know you haven't put it out well enough if you hesitate.

THE COOK KIT

It's confusion time again. Till recently we never used a proper camping cook kit. Sometimes we just dragged some kitchenware with us: a covered, metal-handled pot, a small, lightweight steel frypan, and the bottom half of our drip coffeepot. This explains why we have a two-tone coffeepot. The bottom half is pitch-black, the stay-at-home top burnished aluminum. Still, no one ever refuses a cup of coffee from it. And the first week after we get home from the mountains, the kitchen always has a pleasant aroma of the woods about it as the pitch, pine sap, and other forest goo burn off the pot when we heat coffee.

A one-pound coffee can nests in a two-pound coffee can which nests in a three-pound coffee can. Add a pair of pliers for lifting the cans when hot, and you have a perfectly adequate cook kit for quick soups and stews and such. For covered-pot cookery, add a steel fry-pan to the kit, which obviously you'll also use sometimes on its own merits. The nesting-coffee-can kitchen has the additional advantage of being disposable when you return home. Some old-timers swear the stew tastes better from a can—#10 cans are also used a lot—than a pot.

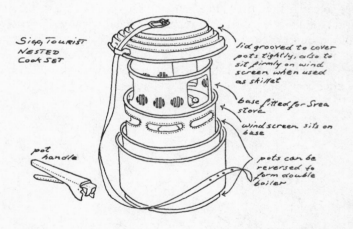

Sigg Tourist Nested Cook Set

lid grooved to cover pots tightly, also to sit firmly on wind screen when used as skillet

base fitted for Svea stove

wind screen sits on base

pot handle

pots can be reversed to form double boiler

A store-bought nesting kit is not too costly and can be a real convenience. Since we got our Svea 123, we've been using a Sigg Tourist set, because the Svea packs neatly inside. The Sigg was designed with precisely the Svea 123 in mind and includes a good wind screen for it. With the Sigg kit, you can bring soup to a boil in the big pot, then cook a main dish in the second pot, nesting the soup pot on top to keep everything warm. The kit cover also works as a frypan. Or is supposed to. It makes a swell cover though.

Smilie also puts out good cook kits, along with, by the way, one of the best selections of outdoor cook gear. There's a two-pot nesting kit which holds the Svea 123, and a two-pot-and-wind-screen combination for the Optimus 00 kerosene stove. There are kits ranging from the one-man mess to the six-man mulepack.

SKILLETS

Teflon has hit the camping market. I don't like it in general, but I thought I'd better mention it. Aluminum is acceptable for pots and pans. But not for the skillet. I'd love to suggesting taking along a cast-iron one. There's nothing better. However, it's a millstone around the neck I wouldn't carry even on a canoe trip unless I thought I might need an anchor. That leaves steel.

There are some good steel frying pans on the market, and if you hope to catch any fish, or like ham and eggs for breakfast, they are a must. A nine-inch model with removable handle will weigh twelve to eighteen ounces, almost twice as much as its aluminum counterpart. But bring steel or none at all, that's my motto. In case you've never used steel frypans before, by the way, make sure to dry them by the fire after use. They rust.

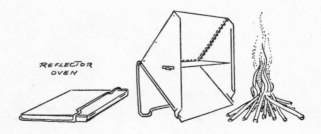

REFLECTOR
OVEN

THE OVEN

On any long trip except a backpacking one, we take a reflector oven. Ours weighs less than three pounds and supplies a seemingly endless quantity of biscuits, trail pies, and even bread. Some of the imported or ethnic-bakery pumpernickels and dark whole-grain breads will easily last two weeks on the trail. After that you're on your own. If, like me, you don't fill up easily living and gadding about in all that fresh country air, want bread for bulk and quick sandwich lunches, and biscuits to mop up the gravy and drippings with, consider a reflector oven. Requires a wood fire.

THE GRILL

I can't be persuaded to give up my oven; on the other hand, I never take a grill to the wilds. But there are plenty of people who do. A light stainless-steel-tube backpacker's model weighs less than three ounces. Usually fifteen and a half by four and a half inches in size, it's good for balancing pots on over an open fire. Not so good for roasting steaks on, since there are only three crossbars, and the steak invariably drapes over the center one, hanging down between the other two and losing all its juices. Hamburgers fall through immediately.

The larger knapsack models, nine by thirteen inches, have wide crossbars on one half for pots, closely spaced ones on the other half for grilling. Usually weigh around eight ounces. Can be packed in the same bag as the reflector oven.

COOKING UTENSILS

If you want pancakes or eggs over light, take a lightweight spatula with you. The G.I. can opener weighs an eighth of an ounce and is well worth having along even if you don't carry any canned goods. It costs next to nothing, and you may decide on a can of sardines before you reach the trail head.

Planning to have baked potatoes? We just toss them in among the coals. If you don't like blackened skins, take aluminum foil.

As a last thought, a pair of pot grippers or tongs is handy. Some kits, like the Sigg, where such a device is indispensable, come with them. Others do not. Rather than a standard camp model, I like a pair of lightweight, long-handled, wire-cutter-equipped pliers. I file one handle tip down to serve as an emergency screwdriver.

CARRYING THE GROCERIES

The invention of the Baggie and other polybags was a real boon to the camper. We pack into them all dry goods—flour, sugar, powdered milk, rice, cereals, dehydrated potatoes, vegetables, etc. The only exception we make is the coffee. A one-pound can just fits in our coffeepot, and that's where it travels.

A number of small bags are better than a few large ones. Double one inside another for added puncture-proofing, fill and tie tightly, and label the things you won't recognize on sight. So filled, the bags in turn pack nicely into odd corners of bigger things, such as the cook kit, outside pockets of the rucksack, the top of a liberal sleeping bag stuff sack. Keep the most often used items the handiest.

Gerry puts out a bottom-loading polytube that is indispensable for the gooey staples like jam, honey, cashew or peanut butter (the nut butters, incidentally, are good protein for meatless days on the trail). It's essentially a plastic toothpaste tube with an open bottom into which you spatula the goodies. Once full, the bottom is folded over and closed with a clip. To use it camping, just unscrew the cap and squeeze out as much as you want. A warning to you middle-of-the-toothpaste-tube squeezers who've never gotten what's coming to you. Squeeze from the bottom, or the clip may well pop open, filling your sleeve. These tubes don't last forever, but they are good for a couple of long seasons.

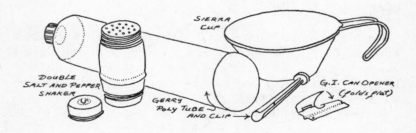

Polybags and polytubes are by now standard on our camping trips. But there are numerous other lightweight, unbreakable polycontainers to choose from—egg carriers (we just use the ones they come in), wide-mouthed bottles, boxes, and vials. Also aluminum provision cans with screw-top lids and hermetically sealing gaskets. These are becoming rare—unfortunately so, for they're really leakproof, and the only thing adequate to the job of containing maple syrup through thick and thin. Buy your maple syrup in tins rather than jars, at least, if you don't buy one of these.

Aluminum combination-salt-and-pepper shakers, double-lidded, come in pretty handy for the lunch bag. We pick up extras for dried herbs, bouquets garnis, and such pinches of this and that for the stewpot.

Last on the list is something big enough to fit most of these items and then some into. You'll sometimes want to hang the food at night (on which more in the next chapter). A net string bag will do in good weather. A coated nylon stuff bag is what we've found handiest. It stows away compactly when not in use, and is an extra all-weather carrier for daytime gear.

THE MESS KIT

It seems strange. People will spend half a week's wages to go to a fancy restaurant and dine on Swiss fondue, each member of the party dipping gamely into the center chafing dish. Yet when you suggest that the only way to dine in camp is for everybody to eat from the same stewpot so there aren't a lot of extra dishes to wash, they look at you as if you are spreading the plague. No matter that you're out in the woods trying to leave the worries of ordinary mortals, including dish-washing, behind. My suggestion is still to leave most of the dishes home.

Our usual dining gear consists of a Sierra cup, a fork, and a fairly generous spoon apiece. Lick off between courses if you don't like peas in your coffee. On extended trips where fresh meat will be available via occasional forays into villages, or where we suspect wild blue-berries might be in season for pancakes, we may throw in a couple of dented aluminum plates. At best they're difficult to hold and don't retain heat well. As to paper plates, well. . . . And then, of course, there are our pocketknives. But that's the lot. However, there are many complete plastic, Melmac, and aluminum sets available if you go for sets. As you spend more and more time camping, though, you'll probably pare down the gear.

DOING THE DISHES

No matter how hard one tries to minimize them, there are those inevitable pots and pans and maybe dishes to wash. Scrape the scraps, if there are any, into the bush for the local wildlife. Well into it if one of the locals is a bear—a hundred yards is not too far for me in grizzly country. Use a biodegradable soap, and don't wash by the river or stream's edge in anything but the remotest areas or where the water flows swiftly. Instead, carry water in your largest pot to a spot well inland and scrub the pots there. Some people like a collapsible water bottle for toting the water. They come in one- to five-gallon sizes and weigh only a couple of ounces, though they are a bit unwieldy to fold into the cook bag.

Sand and gravel make excellent scouring material. A plastic scrub pad is easier on your hands. When grease is the problem, and the fire is still going for the coffeepot or you've plenty of fuel for the stove, boil the pots clean. That's the easiest way of all.

PROVISIONING

Childhood memories certainly run strong, don't they? On any camping trip, except when I'm backpacking and thus more weight conscious, I take along a can of beans and some franks. Just enough for a first meal. Susan swallows the fare stoically, although with amusement. But I can't help it. My early camping as a kid always included franks and canned beans as well as canned ravioli. While I wouldn't choose either under normal circumstances, when the hunger of the outdoors combines with semiprimeval memories, I gobble them down. It's just an aside. I certainly don't recommend lugging around canned ravioli.

What I do recommend—and it's caused more than one jaw to drop —is that if you're a party of four or more heading for regions where campfires are still possible, you take a leg of lamb with you for the first night's camp. Again a feat not for the backpacker, unless you intend to stop over at the trail head before going bush. But if you're paddling a canoe, letting the gear ride on a toboggan pulled behind while snowshoeing, or setting up a base camp, there's nothing quite like a christening cookout.

If you're a good hunter, of course, it's another story. I'm not. In fact I have a certain fear of camping during hunting season. As with anything else, there are careful hunters—those who hunt for food, stay within the limits of conservation, and in fact fill the function of the predators that are being driven to extinction by the other kind of hunter. That's the one who goes only for trophies, doesn't care if the game is in season, and would just as soon shoot a doe in July if he knew he'd get away with it. Or worse.

One game warden was telling me about a couple of Easterners who arrived in Montana a year ago. They laid out hundreds and hundreds of dollars for their equipment, licenses, and transportation. So, to save money, they decided to skip the guide and set out into the woods to get a moose on their own. They were in luck. Lashed the carcass proudly across the hood of the car—a mistake to begin with, since the heat from the engine will spoil the meat—and started back to town. On the way they were stopped at a game-checking station by this particular ranger.

"Morning. See you got one."

"Yeah, on our last day too. Boy, were we lucky. Next year we'll be back to get a bull with a real rack. These females don't make much of a trophy."

"Well that one sure won't."

"Why not?"

"It's a mule, you jackass."

But returning to the leg of lamb. Camping takes many of us back to a lustier, seminomadic existence we were never part of, but would like to have been, for a while at least. And an evening by a fire spit-roasting a leg of lamb can produce one of the most memorable dinners of the year, making the suburban barbecue seem like eating at your local drive-in hamburger stand.

Build up a good coal fire. You don't want many flames, unless you like lamb black on the outside and cold and raw on the inside. The fat from the lamb will drip down, causing the coals to burst into sputtering protest and smoke. But what a smoke, what an aroma. It's like sitting around the steppes with Genghis Khan waiting for the feast to begin. You can't help but salivate a little. Your jaw gets sharp and tense as you turn the spit.

About the only equipment you need for this perfect meal is a long wooden or metal skewer to drive lengthwise through the leg of lamb so it's not too unevenly balanced. If you use wood, it must be green.

When you cut a spit in the woods, do your chopping in a way that helps rather than damages nature. Find two young saplings growing four feet or less apart. As mature trees they cannot both survive. As teenage trees their sibling rivalry will be fierce enough to be detrimental to both. Cutting one down will do no harm. In all probability it will help the survivor.

But make your cut neat and trim the whole thing flat, at or just below ground level. Don't leave a sharp point remaining an inch or so above the fallen leaves. Not only is it unsightly, but you could walk over it a day or two later and have that point driven painfully into your moccasins. So could the camper following you.

Leave a foot or two of the two lowest branches of a sapling spit, if possible. This will give you something to prop another stick against to hold the lamb in place as it roasts. No matter how well you skewer it, perfect balance is almost impossible to achieve. Try to peel the bark off. Not necessary, but it makes things easier.

SPIT-ROASTING A LEG OF LAMB

You'll be hanging the skewer about a foot over the coals on two Y-sticks. A third branched stick can be used to brace the meat when you've got it turned on the spit. Use strong deadwood for the Ys and keep them away from the fire. If it gets very hot, sprinkle some water on them occasionally.

The leg of lamb itself we jab at diagonally with a knife all around, under the skin and fat, stuffing the slits with fresh slivers of garlic. Then sear briefly close to the fire to keep the juices in. Spice to suit yourself. Hang the spit and roast the lamb till you can't wait any longer.

Serve with coal-baked potatoes, onions, and fresh corn in the husk if available. If you really mimic the merry days of Robin Hood and slice the lamb right off the leg in individual bite-sized pieces, there won't be a dish to wash. Licking your fingers will suffice.

BACON BEANS BANNOCK—AND VITAMINS

Tradition calls for the three Bs—bacon, beans, and bannock, or frypan bread—in planning the wilderness menu. And with good reason. They are easy to prepare, filling, provide complementary proteins, don't spoil readily, and just plain taste good in the wilds. The woods-made beans, incidentally, taste infinitely better than the canned. It's true the three don't supply all the vitamins of a carefully balanced diet, yet they supply some, as do the dried fruits in your gorp, the vegetables in the soup, and any number of the other camp staples. Then again, in this well-fed, diet-conscious country, nutrition has become something of a superfad. It pains me to see a camper lug around six months' worth of vitamin and mineral supplements on a two-week backpacking trip. Yet it's not an unusual sight.

No one is going to come down with scurvy or rickets from two weeks of spaghetti. Gustatory boredom, perhaps, but not vitamin deficiency. If you like *cordon-bleu* camp cooking, by all means provision for it. If you're a meat-and-potatoes man, do likewise. The point is, plan to eat what you enjoy—within the sensible weight limits you may have to impose because of your means of travel, of course.

To avoid the boredom of spaghetti for a week straight, a certain amount of planning is necessary. So also is it to reassure you that sufficient provisions are on hand. Again, our overstuffed society may leave you feeling that were you to run out of food you'd starve to death in a couple of days. Far from it. You might trim down a bit, although even that isn't guaranteed. A week's fast would leave you awfully hungry though, and this is supposed to be a pleasure trip, not the woodsman's version of Weight Watchers. Incidentally, should you ever get stuck without food, remember that the first three days are the hardest. After that you're not really hungry any more. (Remember too, when you are presented with food again, the old rule about reintroducing the stomach to it gradually.)

Much too much is usually made of planning the menu for an excursion to the wilderness. Obviously you will have to take into account whether there will be a chance to reprovision along the way or whether you'll have to be totally self-reliant. But except for that factor and knowing more or less the number of meals you're apt to eat on the road, you don't have to go into too much detail. Sitting down to determine to the last spoonful how much sugar you will need, whether to have hash on Thursday and beans on Friday or vice versa, and if each member of the party should be entitled to three pancakes or four—except for the one who will be carrying the grub, which weighs more, and who could thus use the extra 500 calories in five pancakes—is an exercise in minute trivia and rigidity suitable for a prison camp nutritionist, not a camper.

Do plan on eating more than you normally would. Much has been said about the ravenous appetites that develop with fresh air and exercise. Most of it is true. You may not rival Paul Bunyan stacking up his breakfast hotcakes, but the morning cup of coffee, juice, and slice of toast habitual at home won't hold you till lunch noways.

Another thing: Sweet teeth sprout like mushrooms after a summer rain when you're camping. You're burning up more carbohydrates than usual. One of the more readily available sources of carbohydrates is sugar—so you begin to crave sweets. Starches are another source—and another reason why the beans and bannock are there in the traditional three Bs.

A last overall thought on what to take: Most camp food is low on roughage like salads and vegetables. About the only adverse effect this is apt to have on you is constipation. If you're prone to it, take along suitable solutions to the problem, for instance, dried prunes, figs, or apricots that you can soak overnight and stew with sugar or honey in the morning. For breakfast they will help your sweet tooth as well.

HOW MUCH FOOD SHOULD YOU TAKE?

Is it going to rain next Friday? Both questions can be answered with equal ease—it depends. Standard opinion dictates between a pound and a half and four pounds of food, with a caloric value of 2,500 to 4,000, per day per person, depending on the kind of food it is and how lively your camping activities are. The spread is obviously so wide as to make it less than a rule. Additionally there's your own metabolism and weight to consider. One one-hundred-and-fifty-pound individual may eat like a bird; another of the same weight, being a regular jack-in-the-box, puts away enough to shame a truck driver.

The only way I know to gauge your own outdoor appetite is to go there and find out. If you're an experienced camper you already know. If you're just starting out, you want to break into things gradually anyway. To test both yourself and your equipment go on a few weekend and three-day trips. Take more food than you expect to eat. It will give you confidence. And on short trips it's not difficult to bring it back home. Once you've got an idea of what your appetite and those of your companions are like, you'll have no problems gauging for longer trips.

Young children, incidentally, may surprise you. If you thought they ate you out of house and home before, well—suffice it to say that Genevieve, when a year and a half old, could knock down the better part of a two-man freeze-dried dinner.

More on the freeze-dried dinner later. For now let's look at some of the basic camp foods.

MEAT

Meat as you are accustomed to eating it might seem a problem on a camping trip. And it is, for the most part. Besides that leg of lamb at the trail head or a steak the first or second night out, meat is not a readily transportable item. Hamburgers and hot dogs are particularly bad, since ground meat spoils the quickest.

However, there are numerous sausages that trek well. In fact, sausages were probably man's first successful attempt to keep meat. The spices so much in demand during medieval days were combined with salt, a natural preservative, to keep meat edible. If you have access to a European meat or food-specialty store, so much the better. There you will be able to select such delicacies as *Dauernwurst* and the flatter *Landtjaeger,* both expressly designed for the hunter and outdoorsman. They will last for months without refrigeration. Although firm, even hard, they are tasty and soul-satisfying, excellent eaten out-of-hand, equally tasty diced or sliced in stews, soups, and beans. Hard salami and Thuringer sausage are other good buys in this category. Never buy sausage presliced, since this defeats its durability.

Next to the sausages, the all-around best meat for camping is slab bacon. It supplies both meat protein and fat. The excess fat is useful for frying and amazingly tasty solidified and spread on bannock—or even just poured on bread as on a sponge. Although by now Americans are used to keeping paper boxes of sliced bacon in the refrigerator, storage was not always thus, and need not be. Smoke-cured bacon was another successful attempt to prolong the usefulness of meat. Kept merely cool, slab bacon will last many months without refrigeration, so have no fear about its lasting a two- or three-week trip. In summertime it does need to be kept out of the sun and in the coolest spot available.

The problem with bacon is that it molds. You can just cut out the moldy part if it offends you. But the mold also absorbs the flavor. Before you set out from home, wash the bacon slab with a clean cloth. Pat dry. Then wash a second time with a cup of vinegar to which you've added half a teaspoon of salt. Pat dry again and wrap in several layers of cheesecloth for the trip. Don't wrap in plastic or tinfoil. Meat that is not to be refrigerated needs to breathe.

Another thing to watch for is soft bacon. Today's hogs are often fed a diet overly rich in soybeans. This tends to make the fat very soft at room temperature. To avoid the problem, stick with bacon you've used before and know remains firm.

Pemmican, the fabled wonder food of the trapper, consists of lean dried meat beaten to a pulp and then mashed with fat into a concoction about as durable as cannon balls. As romantic as it sounds, it has some drawbacks. If you've never eaten it before, a diet of pemmican can be quite a shock to your stomach. But nowhere near as much as to your nostrils. Pemmican made with beaver fat can be sensed easily at the far end of the campsite, even if you're upwind. Gagging before I'd even had a taste was rather embarrassing until a trapper of thirty years told me nobody besides the Indians could handle it.

But there is a modern-day pemmican with all the good qualities and none of the bad. Wilson's Bacon Bar is every bit as durable and almost as concentrated. Its three ounces of compressed precooked flakes are equivalent to a full twelve ounces of raw bacon. Providing more meat, less fat than any other present-day equivalent, several of these are almost a must on any extended trip. Eat them with eggs, in stews, or simply out-of-hand—but not all at once if you're munching. They're rich.

HOMEMADE JERKY

4 pounds flank steak
3 cups red wine
3 tablespoons salt
2 tablespoons garlic salt
1 tablespoon black pepper
1 tablespoon Tabasco sauce
2 tablespoons Worcestershire sauce

Trim all excess fat from meat. Slice, with the grain, into strips about ⅛- to ¼-inch thick. Mix remaining ingredients in a large glass bowl. Add meat to marinade, making sure it is well covered. Refrigerate for 24 hours, stirring lightly every 4 hours during the day. Drain. Hang meat strips over oven or pan rack. Set oven temperature control on low (no higher than 150°F.). The meat should dehydrate, not cook. Prop door open an inch or so. Jerk for 24 to 36 hours, checking the meat frequently after the first 12 hours. Don't let it dry out too much. Good jerky should be chewy and flexible, not brittle. Store in a dry place. Canning jars make fine storage containers if heated to ensure that they are thoroughly dry before being filled and closed. For trail packaging use plastic bags. If kept properly, jerky will easily last a year at home and several months on the trail.

For base camping, canoe trips, and other endeavors where weight is important, but not *that* important, canned meats are often taken along. Ranging from boneless chicken to ham and roast beef—make sure they're stamped "Needs no refrigeration"—they add considerable variety to your meat courses. The cans also add about 15 percent to the weight, and have to be packed out again—something I always contemplate when eyeing the corned beef, my favorite of the canned meats, on the shelf.

Another commodity that is perhaps best considered under "meats" is the indispensable bouillon cube. As a hot drink or for flavoring stews and casseroles, its weight-to-pleasure ratio is hard to beat.

Winter camping provides you with a greater possible selection of meat, since you are in fact living in a refrigerator. Almost any fresh meats except variety meats, which spoil easily, can be packed along. Just watch that the meat doesn't alternately freeze and thaw. Keep it in one condition or the other. Also don't take along too much. The great outdoors may be your icebox, but that doesn't mean you have to fill it.

CHEWING THE FAT

Bacon grease is good on bread. Butter is better, particularly if you intend to add a layer of jam, but butter will turn rancid. So will margarine, though it lasts considerably longer. Canned butter is still available, and will last for years unopened. Susan prefers it, despite its higher price tag, to the lards and cooking oils because it's more adaptable, serving the pan fry, the blueberry tarts, and the hot pancakes with equal good taste. Polyunsaturate fans may prefer to fill a polytube with sesame or peanut or another favorite oil.

To increase their fat intake, which is vital in cold-weather conditions, many alpine and winter campers drink Sherpa Tea, a mixture of heavily sweetened tea and milk with butter. The original Sherpa Tea was served with rancid yak butter. Your butter may not be from a yak, but try the tea if it goes rancid. Provides lots of long-lasting energy and a taste treat that would wow them back in Katmandu. With fresh butter, the tea is sweet and comforting as well as nourishing.

CHEESE

Of all the dairy products, cheese has the best storage qualities, and it improves with age. The one catch is to keep it from drying out. First, buy it in chunks, which will stay soft considerably longer than the sliced version of the same cheese. Secondly, keep it well wrapped. In the old days this meant using cabbage leaves, with an outside layer of cheesecloth. The moist cabbage kept the cheese pliable. Today plastic is more or less the rule. It does almost as good a job as the cabbage leaves. Almost but not quite—you can't make soup from plastic.

EGGS

There's dried and there's fresh. Fresh eggs can be packed into crushproof egg carriers. If we take eggs, we usually end up simply leaving them in their cartons and being careful. Fresh eggs may also be cracked and removed from the shell before setting out. Pour the shelled eggs carefully, one by one, into a narrow glass jar. They will remain individual even after considerable jolting about. Pour out however many you need. Although this is a popular old trick, I think of it mostly as a nice bit of showmanship. Not much is gained, and they will spoil faster, having been exposed to bacteria. Besides, they don't keep well in plastic, and if the glass jar breaks. . . .

Dried eggs, no matter how you cook them, are still dried eggs. I was told they had improved considerably of late, so I went out and bought a packet. Certainly a braised saddle would have been tastier. Dried eggs are a convenience, however, in pancakes, baking and such, where their desiccated origins are not so noticeable.

MILK

Dried milk is not as bad as dried eggs. Made up a day in advance in order to dissolve it better, it is in fact quite palatable. The skimmed variety is available in any supermarket. Our tastes lean towards Alba, which seems to reconstitute better than most others. Get it packaged in individual quart envelopes for convenience. Also, though it may come as a surprise, there is powdered whole milk. One of the leading brands, and Susan's favorite from childhood camping in Africa, is Klim (spelled guess what backwards). Powdered whole milk is available through the larger drugstores and some mountain supply stores.

FISH

Fresh-caught fish is an excellent source of protein and a scrumptious addition to any camp menu. However, bring food as well. One fellow I know can walk up the stream with his fly rod "beating the water to a froth" for an hour or so and come back with enough trout to feed a party of six every time. Well, almost every time. Still, just because of that "almost," he always brings his regular rations with him. Even if you're a fantastic fisherman, it's something worth considering. If you're on a par with me, you'd certainly never leave the groceries home.

Canned fish really isn't worth its weight for most people. But dried shrimp, squid, cod, and even seaweed are available through ethnic stores in the big cities. Oriental food shops are particularly good for browsing when you're looking for lightweight dried foods. Just be sure everyone that's going has sampled them before you set out on your trip. I happen to like Japanese dried shrimp. Susan is less fond of them, and I admit they bear little resemblance to shrimp of the cocktail-sauce-dunking variety. But in rice, with some slivered vegetables, they are a real treat.

HIGH-ALTITUDE COOKING

Altitude (feet)	Increase in Cooking Time
3,000	20%
4,000	30%
5,000	40%
6,000	50%
7,000	70%
8,000	90%

Over 9,000 feet a pressure cooker saves a great deal of time.

HIGH-ALTITUDE BAKING

Altitude (feet)	Decrease in Amount of Baking Powder
3,000	10%
6,000	25%
10,000	30% *

* And add one extra egg if eggs are called for in recipe.

PASTA AND DRIED LEGUMES

The most filling thing you can eat is good old-fashioned lie-in-the-belly-like-lead starch. Spaghetti is a must for at least one camp dinner. Then there are noodles, in all shapes and sizes, and the dried legumes.

We probably eat more beans than most folks do on a camping trip, but before you shrug your shoulders and pass them by, consider the variety of highly nutritious dried beans and peas available. There are chick-peas, or garbanzos, green and yellow split peas, black turtle beans, navy beans, pinto beans, blackeyes, cow peas, orown and orange lentils, to name a few. With the addition of a touch of spice, small chunks of sausage or bacon bar, dried mushrooms, shrimps, and what have you, it is probably possible to concoct a different bean dish for every day of the year. These dishes are usually referred to simply as glop. Each one is different, and each one is memorable. Why, I remember one split yellow peas/Wilson Bacon Bar/bouquet garni glop we made in Wyoming that would have soothed the soul of Escoffier himself. And there's only one pot to clean for the whole meal.

BREAD

There are numerous varieties of heavy dark European pumpernickels and rye breads that, unsliced, will stay fresh for two weeks. Of course they bear no resemblance to the cellophaned cotton usually sold as bread—which, in case you were considering it, squashes into a gummy mess about the size of a tennis ball in your pack. But their heft is just what makes the dark breads so great. They have substance, flavor, and nourishment, and eating them makes you realize that bread is not only a staple, but a highly palatable one as well.

The other source of bread is baking your own as you go. Bannock, or frypan bread, is simple and nourishing. Great fresh and hot with butter and jam. If you add a reflector oven to your gear, you can bake a steady supply of cornbread, sourdough biscuits and rolls. Make a batch for dinner, save some for the next day's lunch. In berry season, fresh tarts and fruit muffins are a trailside epicure's delight.

BANNOCK

Double or treble the following amounts to make a batter to fit your skillet.

- 1 cup fine-milled whole wheat or all-purpose flour
- 1 teaspoon baking powder
- ¼ teaspoon salt
- 1 teaspoon bacon grease or butter (optional, to add shortness)
- ⅓ cup milk or water (approximately), preferably cold

Preheat your frypan over the coals of the fire and grease it lightly. Mix and sift the dry ingredients together with a fork. Cut in the bacon grease or butter roughly. Stir in enough milk or water to make a stiff dough. Shape into a circle to fit your frypan, making it about an inch thick. Poke a hole in the center if you like your bread crusty. Dust the loaf lightly with flour, place in frypan and hold the skillet over low coals, turning it occasionally to brown the bottom evenly. Then prop the pan at about a 45-degree angle in front of the fire to catch the heat and stir up the coals to make a hotter fire. When the loaf is browned and has a hollow sound if you tap it, probably about 15 minutes from the time you first put the skillet on, the bread is done.

TRAIL BISCUITS

1½ cups fine-milled whole wheat or all-purpose flour
2 tablespoons brown sugar
2 teaspoons baking powder
1 scant teaspoon salt
1 portion dried eggs (optional)
4 tablespoons butter
1 cup milk (approximately)
½ cup to as much as the dough will hold of freshly
   picked, rinsed, and lightly sugared blueberries
   or currants, if available

Get a hot campfire going—you'll want the flames about the height of your oven shelf. Set up the reflector oven and grease the baking shelf lightly. Mix, sifting together with a fork, the dry ingredients. Cut in the butter to a coarse cornmeal consistency. Add enough milk to make a stiff dough that will hold its shape when spooned onto the oven sheet, but just barely so, incorporating as much liquid as possible since baking in front of a fire is a drier form of heating than in the enclosed oven at home. Work quickly, don't worry about small globs or lumps. Fold in the berries with a few light strokes. Drop the dough from a spoon onto the baking shelf of the oven. Set the oven near the fire, controlling the heat by moving it closer to or farther from the flames (6 to 12 inches will be your probable range if you have a good hot fire). Bake, turning the biscuits around occasionally if they are rising or browning unevenly, though this will not usually be necessary, till done and toasty brown outside.

THE SPREADABLES

Honey, jam, better yet, preserves, and peanut or cashew butter will be devoured with fervor in the wilds. The old sweet craving again. Prepack them in Gerry polytubes before you go. Seated beneath blue sky and scented pines, squeeze out on fresh buttered buns for an energy-giving snack or lunch the likes of which will never taste the same at home. One caution: For winter camping you will have to use wide-mouth polyjars instead, at least for the peanut butter, which tends to turn halfway into peanut brittle when the thermometer scratches zero.

DRINKS

Western man has become used to eating his food hot. Whether this is healthy or not has recently come up for some debate. However, conditioned as we are, there's no doubt that a hot cup of something hits the spot on a chill September morn or before slipping into the sack at night. Some hikers even insist on hot soup for lunch. I don't fall into this category because sheer laziness prevents me, but I can empathize with them.

Coffee, cocoa, and tea are the big three. Our one-pound coffee can that travels in the coffeepot lasts us about ten days to two weeks, depending on how many cups we squeeze out of the grounds and whether we run into company or not. Campers who cross paths in the wilds are a gregarious lot. You'll be left alone if you want to be. If not, there's bound to be a long chat and swapping of route information over endless cups of coffee. Instant is popular among backpackers, but personally I wouldn't touch it. When I need to save weight, I take tea.

Tea is a fragrant wonder in the woods. Black teas, green teas, breakfast teas, and numerous specially spiced blends will carry you off to the high plantations of Assam on their steamy mist.

Cocoa and Ovaltine are excellent camp drinks combining the gifts of energy, warmth, and satiation of the sweet craving. They are particularly good for children if they do not take to powdered milk served straight.

Bouillon, a staple of many European coffee breaks, is making rapid inroads on the American office routine. (Apologies for bringing up the subject of the office you left behind.) A good hearty cup of beef or chicken bouillon often hits the spot while you're waiting for the main course to cook outdoors. Instant soups like Lipton's ever popular Chicken Noodle, Knorrs' Leek, and Maggi's Oxtail are even better.

If my previous comments about vitamins haven't entirely put your mind at ease, most of the instant breakfast drinks, fruit or juice crystals, are lightweight and supplied with vitamin C. On the other hand, true fruit syrup concentrates, again available through food specialty stores and European provisioners, are in my opinion infinitely superior. They do weigh more, but by repacking in poly bottles, the weight differential is cut down considerably. Flavors, ranging from raspberry or strawberry to loganberry, are fantastic, almost like those of the fresh berries the wilderness itself may proffer. Great on pancakes—which reminds me of the time, on one long rainy canoe portage, Susan and I guzzled down almost our entire hipflask of maple syrup for energy and warmth. Concentrated grenadine syrup also makes up into a refreshing drink.

CONDIMENTS

Herbs and spices do even more to sparkle up a meal in the woods than at home. They supply more flavor for their weight than anything else. If you want to try new ones, however, do so at home. I think dried dill is great, but you may not agree, and when you've just seasoned a big pot of glop on the trail with it is no time to find out.

Besides salt and pepper, we take bay leaves (for spaghetti sauce), rosemary (for fish), cumin (for dehydrated pork chops), dill (again, for fish), and sage (for just about anything). Any one of these plus a few others may tumble into the glop du jour. The bay leaves travel in a Baggie. The rest, individually or as bouquets garnis, used to go in little plastic pill jars from the local drugstore. Now, so Genevieve doesn't get the wrong idea about eating pills, we pack them into extra aluminum salt and pepper shakers—the traditional camp variety with separate lidded compartments at each end, relabeled from "S" and "P" to the appropriate designations.

If you're going fishing, some lemon concentrate and slivered almonds might be a thought. Then again, it's pretty hard to beat just straight butter-fried panfish.

DESSERTS, GORP, AND CANDY

For us, dessert away from civilization is usually either a fruit soup, fresh picked berries in season, or a healthy slab of bread slathered with butter and a substantial layer of plum preserves. In winter, we treat ourselves to snow ices, pouring fruit concentrate onto the white sparkling snow and then scooping it up in our hands into double-dip extravagances.

Others like to take along instant puddings, which are easy enough to make in a wilderness kitchen. I quake at the thought of Jell-O, but if you like it, mix up and cool some in the snow or an icy stream for a quick dessert.

The instant fruit soups, from Europe, are a little-known boon to campers here. Available from gourmet shops and health food stores, Rose Hip Soup, extremely high in natural vitamin C, and Blueberry Soup, both by Ekströms of Sweden, and Bergene's Mixed Fruit Soup, from Norway, are about as tasty ways to end a meal as I can think of. Serve hot or chilled in a mountain stream. For stream-cooling, anchor the pot firmly with rocks lest it float away.

It has been said that camping involves eating only one meal a day. The meal begins when you get up and ends when you go back to sleep. This is pretty true when you take into account the trail foods and candy. During heavy paddling and long treks, a handful of gorp—the traditional trail food combination of dried fruits, nuts and/or chocolate—picks up your energy to an amazing degree.

There are as many recipes for gorp as there are campers. Some like peanuts. Some like chocolate. Others don't like either. Some insist using tropical chocolate is the way to keep it melting in your mouth instead of on your hands, but there are just as strong advocates of candy-covered M&Ms. The only way to satisfy yourself on the subject is to experiment and make your own mix.

A few campers eschew gorp altogether, sticking with just plain candy for energy. Most candy, however, doesn't have the protein content of a nut-filled gorp, and we find it less satisfying. A good compromise is marzipan, which is ground almonds, sugar, and sometimes egg white, giving you the best of two worlds. Mint cakes à la Kendal are a mountain-climbing tradition, even more so since being gobbled atop Mount Everest.

A European hiking standby to which I became addicted in the Austrian Alps is *Traubenzuckerwuerfel,* or grape sugar wafers. They are straight dextrose, and favored by athletes all over the Continent for instant energy. Dissolve in your mouth in seconds and give you an energy boost just as quickly. Till recently I had never seen them this side of the Atlantic. Now, however, some mountaineering shops are beginning to carry them. The Camp & Hike Shop sells them by mail order.

LANGER'S GORP

2 pounds raisins
1 pound dried currants
1 pound dried apricots
½ pound whole shelled hazelnuts
½ pound whole shelled almonds
1 pound pitted prunes or dates (optional)

Mix well in a large bowl. Then pack by the cupful into individual Baggies. Eat out of hand whenever you need a quick energy boost. A word of caution: Gorp is not suitable trail food for desert country, since it tends to make you thirsty.

THE FREEZE-DRIED LARDER

And so we come to the wonder food for today's backpacker. At least that's what everyone tells me. True, ounce per ounce there's no lighter food you can take with you, even if sometimes the packages are absurdly ungainly. It's also nourishing. Considering the weight saving—it's sold without water, which makes up 96 percent of something like cucumbers—it's not even all that expensive. But there remains the issue of taste, and here it comes in several notches below TV dinners.

Still, there's no squelching the popularity of freeze-dried food, and when it comes to mountain climbing and backpacking, it does save as much as 80 percent of your provisioning weight—provided, and this can be a big if, you're assured plenty of water and so don't have to lug any of that along. In snow season, of course, the water problem resolves itself, although you'll have to melt a lot more snow to get a cup of water than you may realize. If you are going to melt snow, make sure you don't scorch it. As strange as that sounds, it's quite possible. Melt a little bit first over a not too hot flame, so you get a light layer of water in the pan, before you really go at it.

The most popular brands in freeze-drying are Chuck Wagon, Mountain House, Rich-Moor, Seidel, Tea Kettle, and Wilson's. Their products range from individual packets of such things as cottage cheese, hamburgers, carrots, pears—and would you believe ice cream?—to complete dinners featuring names like Turkey Tetrazzini and Beef Almondine. Go ahead and try one. You may like it. And of course after a couple of weeks in the wilderness, almost anything will taste good.

One last warning about freeze-dried products. Their packagers are either midgets or on extended diets. The so-called two-man serving will hold me for a couple of hours. I've seen seven- and eight-year-old kids knock down one of the two-man dinners and still have room for half a dozen rolls and a four-man serving of freeze-dried fruit cocktail. Check out your own appetite against the manufacturer's before you set out with freeze-dried food in your pack.

INSTANTS

Heavier than freeze-dried foods, but almost as convenient, are the supermarket instants. Look over the breakfast cereals, instant oatmeal and the like—Fini is high on our list of staples—gravy mixes, flavored rices, mashed potatoes, puddings, and quick-cooking dinners. A lot of these are dehydrated, a much less expensive process than freeze-drying. Also one that supposedly does not match the freeze-dried foods in flavor. A moot point, I think. In any case, comb your supermarket for lightweight foods, remembering to stay away from those that require half an hour in a 375-degree oven, which you won't have.

If you're camping in Canada, you will find many products that are both unfamiliar and useful. Dried vegetables from England are a particular example. The Surprise brand of vegetables, packaged like frozen vegetables in the United States, reconstitute every bit as well as their freeze-dried counterparts, as long as you use about half the amount of water recommended in the instructions.

BABY FOOD

What the baby's eating at home will be the natural guide for what to feed him or her in the wilds. A baby still nursing is a joy to the cook, because that's half or so of the menu already taken care of. To supply the iron that growing infants need, instant baby cereals are usually iron-fortified. Barley is one of the best. High-protein varieties sometimes comfort mothers. Stock up and repack in Baggies to save weight. Add instant milk and hot water and you have a warm meal. Most powdered milks supply vitamin D, something a baby probably won't lack in the sunny outdoors, but you'll be reassured on the matter. Vitamin C may be a problem on extended trips; Rose Hip Soup, a nice baby-food consistency anyway, is one of the best solutions. Brown sugar or honey will sweeten things; most of the freeze-dried meats mash well for baby protein courses; and the fruits do likewise when well reconstituted and thinned with milk. The dehydrated soups cooked up for the rest of the family make fine baby food. Just give the littlest camper a large share of the vegetables and meat bits mashed in the broth. Babies who have sprouted teeth can probably graduate to your regular camp fare, served in small pieces they can handle.

Probably the only special item you'll have to lug around is vitamin drops. For adults the vitamin situation is not vital. In the case of a baby, however, most pediatricians recommend vitamin supplements even in their normal environment.

If you have questions, check with your pediatrician when you're making out the provisions list. The best advice is that of a professional who knows your particular child.

GARBAGE

There's no garbage pickup in the real wilderness. If you pack it in, pack it out—pack it *all* out. Paper, which you won't have much of, since you've repacked most of your food, burns. So when you have a fire going, toss in the paper. Paper that has an aluminum foil lining, however, will not disintegrate. There will always be some left.

Modern technology has made packaging, cans in particular, lighter

—which is good for the camper. But it's terrible for the wilderness. An aluminum can left behind will be around quite literally for eons. It doesn't rust. It just lies there, an ugly glinting scar, a companion to the discarded snap top that slices into your toe. The old tin cans (really steel), when carefully buried, not only were out of sight, but over the years, as they rusted away, even returned some useful minerals to the soil. The same can't be said for aluminum. Squash cans flat and tote out with you in a large plastic bag brought for the purpose. Don't leave them behind. Better yet, if possible don't bring them in the first place.

Some plastics burn. Others just smolder, choking off the flames with their foul smoke, turning into a sticky mess that clings to the rocks. Pack plastic home.

Food scraps, if there are any, are the only things that can be safely left behind. But don't just scrape them out at the edge of your campsite. Carry them back into the brush and scatter them around. Insects and animals will probably have a pleasant little feast, although I've seen them turn their noses up pretty high at some camp cooking. Oh well, the scraps will rot, adding a little nourishment to the soil.

KEEPING THE FOOD FOR YOURSELF

Although they might not eat everything you take along, animals will make a beeline for the camp kitchen at night. In bear country it's always a good idea to hang your comestibles well out of reach. Put them all together in a waterproof duffel or stuff sack, attach a line to the bag, and throw the line over a large tree branch. It should hang out as far from the trunk as its weight will permit. I used to pull our gear up seven or eight feet in bear country. Now I make it twelve if I can. This past summer a grizzly that must have been trying out for the Olympic basketball team tore the bottom out of our pantry even though it was almost nine feet off the ground.

Never never under any circumstances keep food in your tent when in bear country. Even in regions where bears have definitely been driven into extinction, it's still a good policy to hang your food away from the tent. I remember once many years ago, after an exhausting day of portaging and paddling, I flopped down beneath my tarp and just dropped off to sleep with the pantry as my pillow. Early in the morning, during a strange dream involving earthquakes, I opened one eye when a large bushy striped tail grazed my forehead. A raccoon that had been gleefully devouring a goodly part of my bread and cheese looked at me in a superior fashion as if to inquire where the wine was kept.

FOOD FROM THE WILDERNESS

One of the joys of camping is going out in the morning to pick blueberries for the breakfast pancakes, fresh mushrooms to go with lunch, or some of the other gifts of nature discussed further on. Don't count on the wilderness feeding you—there are too many of us for that now. But always keep your eyes open. Often you'll stumble across unexpected delights.

TOOLS OF THE TRADE

The first tool most people think of when they're planning to go camping is a hatchet or ax. Now a hatchet is a dangerous thing. When you consider a hatchet, consider the fact that the popular term "hatchet job" didn't originate with Lizzie Borden's forty whacks, but refers to the poor quality of work and frequent self-mutilation that usually occurs when the instrument is used for chopping wood. At the entrances to some state and national forest preserves, you will see the three-silhouette sign of a bucket, an ax, and a shovel. It means you are required to have all three when camping in the area. But this is not in consideration of your camping comfort. It's in case of a forest fire. You would be expected to work the lines along with everyone else. And for that you would need the tools.

The standard recommendation is to take along a Hudson Bay style single bit ax with a two- to two-and-a-half-pound head and twenty-eight-inch handle, preferably one of hickory for strength. I have no quarrels with this; it's probably the best all-around ax you can get. The question is, should you have an ax along in the first place? The answer in most cases is no. Axmanship in camping is dying. Which is all to the good. Unfortunately many city dwellers and suburbanites going out into the woods with ax in hand seem to run amuck, chopping here, chopping there, as if they were somehow conquering nature. Felling a living tree simply to satisfy an urge to chop something down is no accomplishment, but rather a sign of lunacy or inability to keep destructive urges under control.

There's no place in North America that I can think of where an ax would be needed to clear a path. Modern tents don't require felled saplings for poles. Green wood won't burn. So you'll accomplish nothing by chopping down these trees for your fire. Clearing a batch of trees to make a campsite is not only terribly destructive, it's an absurd amount of work.

In state and national parks where wood in the form of logs is supplied for each campsite, you'll need an ax to split them. Outside of this one situation and the fire regulations mentioned for some areas, I don't see much point in taking an ax along.

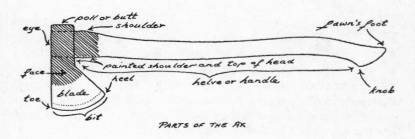

PARTS OF THE AX

CHECKING OUT AXES

If you are going to be camping where an ax is needed, select one with care. The handle, preferably of hickory, should be straight-grained, with the grain running parallel to the blade, not diagonally against it. As with any other piece of wood needing structural integrity, avoid cracks, knotholes, and other deformities. Also avoid wood with a grain of sharply contrasting colors; even small streaks may mean a weak handle. Because of this, although axes painted along the shoulder and top of the head are more visible, this is a safety feature you should apply yourself if you want it. Quite often a painted handle has a fault to hide.

Check to make sure the ax is well hung. This can mean one of two things, depending on whom you talk to. Either that the handle is straight, which you can check by sighting down from the end of the handle towards the head, or that when the ax is held bit and knob against a flat surface, the bit touches at about the midpoint. Both factors are important. But the first is more so, since chopping with a crooked handle is like shooting with a bowed gun barrel—dangerous.

The handle of an ax must fit snugly into the eye of the blade. Traditionally a wedge is driven into the handle, forcing it to grip the eye more firmly. Recently manufacturers have begun to bond the handle to the head with epoxy. This means the head should never come off. The only question then remaining is, what do you do if the handle splits and you have to replace it?

The handle should feel comfortable in your hands when you swing it. A rule of thumb for length is that when you are standing erect, holding the ax in one hand, head down, and letting it swing back and forth across the floor without bending your arm, the blade should just miss the floor.

The head of an ax is made of relatively soft steel. While this means it will bend and dent a little, a hard, highly tempered blade would nick and break, which is much worse. If you've never owned an ax, the best solution to the problem of gauging head hardness is to buy a known brand, such as Collins, Peavy, Norland, or Estwing (made with a one-piece forged steel blade and handle), that has years of experience and reputation behind it. Stay away from double-edged axes. These are for experienced lumberjacks only. In anyone else's hands they're like a loaded revolver in a baby's grasp.

CHOPPING WOOD

Like all real skills, chopping with an ax is considerably more difficult than it appears when done by an expert. That doesn't mean you can't do it. It just means that unless you chop wood on a regular basis, you should make sure you're extra careful when you do.

When you're splitting wood—the only task you'll use the ax for, since cutting down trees is *verboten*—stand with your legs spread but comfortable. Check to make sure the ax head is still firmly attached to the handle. Check too that there are no overhead branches or other obstructions—including people—anywhere near the ax's arc as you swing it from behind, above your head, and down to its target on the chopping block. Children are best taught to keep their distance from the chopping block routinely. Chips fly.

Place the log you're going to split on end so one of its flat surfaces will be at right angles to the descending ax blade. Never put a round log on the block lengthwise and attempt to split it that way. If you weren't to hit it just right, the ax would glance off and you could be in real trouble.

Bring the ax up over your head from behind your shoulders, your near hand down by the fawn's foot, the other about halfway along the handle. This hand will slide down towards the fawn's foot as well when the ax arches overhead. As you bring the ax forward and down for the chop, remember it's the momentum of the ax head that does the work. When the head is just about to hit the log, your arms are loose, merely following the arc of the swing. Don't lean into the blow. It doesn't add any efficiency to the chop. All it does is transmit a lot of wearing vibration through your arms. Keep your eye on the log, not the ax head, when you're chopping.

Don't aim dead center. Splitting is easier if you hit closer to the near edge. Don't aim for the far edge either. If, instead of the blade, the handle should strike the log, it will snap. To tackle a thick log, dig the ax in towards the edge, turn the log and take a crack at the opposite edge, aiming so the two cracks will eventually meet. Then keep digging in closer to the center until the cracks are one. On a big log the first split is always the hardest. Once you've broken the log it becomes much easier.

SAWS FROM JACK TO BUCK

For all the ax's woodsiness, I usually take along with me only a saw. A lightweight folding saw will handle almost all the ground and squaw wood you find. Branches, even ones three inches in diameter, need not really be split in order to burn in a hot fire, and you're not going to find anything much larger. Most of these branches can simply be broken by hand or by a hefty foot stomp. But where the wood is still quite springy, a lightweight saw simplifies the job of reducing whole branches to convenient fire lengths. It also means less wood burned, since you won't be tossing in four-foot-long pieces that wouldn't break easily. As a last thought, a saw is not dangerous even in inexperienced hands.

The lightest and least bulky saw made is a quarter-ounce twisted toothed wire with finger rings at each end. An item for the emergency kit perhaps. Outside of that, it's simply too inefficient. For cutting any considerable amount of wood, it would be quicker to convince some local beavers to give you a hand.

The next size up is the handy jacksaw, its eight- to fifteen-inch blade folding into a wooden or high-impact plastic handle in the fashion of a pocketknife. Get one with at least a ten-inch blade or the strokes will be too short to be effective. Plastic handles are good, but the wooden ones, I find, have a better feel to them. Slow cutting. However, I don't use a saw often, so the jacksaw is usually my preference because it only weighs between six and ten ounces, depending on the model.

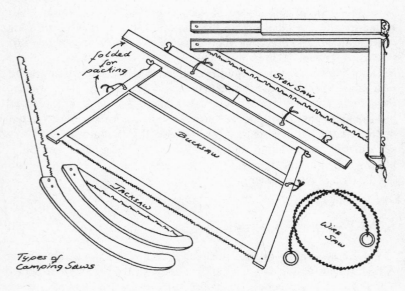

Types of Camping Saws

Probably the most popular folding saw is a triangular-framed version usually sold under the Sven Saw brand. In addition to the wood-cutting blade, a meat-sawing blade is available for hunters. Blade stores in the slim aluminum frame. Compact, but long—twenty-three inches when folded up. Weighs seventeen ounces. A good compromise between weight-saving and efficiency.

It's hard to beat a bucksaw. Although it will weigh over two pounds, a folding version is the best thing to have along if you expect to do considerable sawing. Unlike the triangularly framed version, a bucksaw permits full-stroke cutting of up to twelve-inch-diameter logs without frame interference. It also permits team sawing, which cuts the work more than in half.

SAWING

If you look at a saw blade, you'll see that the teeth are angled out from the blade itself. This is the set of the teeth. The only thing to watch for is that you don't flatten the angle. If you do, your saw's efficiency will fall drastically. Teeth lose their set when squeezed or pinched in a log. Let the log extend over whatever you're bracing it across, another log, for instance, then saw beyond this point. The weight of the overhanging part of the log will widen the cut the deeper you go, keeping the blade from pinching.

You don't have to bear down on a saw when you're cutting. In fact you shouldn't, since this will also tend to make it bind and lose its set. Just pull and push, back and forth.

With a bucksaw two people set to on the job, each one pulling in turn towards his own direction. This is by far the simplest way, since pulling a saw through wood is much easier than pushing it.

ALWAYS A KNIFE

If an ax and even a saw are not necessary on most camping trips, a knife is almost essential even on a weekend stroll. Which really doesn't need saying, and certainly doesn't need explaining, as almost everyone instinctively takes one with him. But, and here's the rub, a large number of the knives taken to the woods should have been left behind. Malayan throwing knives, bowies big enough to kill an elephant in hand-to-hand combat, and commando knives suitable for a submersible attack on Manhattan not only look absurd, they are impractical and in some cases useless.

I have nothing against sheath knives, per se. Most of the hunting models usually sold to campers are simply too big. Also many are hollow-ground, that is, the blade is slightly concave, which weakens it, as does the totally unnecessary blood groove. That's the long channel running along the top edge of the blade which supposedly makes the blade cut through raw unbled meat with greater ease and accuracy. You never see it on a butcher's knife.

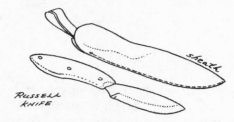

RUSSELL
KNIFE

If you feel you need a sheath knife, keep it small and simple. One of the best all-around models is a skinning knife used by Canadian trappers known by the name of its designer, Russell. You may not find it at a local store unless you're in trapping country, but you can get an excellent Nova Scotia-made one with a smooth rosewood handle and first-class Swedish steel blade by mail from the Ski Hut or Eastern Mountain Sports.

The Russell has a slightly offset four-inch-long beaver-tail blade with a curved handgrip. This means there's no hilt or crossbar needed at the end of the blade, making it a lighter knife. The hilt's sole purpose, in case you're interested, is to keep your fingers from sliding forward and cutting themselves when you stab into something, somebody, or an animal.

My only objection to the Russell knife is that the point is not sharp (a sharp point is no good when you're scraping fat off a pelt, you might cut it). However, it's simple enough to sharpen it up. Should you carry a sheath knife, by the way, try sticking it in your rear pocket instead of on the belt, where it always gets in the way as you walk.

My own choice is a dependable, strong pocketknife of two to three blades, the longest three inches or so. I've had a Buck Stockman for years, and except for a once-dull edge put on it by an itinerant knife sharpener of dubious skill in Kandahar, it's like new. The dull edge has long since been replaced by one sharp enough to shave with. I've

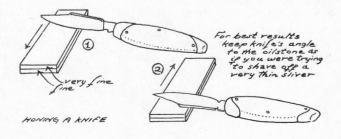

For best results keep knife's angle to the oilstone as if you were trying to shave off a very thin sliver

HONING A KNIFE

learned to sharpen my own knives on a whetstone, and I highly recommend you do the same.

ON THE SUBJECT OF MACHETES IN CONIFER FORESTS

Although Army- and Navy-surplus stores list a great variety of machetes in their catalogs, there's no possible use for a machete in temperate climates, except for trimming a lawn if you like to do things the hard way. A machete is an excellent jungle knife, essential for hacking through dense but tender underbrush. In lush tropical areas, where the water content of most plants is considerably higher than it is up north, it's most effective. If that's the direction in which you're heading, by all means take one. Otherwise forget it.

Also forget, if you do have to use a machete, about those old Jungle Jim movies where they slash once to the right and once to the left, then move forward three or four steps and slash again. Swinging a machete through really dense undergrowth is good hard work; if you're stubborn enough to want to get through, you may proceed at the rate of fifty feet or so a day. That's why river travel is so popular in jungle regions.

THE SHOVEL, TO TAKE OR NOT TO TAKE

A shovel presents more of a problem. Not in choice of models, but in deciding whether to lug it along or not. It's useful for burying human waste and garbage. But it's not essential. Food scraps will feed the wildlife. The inedible paraphernalia of camp cooking should be packed out of the wilderness in any case. Human waste should be buried only a few inches below surface level, a task that a twig or two are usually equal to; buried too deeply, it would not be reached by the bacterial action which is eventually to decay it.

Our decision is usually based on whether a shovel is required in the area to which we're heading. If the fire rules demand it, we take a small folding entrenching camp shovel; if not, we leave it home.

A handy alternative is the Ezee backpacker's trowel sold by Kelty. Made of Cycolac, it's extremely durable and will not rust. At two ounces, it's a convenience to have along for digging latrine ditches and for those rare occasions when you have to put a rain trench around your tent.

PLENTY OF ROPE

Almost any camping trip calls for a length of rope at one time or another—to hang your food up with, to rig a tarp tent, to tow a canoe, or even just for games of tug of war among the kids. On most trips fifty feet—double that figure for canoe camping or tarp tenting—of eighth-inch nylon rope is about right. It has a breaking strength of 400–800 pounds, depending on type and manufacturer, which is sufficient for most purposes. Quarter-inch nylon has a breaking strength of 1,200–1,800 pounds, which you'll need to tow or track a canoe. Braided nylon "parachute cord" with a five-hundred-pound breaking strength, available in hundred-foot skeins, is good for all-around suspension work from tarps to clotheslines.

Nylon rope gives a bit, which means you have to check it occasionally when using it for hitches. But you should get into that habit anyhow. Its strength is two and a half times that of hemp; it frays less; it's easily whipped by holding a lit match to the end, melting it a bit; and it's hardly susceptible to mildew. Even so, keep it dry and clean, and coiled when in storage around camp or at home.

SAFE-KEEPING THE TOOLS AROUND CAMP

Probably more people are injured by carelessly stored tools than by using them. Don't lay your saw down on the ground or prop it next to the chopping block when you're through cutting wood. Hang it on a small branch stump protruding from a handy tree. And if you're camping with kids, hang it high enough so they can't reach it.

Any loose rope that is not in use or packed away should also be coiled and hung. Tripping over it with a hot pot of stew in your hands is no way to wash your face.

Although it looks nice and woodsy to leave your ax or sheath knife stuck in a chopping block or log, sheath it. Put the ax safely away in your tent, the knife in your pocket. Not only is the habit an accident preventative, but it's better for the tools. Dew in the morning will rust your blade. If an ax sits out in the sun all day, the handle will tend to warp and dry out so the head loosens. If you're in porcupine country, you may wake up some morning and find half your ax handle chewed into toothpicks. It's not that porcupines are particularly fond of ax handles, or even in need of toothpicks. They crave salt. And putting any kind of work behind your wood chopping will build up sweat, turning the ax handle into a tasty porcupine pretzel stick.

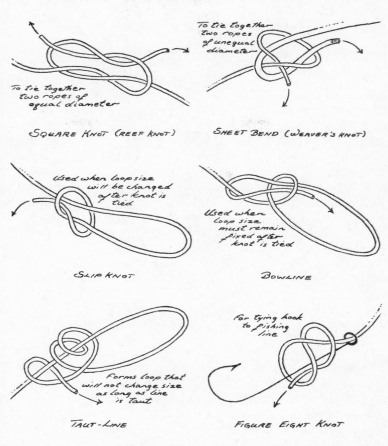

To tie together
two ropes of
equal diameter

SQUARE KNOT (REEF KNOT)

To tie together
two ropes
of unequal
diameter

SHEET BEND (WEAVER'S KNOT)

Used when loop size
will be changed
after knot is
tied

SLIP KNOT

Used when
loop size
must remain
fixed after
knot is tied

BOWLINE

Forms loop that
will not change size
as long as line
is taut

TAUT-LINE

For tying hook
to fishing
line

FIGURE EIGHT KNOT

KNOTS (For tying rope to rope)

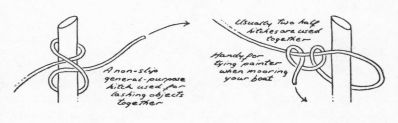

A non-slip
general-purpose
hitch used for
lashing objects
together

CLOVE HITCH

Usually two half
hitches are used
together

Handy for
tying painter
when mooring
your boat

HALF HITCH

HITCHES (For tying rope to pole or other object)

THE PACK ON YOUR BACK

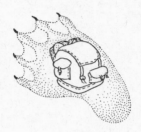

I've used rucksacks for years. For fewer years I've been using back-packs as well. The reason I've been using backpacks on occasion is that presently it's hard to find a good rucksack big enough for the family camper. And the reason for that is, when the modern backpack was swept into popularity by mass-marketing techniques and an under-standable follow-the-leader tendency of bewildered first-time campers presented with a confusing array of packing gear, the rucksack was swept pretty far under the rug. Please, oh please, won't somebody rescue it?

THE RUCKSACK VERSUS THE BACKPACK

At the risk of setting myself up as a target for slings and arrows of derision from backpackers and campers across the country, I'll say right now that in my opinion the frame backpack has been oversold. This came about, at least in part, because the majority of camping gear manufacturers are out West. In open mountain regions with limited areas of close bush, some of its negative features are much less noticeable. On trips lasting three or four weeks without a chance to reprovision, the backpack's larger capacity can be a plus. But for general outdoor use it has some practical drawbacks. Let's look a little closer at it.

The first thing you see prominently displayed in the sales literature and books on backpacking is a panting and exhausted hiker carrying the old-fashioned low-slung rucksack. He's leaning over as if he were charging into a tornado. Next to him is another camper with a high-riding, hip-belt-supported frame backpack, walking bolt upright like a Prussian general, but still managing to look relaxed and cool. In some cases there's a third person shown carrying a canoe. He's also straight and tall and relaxed.

Next, vector lines are drawn in to show how the rucksack distributes its weight further back than the pack, so the wearer has to compensate for it by leaning forward. Thus he wastes energy. This is true—although when the canoeist is depicted wasting no energy because his weight distribution is absolutely vertical, one does get the impression that an eighty-pound canoe weighs nothing. The point is, however, that although it takes a bit more energy to carry a rucksack, its advantages far outweigh, if you'll pardon the pun, this one disadvantage. The backpack's disadvantages, on the other hand, are pretty hard to ignore.

For instance, let's try on the backpack. Although it's cumbersome, it's also comfortable, just as the manufacturer said. And the hip belt does pull the weight in, making the load easier to carry. (You can get a hip belt for a rucksack, but it's not as efficient.) Of course, since the load rides so high on the pack frame, it was a bit clumsy to put on, but you're good at balancing. Besides, it's a minor point.

Balancing on the trail, however, is another matter. For example, there's that icy cold glacial stream with a convenient log spanning it to cross by. The log's a bit slippery from dew and moss. Still, under normal circumstances it wouldn't be difficult to walk. However, your center of balance is now up by your shoulders, instead of your hips as nature intended. Luckily, you do have along a six-foot hiking staff that's been getting snared in the woods all day—along with the top of your high-riding pack, which always seems to be reaching out for low-hanging branches—so you think about balancing yourself across the log with the staff plunged to the river bed. Unfortunately, this would mean bending over rather steeply, which turns the balancing act into somthing for the Great Wallendas. In the end, you take the pack

off and inch it across the log like a toddler with his push toy. Once
you get to the other side you put the pack on and stride away, nice
and upright again. There are a couple more balancing feats to conquer
during steep ascents and descents, but nothing serious.

Time to make camp. You take off your pack, set up the tent for
the night, and put the pack inside in case those low gray clouds decide
to shower you with their presence. Now the fun begins. You can't put
the full pack down on its frame because the frame and clevis pins will
dig holes in your tent floor. It won't balance on its side. If you put it
frame side up you can't get at any of your gear. So you do what
thousands of backpackers across the country do every night. You unpack almost everything, and look forward to repacking it the next
morning. Piles of neatly stacked gear now occupy half of your tent,
and you can just squeeze in a spot for your sleeping bag. In the
morning you pack up what looks by now like a rummage sale. The
guy with a rucksack is of course long gone, enjoying the country he
came to see while you're still in your tent trying to stuff the gear all
back in the way you had it before, thinking maybe next time it would
be easier to get a larger pack. An easier solution is to unpack just
enough of your gear to make a mattress for your backpack, so you
can lay it on its frame and still protect the tent floor.

I'll mention just a few of the other disadvantages, to keep my dia-
tribe to a minimum. On canoeing trips with short portages of only half
a mile or so, it's relatively painless to portage a canoe while wearing
a rucksack. It's impossible to portage a canoe while wearing a backpack; the pack simply sticks up too far. So you have to make the
portage twice even if you're traveling light.

Hitchhiking through Europe, you'll see hundreds of Americans
standing by their packs, while the Europeans sit on their rucksacks.
It's not impossible to sit on a pack, but it's too low for comfort and
the frame on most models will bend, which means you can kiss the
whole Rube Goldberg goodbye. To add insult to injury, when you
finally get a ride, the long pack won't fit into the trunk of most small
cars, so it gets put on the seat, where the clevis pins and frame
promptly tear the upholstery. Oh well, you probably won't ever see
those people again anyhow.

As a last thought, if you want a laugh, wear a high-riding pack
when you go ski touring or snowshoeing: chances are, you'll fall flat
on your face.

But enough. By all means, if you're planning to lug hundred-pound
loads to a base camp with some frequency, get a backpack. Otherwise,

all I'm suggesting is that if you've grown up in the rucksackless generation since the fifties, next time you get a pack try a rucksack, you'll
like it.

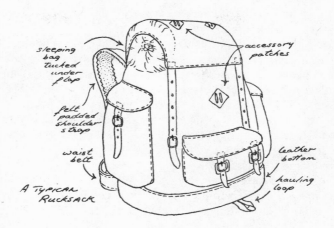

sleeping bag tucked under flap

accessory patches

felt padded shoulder strap

waist belt

leather bottom

hauling loop

A TYPICAL RUCKSACK

WHAT TO LOOK FOR IN A RUCKSACK

Assuming you're trying a rucksack, here's what I would look for.
Several large outside pockets; the traditional standard is three or four.
More and more rucksacks are made with only one back pocket or two
long side pockets. This makes them look sleeker, closer to a pack. It
also defeats the primary purpose of having pockets in the first place.
With three or four outside pockets you can pack your gear so that
everything you might need quickly is easily accessible during hiking.
You only have to open the pack itself when you make camp, and I've
gone several days at a time without having to do even that. An internal
pocket will keep the heaviest gear in place against your back instead
of shifting outwards.

Another thing to look for is leather—good, tough, durable, readily
waterproofed leather—on the bottom, also for the shoulder straps and
accessory straps on the top flap or sides of the back. The shoulder
straps, needless to say, should be padded or so designed as to spread
the load rather than cut into your collarbone. All fittings, the patches
by which belts and buckles are reinforced and attached to the bag,
should be of leather.

You also want good tough fabric—high-quality duck or heavy nylon

—for the rucksack itself. An overly generously cut top flap will permit you to put your sleeping bag underneath, outside the sack but still part and parcel of the pack. This will give you more room, when needed, than the traditional way of packing the sleeping bag inside the rucksack. For maximum stuffability, this flap should have two straps instead of a single center one.

Most rucksacks have a frame, either contoured metal bows or tubular ones, to help make them ride more comfortably on your back. This feature, pioneered by Bergans of Norway in the thirties, although useful, does not transfer the weight to your hips as well as a backpack frame does. By the way, when you're trying on a rucksack or a pack, it won't do you any good to sling it over your shoulders empty. Borrow some fairly hefty gear from the store shelves to weight it with so you'll have some idea of how it will feel packed up for the trail. Don't get one too large for comfort.

Not counting the old, genuine World War II U.S. Army rucksacks, which are wonderful surplus buys if you can find them, there are seven more or less different rucksacks available in the United States today. Not exactly a paucity of models, you say. Perhaps. But they are nowhere near what they could be, and in the case of the European models nowhere near what they were only a couple of years ago. I can only hope that as campers and manufacturers alike begin to realize the limitations of backpacks, designers will turn their imagination to improving and modernizing the rucksack.

Probably the best of the current lot are the Lichenneiger and its larger counterpart, the Mountaineer, manufactured by Class 5 and available through Co-op Wilderness Supply and a few local retailers. Their design is close to being classic. Made of eleven-and-a-half-ounce waterproof cordura, they feature all marine-grade stainless steel hardware. The straps and webbing are reinforced nylon. Full-grain leather bottom and accessory patches. The Lichenneiger has two full-length, zipper-closured outside pockets which would be more convenient and flexible for packing if cut in half to make four smaller pockets. The nylon coil zippers have storm flaps. The Mountaineer is similar to the Lichenneiger in design but 30 percent larger, and comes resplendent with a third outside pocket and a foam-padded waist belt with quick-release buckle. I'd like to see a larger top flap. Otherwise they're excellent modern rucksacks.

Second in line are the French La Fuma rucksacks. You won't find one with a leather bottom, unfortunately, though the synthetic one will be sturdy and flexible. The substantial outside pockets are closed with leather straps on most models. I personally prefer the straps to zippers. But with this arrangement you must learn to pack so that no small objects will work their way out of the top of the pockets as you wander or put your pack down. The Flexframe model, smaller than the standard Super AR-11, comes with somewhat diminutive waist straps. Luckily they are removable so you can replace them with wider, more comfortable ones. A waist strap, incidentally, keeps a rucksack closer to your body when you're active, and thus improves your balance for skiing, snowshoeing, and so on. It does not really do much to shift the load the way a waist belt on a pack does. The top flap of all the La Fumas is laughably small. But in spite of its faults, the Super AR-11 is one of the few rucksacks presently on the market with any substantial carrying capacity.

Next on the list is the Alpine Designs Eiger Pack. Hopefully Alpine will soon come out with a larger Eiger Pack, maybe even complete with a third outside pocket. Except for its size—good for a comfortable week's trip but no more—the aborted third pocket, and the abbreviated top flap, the Eiger Pack is a fine rucksack with leather bottom, generous straps, and zippered side pockets. The ski touring model is handy for nonskiers as well, having extra accessory straps and a convenient spot to tuck the ax if you carry one.

The Sierra Designs Summit rucksack suffers from the same drawback of being too small for any extended trips. Its third pocket is on the top flap, which I find makes the rucksack high, particularly if a sleeping bag is tucked under the generous flap. The old concept of having a map case there instead is much more convenient. The bottom is tough leather, and the sack itself is a heavy-grade waterproofed nylon. Nylon straps.

Millet makes a nice medium-sized, two-pocket canvas bag, available from Recreational Equipment, Inc. Unfortunately it has a nylon bottom. A good synthetic bottom will often wear as well as leather, but it certainly doesn't age as attractively. And the esthetic quality of nylon and its ilk when used to mimic leather is just plain poor. Synthetics have their place—as honest synthetics.

Then the hybrids begin. Some manufacturers, notably North Face and Bergans, are trying to flow with the tide of backpacks by modifying the rucksack. As with most compromises, it doesn't seem to be working.

The North Face Ruthsac uses three riveted aluminum bows on which the sack is hung in such a manner as to transfer the weight of the load to the wearer's hips. It's a comfortable sack; however, it's too small. And the novelty of having the whole back zipper open so things are packed and unpacked as in a suitcase is to me just that, a novelty, not very practical, since with this design you can't really "stuff" when you pack.

The new redesigned Bergans knapsack is a very good rucksack—on a not particularly good frame. It's essentially a low-slung pack frame with a bottom ledge for your sleeping bag. The old Bergans are classics if you can find them. The new ones—well, they're certainly better than a backpack when it comes to keeping your balance, but that jutting low frame just gets in the way too often for my taste.

BACKPACKS AND THE SOLITARY FRAME

With the scarcity of rucksacks to choose from, you may not be able to find one comfortable for you. That's one reason for looking over the backpacks as well. Another is for extended trips when you must carry above-average loads in order to be fully self-sufficient. And thirdly, they're the only sensible kind of pack for those who develop the charging bull syndrome of camping. This, if you're not familiar with it, is usually manifested by such campfire talk as, "Yeah, I made twenty-three miles through the bush today. There's three swamps on my route tomorrow and a 2,000-foot sixty-degree gradient, but with an early start I still should crack twenty miles."

One of the most important things to keep in mind when buying a pack is getting one the right size. Don't buy a large one just because you think it's more impressive if a medium will do. Probably more difficulty is encountered by carrying too large a bag than by any other single factor.

A pack frame should be body-contoured for comfort, and is best made of lightweight tubular aluminum or aluminum alloy, preferably with heli-arc welded joints. Stay away from angle iron construction; it twists out of shape very readily.

Most people agree on a strong, abrasion-resistant nylon bag. However, whether it should be waterproofed on the inside like the Mountain Master ones, or on the outside like the Alpine Designs, or not coated at all, like our old Kelty packs, is a bone of contention. If you use an uncoated one, get a rain cover; with a coated one, any moisture that happens to get inside stays there. Take your pick.

A SAMPLING OF BACKPACK AND RUCKSACK SPECIFICATIONS

BACKPACKS

Pack	Length	Width	Top Depth	Bottom Depth	Volume of Main Compartment (cubic inches)	Number of Pockets	Total Volume (cubic inches)	Weight without Frame (ounces)
Alpine Designs Expedition	22	14	7	7	2150	6	2700	17*
Camp Trails Horizon Medium	18	15	9	6¾	2160	5	2700	24*
Eastern Mountain Sports Backpacker Large	20½	16	7½	7½	2470	4	3040	20*
Kelty B4 Large	20	15	9	6	2460	4	2800	19*
Universal Loadmaster Large	20	14	8	8	2240	6	2870	25*

* *Average frame weight 38 ounces.*

RUCKSACKS

Pack	Length	Width	Top Depth	Bottom Depth	Volume of Main Compartment (cubic inches)	Number of Pockets	Total Volume (cubic inches)	Total Weight (ounces)
Class 5 Mountaineer	24	16	9	6	2600	4	3600	46*
Eiger Pack	19	14	7	7	1525	3	2000	38*
La Fuma Expandable	17	18	10	10	2970	3	3320	62*
North Face Ruthsac	20	14	6	6	1680	2	2160	58*
Sierra Designs Summit	20	14	7	7	2000	3	2600	41*

* *Includes internal or external back brace/frame arrangement.*

The bag should have a minimum number of seams and be reinforced at all major stress and attachment points. If the bag tears off, it's possible to continue using the frame as a true pack board, but it's much simpler just to keep it all together. Clevis pins are used to attach the bag to the frame. These are easier to work and keep the bag more firmly in place than the old tie-and-strap method you may still see around on some models. If you're hard on packs, incidentally, pick up a couple of extra clevis pins when you buy your bag.

Pocket arrangement and compartmentalization, if any, are matters of convenience to you. My own experience has been that a bag compartmentalized into what amounts to several bags on one frame defeats the very ease of packing rucksacks and backpacks were designed for. I like one big bag. But I also like it to have several outside pockets.

Make sure zippers are nylon rather than metal. Check that flap covers when closed extend well below the zippers to keep out dirt, dust, and rain.

The harness for a pack, including a hip belt as well as shoulder straps, should be fully adjustable in all directions so you can custom-fit each load and compensate for your own weight loss or gain. The hip and shoulder pads should be firm. Nice soft ones may feel luxuri-

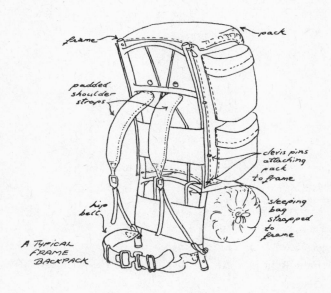

frame

pack

padded shoulder straps

clevis pins attaching pack to frame

sleeping bag strapped to frame

hip belt

A TYPICAL FRAME BACKPACK

ous in the store; on the trail they'll begin to develop Vs with a sharp cutting-into-you edge from the strain.

There are a lot of well-made backpacks around. When it comes to choosing the one for you, keeping these basic points in mind and buying from a reputable manufacturer—Kelty, Mountain Master, Gerry, Recreational Equipment, Inc., and Jan Sport, to name just a few—it's pretty hard to go wrong. Find the pack from among the established makes that has the specific features that appeal to you and that is the most comfortable.

PACKING IT IN

There's no doubt that the backpacker can carry more equipment than the rucksacker. But besides the problems a pack frame causes, the question is, should you have all that equipment along in the first place?

Up the Abitibi River in Ontario one time, I ran across a man traveling with his twelve-year-old son. They had been canoeing for over a month. Their equipment consisted of a lightweight tent, two sleeping bags, one rucksack, a set of spare clothes for each of them, and two fishing rods. You'll notice there are several items missing, to say the least, from the average camper's check list—and that certainly includes mine. This man knew how to fish; it was the end of August, with boletus and berries plentiful; on occasion they caught assorted fowl by hand. Now I wouldn't recommend to anybody (except the twelve-year-old son and eventually, hopefully, the son's son) that they set out on a camping trip this way. On the other side of the fence, I once met a group of hikers on the trail with a portable TV. They were complaining about the poor reception. . . .

The point is, the more experienced a camper you become, the less you should and will take along. If you're going out into the wilds to escape from civilization, why drag it all painfully along with you?

Well, then, what should you have along besides the big three—rucksack, sleeping bag, and tent (or tarp with ground cloth)? I'd start with the Mountaineers' Ten Essentials, a check list compiled by the West Coast organization of climbers, conservationists, and outdoorsmen.

(1) At least one complete change of clothing, including extras for such contingencies as rain and cold weather.

(2) Extra food. A mystique has surrounded the weight factor in backpacking. Some members of the fraternity sit around with everything short of a calorimeter estimating how many raisins to take or how few grains of rice they can get away with. By all means pare your weight down, but include extra rations in your minimum. On any hiking trip in which things go as expected there *should* be food left over. This is your insurance policy in case something goes really wrong. If you're lucky in fishing, and the berries and roots are plentiful, you might even come home with more food than you started with.

(3) Sunglasses. This one I could quibble with sometimes, but that's what makes a horse race. In the northeastern United States and Canada where we camp most frequently, one seldom needs sunglasses, because of the forests' density. However, every time you set out for a strange area it's good to have a pair along. And if you're planning on desert, alpine, or winter camping, it's a rare pair of eyes that doesn't fatigue under those conditions, particularly after the subdued smoggy light of city living. Even the Eskimos worry about snow blindness.

(4) A knife. A substantial pocketknife is the order of the day. You don't need a bowie knife to whittle kindling. And leave the big sheath knives for people who are out to tackle bears with their bare hands.

My old three-bladed Buck, given to me by a friend years ago, has been used to tear off coconut husks in Moorea, gut fish in the Yukon, and skin snakes in Thailand. It isn't perfect. The main blade is a bit small for some of the jobs I ask it to tackle. But it works, keeps a great edge, and is compact. Susan uses a small red Swiss Army knife with two blades, can opener, scissors, screwdriver, tweezers, and file. It's also a very handy knife, although the blades are shorter than those of my Buck and it's poorly balanced for mumbletypeg. Between us we have a mini tool shed.

(5) Fire starters, jelly, ribbon, tablets, or impregnated peat bricks. While I feel strongly that the age of the seven-foot bonfire casting long shadows into the woods is no longer with us, the occasional small evening campfire is hard to forsake entirely. And there are emergencies where a fire is both necessary and difficult to start. To this end every kit should include a supply of starters of one kind or another. They can raise the flames in some pretty thoroughly drenched wood. I still have some old peat bricks from the now defunct Camp & Trails in

New York (not to be confused with the still very much alive and thriving Camp Trails). One early fall in the Adirondacks, after we'd been paddling for four hours in pouring rain—don't ask what we were doing paddling in the rain all that time, those things happen—the fire starters coaxed flames out of some completely soaked pine, probably keeping us from nasty colds, if not pneumonia.

(6) Emergency matches. Fire starters alone do not a fire make. You need matches. Yes, you can start a fire with flint and steel or even a fire drill if you really want to. A fire drill will keep you warm as you pump away trying to get the tinder started. But carry emergency matches, in addition to your regular cook kit supply. Get the long, strike-anywhere kitchen ones. In some cities, like New York, these have been banned as a fire hazard; when it comes to camping, however, the strike-anywhere feature is a very real boon. I always pick up a couple of boxes when I'm in a store where they're sold.

Not only should the emergency supply of matches be kept in waterproof containers, but the matches themselves should be waterproofed as well. All the waterproof containers I've tried keep water out, it's true; nevertheless moisture still seeps in. Dip the match heads in paraffin heated slowly just to the simmering point in a double boiler at home. Don't let the paraffin get too hot, or you'll end up with a cozy little fire on the range.

A simpler and safer method of waterproofing is to paint the match heads with spar varnish. Two points to remember if you do this, however: you'll have to strike them harder for a light, and varnish does not contribute as much to the overall combustion as paraffin does.

(7) A first aid kit. My first time out, the kit I carried was a four-pound minihospital that could handle anything short of an epidemic of cholera or plaster-casting a greenstick fracture. With the passing of time, it has been scaled down to more manageable proportions. And even though I've never had to use any of it (I'm keeping my fingers crossed) except to help other people caught without one—or perhaps for that very reason—I would never set off on any extended trip without it.

That goes for my faithful Cutter snake bite kit as well. It's self-encased in fit-together rubber suction cups. Every ten years I throw it out and get a new one just in case the rubber's getting a little less resilient.

What you put into your first aid kit depends on your own needs, the conditions under which you travel, the number in your party, and so on. Although there are some good prepackaged kits, most of them contain too much unnecessary junk. If you don't want to assemble your own, Recreational Equipment's Mountain First Aid Kit, packed to measure one and a half by four and a quarter by seven and a half inches, and weighing ten ounces, is about the best. It includes the *Mountaineering First Aid Book*, adhesive tape, adhesive bandages, sterile gauze pads, butterfly Band-Aids, roller gauze, moleskin, sewing kit, safety pins, antiseptic soap, aspirin, salt tablets, merthiolate swabs, razor blade, antiseptic first aid cream, and ammonia inhalants. With a little coaxing you can squeeze in a few pain-killing tablets, antibiotics, and some Halazone as well. Put half a dozen rubber bands around the outside. They come in handy at the strangest times. If you're traveling with kids, you may need some extra bandages. Reading over the latest edition of the standard Red Cross first aid manual —do your studying before you set out—is also a good idea.

(8) A flashlight. Everyone should carry his own. If your trip is to be of any duration, add extra batteries and bulbs, just in case.

You can get supercharged monsters whose beam will carry half a mile and blind you at a quarter, but I see no reason to. Probably the best, almost the cheapest, and easily the handiest flashlight is the Mallory Compact that uses a pair of AA-cell alkaline batteries. It weighs only three ounces and can be used continuously for four hours. With intermittent use, the battery life is considerably longer. Durability is not its forte. Still, many campers prefer to carry two of these to one of the larger C-cell type. Susan and I carry one Mallory apiece. They've always seen us through. Fits handily in your mouth if you need both hands to work with in the dark. Put a piece of adhesive tape over the switch when you pack it. Otherwise it's apt to jiggle on as you walk, running down the batteries. Taping it down—or up when it's flicked on, just to ensure the tape sticks around—is simple enough, but let's hope Mallory comes out with a locking switch model soon.

(9) Maps. You should have a map when going to all but the most familiar places. It's not only a safety factor, but can add a lot of enjoyment to your trip, helping you to find the best camp spots, scenery, and sights.

(10) A good-quality compass. Goes hand in hand with the map. More about both in "Getting Lost and Unlost."

(11) A space blanket. The original mountaineers' list was drawn up

four decades ago, and the eleventh item I'm taking the liberty of adding was not included because it didn't exist at the time. Today it is an invaluable safety precaution. Weighing only two ounces, its folded size is two by four inches by one inch thick. It opens up to a full fifty-six by eighty-four inches. Its space-age-developed crinkly material reflects up to 90 percent of a sleeper's body heat, while at the same time keeping out wind, rain, and snow. It will rip easily, but not as easily as its flimsy looks suggest. Since it works on the reflector principle, you'll have to leave a crack open along the edge or vent it open occasionally to let moisture out. Not to be used as a camping blanket, but essential emergency gear.

ODDS AND ENDS AND PERSONALS

For your toilet kit, set out whatever you feel you need—then try to cut it in half. Don't leave out the toilet paper, but take the smallest possible toothpaste tube. In the same vein, take suntan lotion, lip balm, and insect repellent in simple containers, not bulky aerosol cans. For the males: Consider leaving your shaving gear behind. If you've ever wanted to grow a beard or moustache, this is the time to get a running start without appearing stubbly in civilization. If you haven't, consider growing one just for the occasion. For the women: Why not leave your cosmetics at home? Fresh air and exercise offer you that healthy, young blush of beauty only the outdoors can give.

However you pare the check list, you'll always think of some other necessity you'll want to bring along. Try not to. One that I do tuck in for youngsters old enough to be taught that I'll tan their hide off if they use it when they aren't lost is a whistle. The shrill blast of a whistle requires less effort and carries further than shouting. Three whistles—as is three of anything—is a universal distress signal easy for lost people, be they children or adults, to remember and execute. It gives little John and Mary extra security.

PUTTING IT ALL TOGETHER

Pack everything you need into your rucksack or backpack once. Then unpack it. Pack it again. Everything in its place and a place for everything, as the old platitude goes. You should be able to find anything you want blindfolded. This way you'll minimize your work and forestall problems, the better to enjoy your camping.

How you pack is up to you. Besides such obvious things as putting the most needed things in the most accessible places and keeping heavy objects in the pack, close to your body—so they will bear down less on your shoulders, but not so close they poke into your back, there are only a couple of tips to consider. Traditionally the sleeping bag goes inside a rucksack; if you're using a backpack, on the other hand, the sleeping bag is lashed to the outside frame. This difference in packing technique, incidentally, has a great deal to do with the backpack's larger load capacity—its inside dimensions often being more or less the same as an equivalent rucksack's. By rolling your clothes instead of folding them, they take up less space. Don't keep all your matches in one place. Some should go with your kitchen gear, others in their waterproof container at the opposite end of the pack, maybe even a third cache in an outside pocket by the first aid kit.

While I don't like my bags precompartmentalized by the manufacturer, because that way they lose their versatility and ease of stuffing, keeping such things as cook gear, underwear, breakfasts, and main meals separate can be very handy. To this end, consider getting a few extra nylon stuff sacks of different colors so you can tell at a glance what's inside, turning your pack into a mini container ship.

However you pack, once you hit the road you'll make some changes. It's not until you've been living out of a pack for a while that a-place-for-everything-and-everything-in-its-place becomes ingrained.

THE LITTLEST CAMPER

"She's not even a year old, how can you take her camping?"

Later.

"What do you mean you're taking her up to the Yukon with you? She's not even a year and a half old. How's she going to live in a tent when there's snow on the ground?"

Those were the softer questions asked of us when we began camping with Genevieve. The fiercer statements threatened to have us locked up for child abuse. You'd think children had always been raised with central heating, running water, and the supermarket around the corner. Yet today's high-quality camping gear makes it almost easier to care for a child, even an infant, in the great outdoors than in the wilds of the city.

For camping purposes, kids can be divided into three distinct classes, depending on their mobility: carry-alongs, anchors, and catch-me-if-you-cans. As infants they ride and even fall asleep in a Gerry or similar kiddie pack with such ease you almost have to force yourself to remember they're there when you duck a low-hanging branch or sit down for a rest and start to lean back against a sun-warmed boulder. Your partner will remember better, since he or she will be carrying most of the gear for all three. I once tried to talk Susan into toting a knapsack behind, the baby in front in the frameless Peterson carrier, to keep nicely balanced all around, but she didn't go for the idea.

The second, or anchor, stage is the only one that limits your mobility to any real extent. Roughly between the ages of two and five, children become both too heavy and too restless to be carried for prolonged periods; at the same time they're not really self-propelled enough for treks over appreciable distances. It's a great time for base or canoe camping, but not for backpacking. When canoeing, by the way, put the kids in life vests and give them the run of the boat except when you're in white water. They'll get their sea legs before you do. But learn how to swim first, both of you parents. And give the kids lessons as soon as they seem eager for them.

After the riding-at-anchor stage, it's catch as catch can. Developing a plan of tactical exhaustion simmers things down, but make it one that gives the junior camper a sense of accomplishment and belonging to the group. Don't force your child on, you yourself walking into the trap of bragging, "He's only seven, but he can carry a twenty-pound pack all day." Maybe he can, but that's no way to teach him to appreciate the great outdoors.

Start by letting the child assume some responsibility for his or her own gear. Any time a child takes the initiative, encourage it. Genevieve carried a small blue knapsack around camp with her toy lambs in it. Sometimes on her back, sometimes clasped in her hands, no time for very long. But she knew it was hers.

As every mother knows from endlessly emptying out boys' pants pockets, children collect things interminably. This can be channeled in the direction of gathering twigs for the fire, picking berries, bringing water, and cleaning up the camp site. Genevieve became quite adroit, if somewhat irregular, at wood gathering as soon as she could toddle. Unfortunately, her harvesting spilled over to collecting pine cones, the favorite repository for said prickly bundles being Daddy's sleeping bag. Never Mommy's. I'm sure there's some deep hidden Freudian significance in that, but even when pulling out half a dozen cones in one night, I've never been able to discover it. Besides, she giggles a lot as I make a somewhat extravagant project of mining my bag.

BACKPACKING A BABY

Probably no one knows how much infants who are a year old or younger absorb of their wilderness surroundings. Communication at that age is somewhat elementary. Babies of camping parents we know almost invariably seem to make a leap forward in development both when they arrive in the wilds and when they return home. Maybe it's just the change in environments. Nevertheless, there it is. So if your only reason for not taking the baby camping is a fear he can't adjust to the woods, relax. With a little care and planning, it will be a great experience for all of you.

For a big baby, take a Gerry or similar kiddie pack; a very young or a lightweight baby may be more secure and protected in a Peterson or Snugli model that can be strapped on in front. Start out with short trips to areas you are familiar with before you tackle a long journey. And a small point, but one easily overlooked: backpacking a baby usually lulls the little tyke to quiet murmurings or even sleep, so you may have to remind yourself to check that he's not getting too much sun or wind back there.

THE WILDERNESS NURSERY

Baby food, sleeping accommodations, and clothing have been discussed in the earlier chapters on outfitting and provisioning. That leaves the traditional nursery topics of diapers and, for the bottle-fed baby, formula still to deal with.

The Crees have the easiest solution I've heard of to the diapering problem. They use a highly absorbent and skin-soothing variety of tree moss as an all-day diaper liner. Unfortunately I haven't been able to discover where the moss is to be found. So for us the gear still has to include a fair-sized diaper duffel. Some mothers find Pampers a real boon in the city, but in the wilds these diapers are something else again. They can't be buried, since the plastic outer linings don't decay and would be around for at least the next sixty or seventy generations. And burning wet Pampers is not my idea of a cozy fragrant campfire. So you end up lugging a lot of extra plastic out. By the sopping bagful.

For the sake of convenience, do stick with the type of diapers you use at home. Just remember, if Pampers are your choice, in the wilds they are no longer disposable. We use cloth diapers because Genevieve is more comfortable in them. We wash them out by hand as we go, drying them in the sun, which both bleaches and sterilizes them. Using paper diaper liners takes care of the problem of really messy diapers. The liner can be buried in toto beneath a three- to six-inch layer of soil in a remote spot. Be sure it's well covered, and roll a rock over it as an added measure. Unlike a Pamper, it will disintegrate completely in a year or so.

Formula should be no particular problem in this day and age, with all the canned varieties. Buy in single-feeding size, even though it means more flattened cans to pack out, so you'll be using up what you open right away.

Unfortunately, there's no getting around the weight factor completely. But powdered formula, and to some extent the concentrated liquid, will save a lot of pounds. And there's always the evaporated and dried whole or skim milks. However, with the liquid concentrates or powders, you'll need a boiled water supply for mixing; the premixed formula, if you have room for it, saves time and bother. Naturally, as with the baby foods, you want to check with your pediatrician if you have any questions about formula feeding.

The presterilized nursers on the market today make hygiene simple, even though you're packing out the used refill containers. All you have to worry about is boiling the nipples. Mother's milk is, of course, easiest of all.

For the baby just going on solids, a handy puréeing device often available in local infant specialty shops is the Happy Baby Food Grinder. It does almost as good a job as the blender back home, and will save the cook's wrist a lot of busy mashing activity at feeding time.

HOME IS A LOVEY

All through the first day it's fun and games, everything is new and exciting. Then suddenly comes night and it's time to go to bed. To go *home* to bed, to security. This can be a problem, but need not be if you prepare for it. Take along the littlest camper's favorite lovey, be it the teddy bear, lamb, blanket, or the huge gingham dog with floppy ears you know are going to flap into the cereal. Take several of the next-favorite toys—these can be kept to the small-size variety—on long trips, hiding one for a couple of weeks and bringing it out again as something both old and new.

Even six- or seven-year-olds appreciate having a favorite toy with them. It may be as unrelated to the wilds as a small dump truck or airplane, but it's something to fall back on.

Letting a baby or young child sleep in his own bag at home for a couple of days before you set out will convince him he's got at least a chunk of the real thing with him when he hits the road. If it's a down bag, it will be too warm to sleep inside of in the house. Sleeping on top of it, however, breeds the same familiarity.

GET THERE BEFORE THE TODDLER DOES

Once a kid is weaned and out of diapers, the adjustments and modifications of your camping routine are pretty similar whether he is in the anchorage or catch-me-if-you-can stage. I trust it goes without saying that you'll childproof your campsite as you would your home, and be especially watchful about where you leave the fuel and stove, matches, ax, first aid items, and all such potential hazards to young children. And we've covered the practical details of children's sleeping bags and possible tenting arrangements earlier in the book. But there are a couple of suggestions I would make on planning where to go. Keep to familiar areas on at least some of your trips. Children like to go back to favorite haunts, and parents rest easier knowing the lay of the land and its trouble spots. You may want to stalk out the new places before you let the family loose in them, so you'll be aware of any local hazards as well as the convenient rest spots for a hike, the perfect frog pond to camp near, or the spot up in the mountains that has snow banks still clinging on through late spring. Snow and children go together like ice cream and cones. Finding snow when it's totally unexpected is almost as good as having an extra Christmas.

Knowing about an area does wonders to keep kids amused and interested. And if a camping trip isn't fun, what good is it? A couple of lightweight handbooks, such as the Peterson series, which covers nature from minerals to birds, are handy for reference if you're rusty on your flora and fauna and such. Maps and adjunct reports on the geology of the region will have you telling the kids about the massive glaciers that once moved down that particular valley, or the volcano whose fiery lava now lies still and fertile beneath their feet—and it's amazing how fascinated you yourself will become with it all.

Oh, by the way, it pays for you to be familiar with your equipment too. "That's not the way it goes, Daddy," from a three-year-old is no morale booster, especially if he's right.

NATURE IS A TOY CHEST

Keeping a child busy and active is not much of a problem. The real problem is more apt to be toning things down. I still remember Genevieve, whose animal vocabulary at the time was limited to city creatures, running after a 1,200-pound bull moose that edged towards our camp in Alaska, shouting delightedly, "Doggie! Doggie!"

Almost any child will play for hours with "boats" in a stream or by the lake shore. He'll stick a small leaf into a bigger one and watch the ship sail with its bounty all the way across a pond to China. Again I trust it goes without saying to parents that water play time is a time for keeping noses constantly, vigilantly counted.

But sometimes a child not brought up in the country needs a little help to enter his new world of the wild. Give him a hand, and he'll carry you through with him to a universe you may have long since forgotten. A small fallen log laid across another becomes a seesaw the likes of which no playground at home can match. And a pile of pine needles, well, have you ever seen such a wonderful cargo for loading in and out of trucks? A few pipe cleaners tucked away in anticipation will turn pine cones into a menagerie. Then there are always snail races, frogs and salamanders found and returned to their proper place, and of course that most wondrous of outdoor Pied Pipers for a child—the willow whistle—to make. And they can bring home a piece of the wilderness as well, as you'll discover in the last chapter.

THROUGH A SMALL CHILD'S EYES

The world's not the same when you're three feet tall. Vistas of Grand Canyon splendor can't compete with walking along a log, carefully balancing so as not to fall over its six-inch precipice, nor

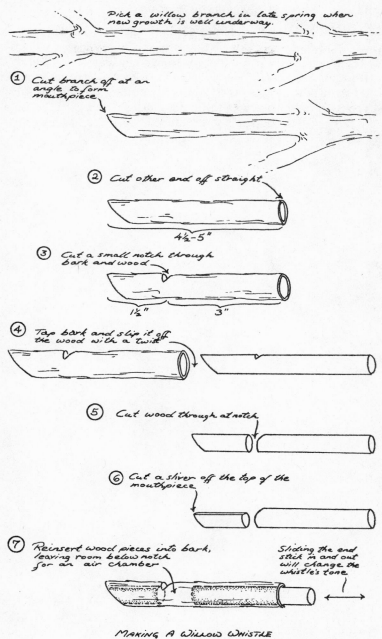

Pick a willow branch in late spring when new growth is well underway.

1. Cut branch off at an angle to form mouthpiece

2. Cut other end off straight

   4½–5"

3. Cut a small notch through bark and wood

   1½"   3"

4. Tap bark and slip it off the wood with a twist

5. Cut wood through at notch

6. Cut a sliver off the top of the mouthpiece

7. Reinsert wood pieces into bark, leaving room below notch for an air chamber

   Sliding the end stick in and out will change the whistle's tone

MAKING A WILLOW WHISTLE

the wide Missouri with a foot-wide creek that can be dammed. A winter landscape stretching like a vast vision of Siberia is hardly noticed while a dozen icicles hanging from a low branch to the ground is a magnificent castle. When you camp with children, look at the world through their eyes occasionally. It will turn those frequent rest stops you have to make with them into a delight rather than a chore.

So there you are, all ready to take the kid on his or her first camping trip. Go to it. It'll be a great experience for all of you.

MAKING CAMP

A number of years ago, having crossed the High Atlas, a college friend and I passed through the village of Erfoud for a dinner of charcoal-braziered lamb and then continued on into the desert. Several hours after sunset, we were still searching for a place to lay out our sleeping bags. It was an unusual night on the eastern Sahara, for it was dark and clouded. Not to the point where it would do something absurd like rain, just dark enough so we should have made camp a long time back. The problem was that this was a countryside of talus and large pebbles. We hadn't passed a smooth area large enough to put our heads on, much less the rest of us. But it was really too dark to go on. Besides which, we were getting dog-tired. At the moment of imminent collapse, when even sleeping on a field of golf balls seemed possible, we came upon a hard-packed, smooth depression right at the side of our path. It was even level for the most part, besides being big enough to sleep half a dozen elephants. And sleep we did.

Came morning, we rolled out shortly after dawn. It was then that we discovered we were sleeping on an old Texas bridge. A Texas bridge, in case you're not familiar with the term, is simply a slab of continuous concrete laid down across an occasional river bed, so that in those rare instances when there's water present vehicles can ford the stream if it isn't too deep. It's a good, cheap way to ensure a river crossing when the river's around only a couple of times a year. Now the idea of traffic didn't bother us because there wasn't any. But as we sat up in our sleeping bags, we came to the realization that if there had been one of those sudden unaccountable rains up in the mountains the previous evening, we'd probably have been floating down in the flash flood like a pair of dead logs.

FINDING A CAMPSITE

Choosing a camping spot requires a bit of observation. More so if you're off the beaten track than in a national park or forest, where locations are usually restricted to fixed campsites. Even there, when on remote trails and waterways, away from these fixed sites, the considerate camper picks a previously established location wherever possible, in order to minimize man's intrusion into the wilds. Not only does this practice preserve the same unspoiled beauty that you found for those who follow and who in turn are followed, in most cases it also assures you of one of the best spots available.

The campers of the past—the woodsmen who unleashed their weapons upon arriving to make tables, dingle cranes, kitchen racks, bough beds, and sapling tent poles, all from native material—seem in the camping world of today very destructive indeed, but fools they weren't. They picked the best spot to be found within any given area —sheltered, close to water, and usually with the grandest view around as well.

The only problem is that the natural advantages of these spots often lead to their becoming minislums. Without trying to sound like a platoon leader assigning KP, let me suggest that if you come to a campsite where the previous occupants apparently reveled in leaving paper, cans, and other garbage scattered all over the "floor," help clean it up. It only takes a couple of minutes, and isn't asking much in repayment for the free use of nature. Hopefully, if everyone does the same, in a few years there'll be no need to continue the *pro bono publico* cleanup.

DOWN BY THE RIVERSIDE

One of the keys to a comfortable, nay even a bearable, campsite is water. In the desert, salt marshes, and some mountains, water is inaccessible. There you must pack it in. But in most locations water will be available from one source or another—hopefully not too polluted.

To help minimize pollution, some national parks and forests are beginning to forbid people to set up camp closer than a hundred feet from a lake. Another tragic sign of overcrowding in parts of our wilderness. These national recreation areas are so popular that were everybody to camp by the water, the shores would become a trampled carriageway; and this most crucial strip of the ecosystem would no longer be able to sustain itself. Trees would not shade the pools where fish play; insects would not fall into the water to feed the fish; the trampled banks would erode, caving in to fill the streams and lakes more quickly than they could assimilate the material, eventually turning large numbers of the most scenic and thus most desirable camp spots into hog wallows. You will want to be close enough to the water to use it; but in those areas where it's necessary to camp a bit away from the source, you will find it a pleasant task to stroll down for your supply.

There are other things to be said for camping some distance from streams, rivers, and even lakes. They do rise unexpectedly. Most of the time you can spot the high-water mark by mud and other stains on nearby trees. But there's no such thing as the ultimate flood record. For the same reason, although that grassy sandbank with a cozy ring of little pines in the middle of the river may seem the perfect place to pull the canoe in for the night—what could be better than one's own island?—it could be mighty dangerous. A fine place for lunch, but not for an overnight stay. Although the rise of water will be small in most places, given the right conditions, water levels have been known to rise five to ten feet overnight. Also, keeping away from the very edge of the water, and preferably up from it as well, lessens discomfort from dampness, mist, and often mosquitoes.

FINDING WATER

There are no handy kitchen faucets in the wilds—except in the larger campgrounds with their trailers and recreation vehicles bumper to bumper, and six-man tents guy line to guy line. If you're not in one of these, and don't happen to be hiking along the course of a river or canoeing over chains of lakes, where do you find water?

Your map will help if it's detailed enough. Almost any water source of any size, including annual spring freshets, will be marked on a geodesic map. Even so, it's a good idea to be aware of where water is most likely to be found, just in case you left the map at the last log rest stop. Besides, knowing nature, being familiar with its habits, gives you a real sense of understanding and accomplishment that is very much a part of the joy of camping.

In mountainous and forest regions such as Eastern and Western Canada, and the United States, and most of Northern Europe, water rarely presents a problem. Almost any downhill country, be it a long slow valley or a deep gorge, will lead to it. These natural formations developed through water erosion, and the sculpture tells the tale.

As you walk, keep your eyes open for a change not only in terrain but in vegetation as well. If you see a crooked line of willows or willowlike trees in the distance, it's an almost sure bet you'll find a stream when you get there.

The mountain ahead is bare, with no water or greenery in sight. One side comes down steeply to a heavy rock formation; the other side slopes gently down to a valley and gently up to another mountain. Head for the sloping side rather than the steep escarpment. It has a much slower runoff, larger surface area, and thus a greater likelihood of retained water.

Cottonwoods in arid country serve much the same purpose as willows in country more hospitable. A chain of cottonwood in the distance indicates a river bed. Whether that bed turns out to be wet or dry is another question. But if it's dry, examine the ground by one of the largest and most ancient of the cottonwoods, on the inside bank of the old river's curve; you'll usually find a small pool of water. At least there should be enough ground moisture so that if you really need water you can dig down a foot or so and find seepage. Remember though that usually it does not pay to dig for water. With the amount of energy used, the moisture lost in sweat usually far exceeds that gained from the hole you've dug.

Any lush vegetation in arid terrain indicates water in one form or another. Birds, such as doves or blackbirds, in flocks, and, on the ground, quail in any quantity, are other signs of a water source nearby.

All handy bits of information, but if you're anticipating trekking where water may be in short enough supply that you might have to make use of them, the best thing is to take your own water along. You'll need two quarts a day under average conditions. In the desert, or during periods of heavy activity, this rises to four quarts or more per person per day.

WATER PURITY

Once you've found a water source, you have two old drinking rules to choose from, depending on how healthy you are, how cautious you are, and where you are. The first is, when in doubt about water, purify it. The second is, a lively bubbling stream cleans itself in thirty feet of flowing over rocks and sands. Or as one old codger I know, referring to the same quality of stream bed, put it succinctly, "If the cow's around the bend, the water's fit to drink."

Which rule you follow is up to you. We tend to use the second when in mountainous, wooded country. Our stomachs might not be cast iron, but they are pretty resistant to Montezuma's Revenge and *La Turista*. Also, because we travel a fair amount, our inoculations, ranging from typhoid to yellow fever and plague, are usually up to date. However, as pollution keeps increasing, we lean more and more to the first rule.

Following the first rule adds little work, if some odd tastes, to your camping. Water can be purified by boiling, although it takes time —boil for at least five minutes—and consumes a lot of fuel. It takes even longer for it to cool. In regions where the water is definitely unsafe, we drink a lot of tea rather than wait for the water to reach a drinkable temperature plain.

Water can also be purified with Halazone tablets. Add one tablet to a pint of water. If you're seriously in doubt, add two. After standing for half an hour or more, the water can be drunk, though it will taste like a swimming pool. Aerating the water by pouring it back and forth between two containers several times will eliminate most of the chlorine taste. This chemical is quite volatile, and a large part of its taste comes from smelling it. If you hold your breath while drinking it, you will hardly taste a thing.

Should you be in a situation where you have no Halazone tablets handy, reach for your first aid kit if it has iodine in it. Iodine at the rate of two to four drops per quart will do the job.

To avoid worrying, waiting, and a chlorine taste, when you're heading for a region where you know the water is not potable, bring your own supply. Unless you expect to do extended desert camping, however, water should not be a major problem.

THE LAY OF THE LAND

The three traditional requirements for a campsite used to be water, wood, and a flat area on which to lay out your sleeping bag or pitch your tent. Wood is no longer a prerequisite, with the handy and convenient stoves on the market. Water is still necessary. So is the relatively flat stretch of ground.

Flat ground can be as difficult a thing to find as water, if not more so, particularly in the mountains. There you may have to settle for a spot that slopes. If you do, make sure you set up the tent or lay out the bags so that you will be sleeping with your head up. Sleep with your feet higher than your head, and you'll wake up in the morning feeling you have a nasty hangover. Sleeping sideways on a slope will have all the occupants of a tent piled on top of each other on the downhill side before the night is halfway through. If you're not in a tent, you don't know where you'll wake up. The only certain thing is that it will be far from where you fell asleep.

So why not pitch camp at the bottom of the hollow? Well, usually because that's the wettest, coldest, foggiest spot around. In the case of a heavy rain it usually also means the morning will greet you with a small quagmire all around.

The top of a knoll avoids these problems. Its more positive advantage is ventilation. A good breeze will keep the bugs to a minimum.

Speaking of bugs, there you are in the middle of a beautiful mountain meadow, fragrant summer blooms swaying in the breeze. A perfect spot. No—for several reasons. Tall grass is where the chiggers, ticks, and other bugs like to camp. Also alpine meadows are fragile. Setting up a tent there for a week may leave a visible scar for years. For your own comfort and that of the meadow, pitch your tent at the edge instead of the middle. It will be just as fragrant and the view will be better.

At the edge of a meadow is also where you find bushes and trees to provide wind shelter and shade for the heat of the day. For best results, pitch the tent or lay out your sleeping bag on the east or north side of shade trees. This way you will be greeted by the warmth of a cheering sun in the morning. Yet during the heat of the day you will be shaded from its harsh rays. If prevailing winds are known, take them into account the same way. Camp on the lee side of rocks and trees when it's cold and you need protection. When it's warm, make camp on the windward side so the breezes help cool your wilderness home.

But check the trees out. Never camp beneath a lone tree if there's any chance of a thunderstorm. With its limbs reaching higher in the sky than anything else around, it makes a natural lightning rod.

Dead trees are also a hazard, the heavy waterlogged birches in particular. One moment they stand tall and serene against the sky, the next moment, sometimes without even the lightest zephyr having whisked across the ground, they lie uprooted and prone. Should your tent have been pitched beneath, well. . . .

The same holds true, if to a lesser degree, for dead branches. Don't camp beneath them. Chances of a dead branch killing you in its fall are very slim indeed. But an injury is far from out of the question, and the least it will do is ruin your tent.

When pitching your tent above the timberline in mountainous regions, look up before you set up. Landslides are not a common occurrence statistically. But why become a statistic? Slopes of loose rock slabs, round boulders, or what looks like a frozen stream of smooth rocks down a gully may decide to move during a heavy rain or in the alternate freezing and thawing of the cold of night and warm of day. Give all of them a wide berth.

Do pick a spot that is sheltered as much as possible from the wind. A firm outcropping of rock or large, well-entrenched boulders are probably the best shelters you'll find to pitch tent behind. But take advantage of whatever you can. A determined mountain gale may hit a hundred and fifty to two hundred miles an hour.

A good campsite is not that difficult to find, I hasten to add before proceeding with one more small caution: know what poison ivy and poison oak look like. Now I pride myself on never being affected by the stuff, and I've passed unscathed through a lot of it over the years. Suddenly last year these little blisters appeared from nowhere on my fingers. Me, the guy who never gets poison ivy. . . .

SETTING UP THE EASY WAY

To really enjoy camping, the trick is to make it as little work as possible. In pitching and breaking camp, each person doing specific tasks is the key. Susan and I both know how to do everything that needs to be done, although my bread never comes up to hers. When we find a campsite, we divvy up the jobs and go to it. One time I pitch the tent while she gets the fire going. Then we reverse the procedure, and I put the grub on while she lays out the sleeping bags. Sometimes we follow the same routine for weeks; other times we alternate daily, depending on who's in the mood for what.

Certain tasks are primarily in one or the other's domain. For instance, since we use smaller-than-normal stuff sacks for our sleeping bags to save space, the job of stuffing them is traditionally mine, and I build up a good appetite for breakfast doing it.

If you haven't camped before, to make your first night on the trail the pleasure it should be instead of a trial-and-error guessing game, go through the whole routine of setting and breaking camp in your backyard, or if need be, your living room, before you leave. If you're gearing up for extended camping, take a couple of overnight break-in trips. They will more than pay for themselves by instilling a rhythmic efficiency in your camping party.

Don't leave out the kids. Making them part of the team is worth more to them than having a free rein. It also helps wear them out. Of course it may not always save time. Genevieve started helping to pitch the tent when she was fourteen months old. Getting the tent up took three times as long, but she was proud as could be. Camping with five-year-olds and up, take a night off occasionally and let them do all the work while you sit back and relax. It's amazing how much a young child can handle in the wilds—and what a sense of accomplishment it gives him.

On one of your practice runs, incidentally, have a crack at setting up camp in the dark with a minimum amount of light. That's one flashlight or less. No matter how well planned a camping trip is, at one time or another you're going to reach your campsite after sunset. It's really not such a tragedy. Once you've done it a couple of times, setting up camp at night becomes automatic. In the morning it's always interesting to see exactly where you landed. Waking up in a place you've never seen can be a lovely surprise. But not if you spent three or four hours bickering the night before as you tripped over the tent, couldn't find your sleeping socks, and not only burned the dinner but ended up eating it stone cold as well.

PITCHING THE TENT

Clear the spot for your tent of any sharp rocks, twigs, or other debris. If a live root pokes up somewhere, don't try to dig it out. The more you dig, the thicker it always seems to get and the harder it is to break. Sawing in a hole is not only difficult, but you'll usually damage the blade as well. You won't injure the tree much by pruning a root, but you'll certainly wear yourself out. Better to move your future tent location a bit. If that's not possible, set the tent up so that the root is where your sleeping bag won't be, and pad it on the inside if you're likely to crawl over it.

Next, if you have a self-supporting tent of the Draw-Tite variety, all you do is roll it out, put the pole sections together, and lift the tent into place on them. If you have a peg-and-pole tent, you start the same way. Roll out the tent. Stake down the four corners, making the floor snug and squaring the corners. Position the poles and stake out the guy lines, leaving enough slack so you can make the fine adjustments with the line tighteners later. Next stake out the side pullouts. Once the lines are all out, adjust them so the tent is taut and wrinkle-free. The key is balanced tension, not just tension. Although the lines should be taut, excessive tension deforms the tent, adding unnecessary strain.

If you're using a rain fly, lay it over the tent poles. Stake it out, unless it's the exterior-frame-supported variety, so it doesn't touch the tent itself anywhere or it will cause capillary leaks. You can tie the end lines of your fly to your tent stakes. But on windy days it's an added safety factor to use separate stakes for the fly. By the time you're done with this your partner should have dinner well under way. Lay out the sleeping bags so they can maximize their loft before you crawl in. Then head for chow.

SANITATION

One would think that man had at least as much sense as a cat or dog. Unfortunately he doesn't. While animals scratch and bury their waste (futilely, needless to say, on hard city pavements), many a camper will, to put it bluntly, simply drop his pants and leave a souvenir complete with wrapping paper. Not a pleasant thought. Even less so when you arrive at a campsite and find someone's left it right in front of you.

If you are in an established campground with latrines, use them; they are obviously there for a purpose. If, as is more likely, there are none around, head for the woods. Go a reasonable distance from camp and dig, scratch, or kick a hole in one of the less accessible spots where you would not normally be walking. The hole need not, in fact should not, be deep. Most bacterial action occurs in the top six inches of the soil. So although a shovel might be handy, it's not really necessary. Toilet paper may be buried as well. Usually it will break down in less than a year if covered by a layer of soil. Biodegradable toilet paper is even better. Cover everything well and stomp it down. If you're squeamish about stomping it down, you haven't covered it well enough.

For a party of several people on an extended stay, a longish trench, again only six to eight inches deep, is usually dug at an agreed-upon spot. As it's used, it's covered up with dirt bit by bit. Leave toilet paper hung on a branch, an empty coffee can over it to keep it dry, conveniently nearby.

Aside from human waste there should be no sanitation problem. Anything that's not eaten is given to the animals. Anything that *can't* be eaten is packed out in those handy plastic garbage-can liners you have brought along for the purpose (in some Canadian provincial parks they now even check to make sure you have them with you). Nothing gets left behind. It's as simple as that.

BASE CAMPING

You wake up at sunrise and the campsite looks even better than it did before. It's a beautiful day, you're musing as you sip your morning coffee. With some regret you think about breaking camp and moving on.

Why? Why not linger awhile instead? The go-go-go of urban living is hard to leave behind. Too many campers set up, break down, and move on, day after day, charting how many miles they've covered on foot, on skis, by canoe, as if they were in a race.

Certainly if there's some quiet little place you really want to reach, this is the thing to do. But if not, and you've found a good camp spot, force yourself to stay. Consider it a base camp for a while. Take leisurely strolls during the day, packing a light lunch. Go climb a small mountain. Look around, not just at the panoramic vistas, but close up, at an individual flower or tree. Sit and watch an ant hill for an hour of amazing revelation.

That mysterious old art of hunting by "sitting on a log" that Nessmuk recommended so highly is a hard one to perfect. Yet it is one of the best ways to learn the woods and see the animals. It consists of, obviously, sitting on a log. But not just for a full minute's rest, nor on just any old log. Once you learn how to spot an animal runway, choose a log a couple of feet from it. If you're just starting to learn the woods, pick a log close to a stream, or an inlet on a bog pond. In either case, take a pair of binoculars if you have them. Sit yourself down—for a couple of hours. Don't smoke, don't make any noise, and move as little as possible. Simply look around. Traditionally four o'clock or so is tea time for many animals; and deer, elk, rabbit—what have you—which would be unseen a thousand yards away in the bush if you were strolling along, will sometimes walk by only a couple of body lengths from you. Their sense of smell and sight and sound are as keen as ever. But somehow they refuse to believe that a human being can sit still like a bump on a log. And indeed most of us can't anymore.

Keep practicing. As you do, look about you, watch the leaves in action, the insects, the birds, the movement of the wind. Smell the damp earth, the pine needles. If you sit by the side of a young mushroom for the better part of a dewy night—which is surely the ultimate test in log-sitting endurance—you can actually see it growing.

Getting About in the Wilderness

COME PADDLE
YOUR OWN CANOE

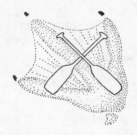

From spring breakup of the waterways to winter freezeup, canoeing is the best way to escape into the wilds that I know. The American Indian craft, fleet of keel as its designer was fleet of foot, goes where the city mortal dares not, and his motorized transport cannot. In the Southwest, canoeing is limited by the absence of suitable water in many places. But elsewhere, particularly in the northern United States and Canada, it affords a mode of camping with more variety, flexibility, and to me pure enjoyment than any other.

Canoes as we know them, like snowshoes, are strictly North American in origin, and largely remain so in current use. The Arctic equivalent, the kayak, is found almost worldwide today. Popularized by Klepper, it is *the* form of light river and lake transportation in Europe, although the Eskimos, originators of the craft, never used it much for river travel. Dugout canoes dot the Pacific and tropical waters, but they are heavy, cumbersome juggernauts beside the light shell and rib construction of the Indian canoe.

The birch-bark canoe, which the modern canoe emulates in every respect except materials, was designed to take advantage of the highways of water—the thousands of rivers and lakes—that constitute the watershed of the glacial shield of North America. The canoe has a shallow draft, permitting it access to waters forbidden all other craft. It has a phenomenal load capacity for its size, is highly maneuverable nevertheless, and is light enough to be carried by one man across those junctures where the waters fail to meet.

The highways it claims as its own spread to the four corners of the compass, covering immense distances, often with remarkably few portages. The Taylor-Pope route of the late 1930s, for instance, stretched nearly seven thousand miles from New York City to Nome, Alaska, with only a hundred and fifty miles of portage in all. A trip we hope to make someday—when Genevieve is old enough to paddle.

If seven thousand miles seems too long a voyage—and it took Taylor and Pope two years—consider the very real possibility that even a couple of days on the water may have you feeling like Lewis and Clark, or the northern fur traders, or *voyageurs,* singing *"Auprès de ma blonde"* as they brought their beaver pelts in to a Hudson Bay post with spring, or Mackenzie on his way to explore the legendary Arctic. The dip of the paddle, the changeable waters, from quiet lakes to rushing streams, the terrain beyond the gunwales—all make one's cares vanish more quickly than sandwiches offered on an outstretched paddle while resting on a bay after a good morning's run. You can imagine, then, what it does to your sense of time.

EVER SINCE BIRCH BARK

Although I am a traditionalist, when it comes to canoes, no matter how much I love the varnished beauty of a wooden canoe—canvas-covered, for birch bark went out with the freedom of the wilds and the birth of conservation—I almost always use an aluminum one. It's a matter of upkeep, care, and weight. A canvas canoe is not as fragile as you would think, and for those whose travels are limited to lakes, they are the most beautiful and silent watercraft devised since the Indians ruled the American waterways. They take the battering of rivers, rapids, rocks, much more gamely than suspected. Still, there comes the time when they must be recanvased, a task that is arduous and demands skill. Besides, even if recanvasing is necessary but once in three or four years, before each new season all the exposed ribs, the gunwales, thwarts, and seats should be taken down to the wood and revarnished. And woe is me when that wooden canoe weighing eighty pounds at the beginning of the first season absorbs enough moisture to tip the scales at over a hundred by the end of the second.

So, with the wistful hope that the wooden canoe will always be around for some braver soul to lug and for me to admire, I've deserted beauty for functionalism. Our *Kinabalu Queen* is an eighteen-foot lightweight Grumman painted dead-grass green, and complete with carrying yoke and gunwale covers. It weighs in at sixty-seven pounds.

The main objections to aluminum have been its color, heat problems, and sheer noisiness. Shiny aluminum stands out in the wilds like a nude at the Vatican; and if your paddle hits the gunwales as you stroke, it's about equivalent to hitting the Liberty Bell with a tennis ball. The paint and gunwale covers don't solve these problems completely, but they do minimize them.

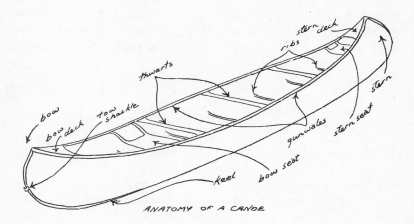

ANATOMY OF A CANOE

Fiberglass would seem at first glance ideal for canoe construction. But when it comes to synthetics, the aluminum canoe is still way out front in popularity. This is mostly a matter of craftsmanship. So many poorly designed and constructed fiberglass models flooded the market in the early days that canoeists became wary of the stuff, even when from high-quality manufacturers. Things have improved considerably since then. If you're thinking of fiberglass, reputable old-line firms like Old Town turn out some fine canoes.

Fiberglass craft tend to be heavier than either their wooden or aluminum counterparts. To compensate for this tendency, many manufacturers produce a design narrower than usual at bow and stern. Not only does this save on weight, it gives a canoe very racy-looking lines and makes it easier to paddle. However, it cuts down on handling ability in rough seas—except in white water, where the narrowness can be a distinct advantage—and more importantly, severely curtails buoyancy and cargo-carrying capability. Unless all your canoeing is going to be on white water, don't get a canoe that tapers sharply towards the bow and stern.

BOTTOMS UP

Viewed from the bow (or stern, for that matter), a canoe hull has one of two distinct looks: flat bottom or round bottom. The sides of a flat-bottomed canoe rise vertically or sheer in slightly in what's called a tumblehome. Those of a round-bottomed canoe usually flare out slightly. Again, the round bottom is fine for racing. For canoe camping, where shallow draft, stability, and carrying capacity are important, the flat bottom is much preferred.

THE KEEL

Most canoes have a straight line keel, which is what you want for canoe camping. A rocker keel line curves up, and again is designed for white water racing. Its maneuverability is excellent; on a windy lake, however, you're hard put to keep it from drifting sideways.

Keels become most important on the high-riding lightweight aluminum canoes, whose side drift in a gale can be disastrous if the canoe is not loaded. One time on Lake Jean-Péré, a storm picked up while I was fishing from the *Kinabalu Queen* in a sheltered cove about a mile downwind from camp. When I paddled out, the wind grabbed my canoe, and even though she had a keel, spun her around, and sent her back into the cove. That happened three times, even with me kneeling almost amidships. I finally had to beach my nervous craft and take on a cargo of some two hundred pounds of rocks before I could coax her out of the bay and back to camp. If nothing else, I ate well that night.

The standard center, or straight line, canoe keel is from half an inch to an inch deep, and anywhere up to three-quarters of an inch thick. It should run the entire length of the canoe. Bilge keels are common on wooden canoes. They are in addition to, not substitutes for, the center keel. Mounted on either side of the bottom, in the proximity of the chine line, and running for about five or six feet, they aid in protecting the canvas when the boat is dragged over beaver dams and other such obstructions. They also make the canoe turn like a water-soaked log.

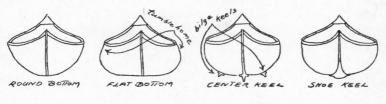

CANOE HULL SHAPES AND KEELS

The shoe keel is a flatter, broader version of the standard center keel. It makes for a quite maneuverable canoe with lateral stability considerably above that of keelless or rocker keel models. At the same time it affords hull protection over a broader base, making it excellent for white water.

HOW LONG?

Within reason, the bigger the canoe, the better. The longer it is, the easier it is to paddle. Currently there are several canoes being made in the eight- to twelve-foot range. They may be fine for the proverbial butcher, baker, and candlestick maker. But anyone seriously considering canoe camping should stay away from these tubs.

A fifteen-foot canoe is the minimum practical length for two persons. The same holds true for one person, if you discount the small duck shooters intended only for paddling short distances in the marshes. And while I would heartily recommend a seventeen- or eighteen-footer instead, the fifteen-foot model has one distinct advantage in portaging. Surprisingly enough, this advantage is not its weight, although of course it is lighter than the longer canoes. The real advantage is carrying comfort. The yoke is always attached to the center thwart of a canoe, its natural balancing point when riding on your shoulders. On most fifteen-foot canoes the bow thwart is so located that when you shoulder the craft with your arms comfortably outstretched, your hands rest easily on it. Portaging a longer canoe, one ends up holding onto the gunwales instead—and they're mighty narrow on most aluminum and fiberglass models.

Once your party goes beyond two, a seventeen- or eighteen-footer is unreservedly the best. Not only will it cut through the water more easily, it will have plenty of room for passengers and gear without lowering your freeboard—the distance between the waterline and your gunwale at its lowest point, that is, the amount free and clear of the water—to dangerous proportions. The minimum freeboard advisable is six inches. Eight inches on a choppy lake certainly doesn't hurt.

WHAT TO PADDLE WITH

Synthetic materials have made definite inroads on the traditional wooden hull. When it comes to paddles, however, nothing beats good old-fashioned natural maple or ash. Maple is the heavier of the two, also the stronger. Both are springy, as they should be. Your choice can and probably will depend on which of the two is more readily available.

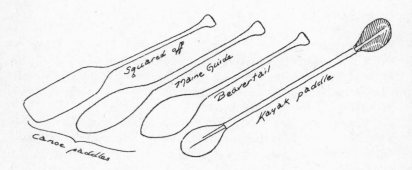

Advice on paddle length is usually rule of thumb: eye level from the floor for the stern paddler and chin level for the bowman. If you have to have a rule, this one's about as good as any, though if in doubt you should choose a longer paddle over a shorter one. The basic thing is to feel comfortable with it. To this end, renting a canoe and testing out various paddles before you buy is a good idea.

Finding the paddle width comfortable for you is the same sort of thing. The wider the blade, the more energy it takes to stroke with it. A parallel observation: the wider the blade, the faster you'll get where you're going. That doesn't mean you should use a snow shovel for the job. But do get a paddle that takes a decent bite. The beaver tail and Maine guide have a rounded bottom edge. Most other paddles are nearly squared off. Squared-off paddles tend, although not infallibly, to stand up to more abuse without major damage. Speaking of which, when you go to buy paddles, buy two.

That paddle we're talking about is going to be in your hands a long time once you hit the water, so check that the grip fits in your hand comfortably. It should not be varnished. You'll be raising blisters on your hands easily enough the first time out—varnish on the grip will only help them along. The blade of the paddle, however, should have a light coat of protective varnish. Not paint. A painted paddle is covering up something, usually a fault in the wood.

Sight your prospective paddle for straightness. Check to see that the length runs with the grain and that there are no knots or burrs. The blade should be evenly feathered. If it's thinner on one edge than the other, you'll have extra kindling before the trip's over.

A YOKE FOR THE TENDER SHOULDERS

Hudson Bay Crees will carry a hundred-and-fifty-pound canoe, the midship thwart plunked right down on their shoulders, one hand on the gunwale for balance, the other hugging a twenty-five-horsepower Johnson outboard. All without breathing heavily. Carrying yokes are for children, they say.

Well, just call me a kid. I wouldn't own a canoe without a yoke. After you've taken a couple of portages, in all likelihood neither will you. The yoke is by no means a necessary appendage. But it is certainly a comforting one to have between thwart and shoulder. And somehow I've yet to manage to take a canoe trip that doesn't require at least one portage.

On most canoes the yoke is simply bolted onto the center thwart, which is the natural balance point for the canoe when carried. Probably the most predominant yoke is the double square pad made by

Grumman for its canoes. The bolsters are serviceable, but not entirely comfortable. The edges still tend to dig in. So I drape a shock-absorbing horse collar in the form of a heavy shirt or jacket around my neck before I loft the canoe. I suppose as an alternative I could gain a bit of weight so my shoulders would be less bony.

A quite efficient temporary yoke can be made by lashing the paddles blade end to the center thwart in a wide V, leaving room between them, obviously, for your neck. The blades are broad enough to distribute the weight well. Wear a heavy shirt, though, for the carry.

Lashing the paddles in place takes a bit of time. So does unlashing them at the other end. Also, although in all likelihood you'll never fall when portaging, with this yoke you nevertheless have a pair of sharp paddle edges at your throat.

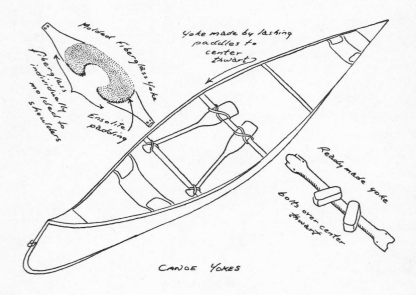

Molded fiberglass yoke

fiberglass individually molded shoulders

Ensolite padding

Yoke made by lashing paddles to center thwart

Ready made yoke

bolts over center thwart

CANOE YOKES

The most comfortable yoke I have ever seen was a homemade one of fiberglass. The owner had a friend make a plaster cast of his shoulders. From this he molded a yoke in fiberglass, then added an Ensolite lining. With this rig, carrying an eighty-five-pound canoe was easier than toting home the groceries. One of these days I'm going to get me some plaster. . . .

CASTING OFF

Once you've picked out your canoe, you've got to get it into the water, and then you into it. Then, provided you're both still intact, you want to propel yourself someplace with the paddles. Not too far, probably, the first couple of times out.

A canoe must be floating when it's loaded—that means loaded with with you, as well as with your gear—in order for the weight to be distributed both for balance and to avoid damage to the hull. If you're beached, ease the canoe into the water slowly and bring it around broadside, but not too close. You want to step into it without letting the bottom scrape the beach. This is easier said than done, and you will no doubt get at least one foot wet. I usually take off my shoes and roll up my pants, weather permitting. Starting from a dock is much simpler. You just step in.

Standard rules call for stepping right on the center line of the canoe and lowering yourself gingerly into a sitting position. Now caution is rarely a dangerous commodity, but too much has been re-iterated about the instability of a canoe. I wouldn't advise anybody to try standing in a kayak. But in a canoe, why not? Lots of people do it safely all the time. At first, of course, you want to develop a feel for the canoe from the orthodox sitting position. And when a storm springs up, it's best to kneel for added stability. Do so in front of the seat, resting your rear on its edge. By all means put some padding beneath your knees.

But for a start, the object of the game is to get a comfortable feel for your craft on the water. Period. You'll never get that while sitting ramrod-straight in the middle, or kneeling in fear all the time, as if you're on a log about to roll over. Hang loose.

So there you are, or there the two of you are, sitting in a canoe, two paddles apiece at hand. The old saying about being up the creek without a paddle has its origin in the fact that a paddle will break at the most uncalled-for times. Knowing this, you always carry a spare for each man.

Pick up a paddle, one hand over the grip, the other around the shaft a short distance above where the blade flares out. Keep your hold relaxed.

Reach forward with the lower arm. The upper arm should also reach forward, but not as far; keep a bend in the elbow. Now dip the paddle into the water, and pull the lower arm back, keeping it semi-rigid. At the same time, push the upper arm forward. To get the most out of the stroke, your torso should follow the upper arm forward slightly. The main force comes from your upper arm and your back. Keep the paddle vertical; don't bring the shaft in over the canoe like an oar. That's it, you're paddling. Remove the paddle from the water, reach forward. . . . This is what's known as the cruising stroke, and is the one used almost exclusively by the bow.

With two to a canoe, the bowman sets the pace—one that's comfortable for the stern as well—and paddling is done in rhythmic unison. After a while you find yourself falling into a natural tempo with a fractional rest break between strokes, just before you plunge the paddle back into the water. The whole thing becomes as unconscious as walking.

Switch sides every now and then; you'll soon be able to flash the paddle across without breaking rhythm or missing a stroke. It's best to get into this habit early. If you don't, you'll find that as time passes you develop a distinct preference for paddling on one side. Not a serious problem, but somewhat limiting.

GOING STRAIGHT

You'd never think there were as many different ways to paddle a canoe as there are. Actually, a number of the strokes are simply variations on each other. But this past summer I discovered an entirely new—to me—way of paddling a canoe that, as far as I'm concerned, relegates the J stroke, the pitch stroke, the Canadian stroke, and most of the rest of the stern strokes to oblivion. To my knowledge it doesn't have a name, so I'll just name it after the people who showed it to me, the Rupert House Crees of Hudson Bay. (They are the Rupert House Crees, as opposed to plain Crees, because they're outcasts the rest of the tribe won't associate with. And the village Rupert House is where they settled when banished.)

Here's how I happened to chance on the stroke. A couple of self-proclaimed professional canoeists had made their way down the Rupert River to Rupert House. For some reason or other they decided to put on a demonstration for the Indians to show them what real team paddling was all about. Churning the waters around the town seaplane dock, and chanting to each other, they kept up a clipped military advance. The local Crees deserted their checker boards momentarily. It wasn't as much fun as when the planes landed. Still, it was a diversion.

Ignorant of the event, Jimmy (the only name I knew him by) was heading into town to get some raisins for his home brew. It was late Friday and the Hudson Bay store would be closed all weekend. Perched high on the square stern of his red twenty-two-footer, as is the local fashion, he paddled obliviously up to the dock with short choppy strokes, leaving the two "professionals" in his wake. A cheer rose from the spectators. Satisfied with the finale of the show, they returned to their blitz checkers. Jimmy got his raisins. The two canoeists went over his boat looking for a hidden motor. And I got a new stroke.

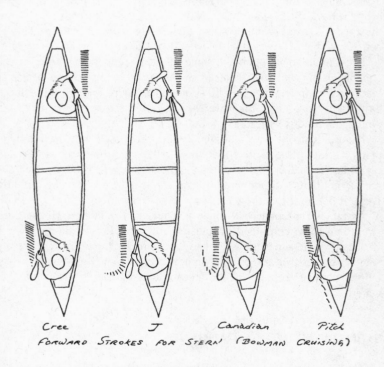

Cree   J   Canadian   Pitch

FORWARD STROKES FOR STERN (BOWMAN CRUISING)

It's so simple it's obvious. One of those things you keep saying "but, of course" to and wondering why you never thought of it. The Rupert House Cree stroke consists of digging the paddle in with the blade at a slight outward angle to the direction of the pull, rather than perpendicular to it, as is customary. This automatically compensates for the torque normally produced by the stern paddler's thrust being offside. And it does so without the slightest bit of drag, since the paddle is not trailed as a rudder.

Unlike all the other torque-compensating strokes, this one delivers nothing but power. It is also the most difficult of all strokes to master —and I admit to still having problems with it on and off: since the paddle blade is at an angle while passing through the water, it tends to slip constantly sideways. However, it's well worth practicing till you can control it, for it is probably 50 percent faster than the standard strokes, with no more work.

The most common stern stroke is the J. After the paddle has been brought back in the water, the blade is turned and pushed away from the canoe, the full stroke forming the characteristic J pattern. This of course produces drag, which slows down the canoe while steering it.

The Canadian is much the same affair, except in this case, at the conclusion of the stroke, instead of the blade being pushed out, it is feathered, or pitched, at a slight outward angle, and brought about halfway forward again underwater. The return stroke acts as a rudder. And again it adds unnecessary drag.

The pitch stroke uses a similar rudder technique, but the pitching, or feathering of the blade starts about halfway through the stroke and continues until the paddle drags behind like a real rudder. Then the paddle is lifted, still feathered, out of the water and brought forward. Reset it before it hits the water on the next stroke.

As far as I'm concerned, once you master the Rupert House Cree stroke, all these combined propulsion-and-direction-maintaining stern strokes become superfluous, not to say inefficient. However, there are some steering strokes for rapid maneuvering which you should master before you ever venture off the lakes onto even mildly turbulent river water.

STROKES TO STOP A CANOE BY

The simplest of these is the backwater stroke, used to stop a canoe's forward motion or to reverse its direction completely. All you do is paddle backwards.

Almost equally effective in stopping a canoe is the jam stroke. In reality it is no stroke at all, since it consists merely of thrusting the paddles into the water with the blades perpendicular to the direction of progress and keeping them there.

Both the jam and the backwater stroke require strong arms, wrists, and back if the boat is well under way. Practice them at slow speed first to get a feel for what's happening to the canoe—and your muscles. If you're going full steam ahead and apply the jam stroke for the first time, you'll probably find yourself paddleless, with a bruised wrist to boot.

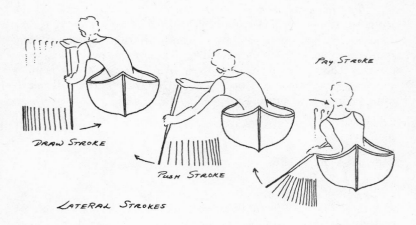

PRY STROKE

DRAW STROKE

PUSH STROKE

LATERAL STROKES

SIDLING OVER

Now that you have the canoe going forwards and backwards, it's time to consider going sideways. Paddling downriver, it is necessary to keep the keel of the canoe always almost parallel to the water flow. If the stern swings too far from this direction, the current will grab it and turn the whole canoe around. And should there then be a rock in your path while you're traveling broadside, you'll end up with a U-shaped canoe.

The two most-used lateral pulling strokes are the draw and the push. A couple of moderately experienced people using the draw stroke can slip a canoe sideways over the waters ten feet in ten seconds. If stern and bow paddler stroke on opposite sides of the boat simultaneously, they can literally turn on a dime. All you do is reach straight out with your paddle as far as you can and dip it into the water with the blade parallel to the keel. Now pull the boat over to the paddle.

The push stroke is the reverse of the draw stroke. You start with the paddle next to the hull and push the boat away. Since it's easier to pull than push in the water, however, the draw stroke is the more effective of the two.

An easier-to-handle modification is the pry stroke. When the paddle is put in next to the hull, the shaft is brought to rest against the gunwale. Then the grip is pulled sharply inboard, the gunwale acting as a fulcrum, the blade consequently pushing out with more force and setting the canoe over.

Wherever possible, stick with the draw stroke. The pry stroke is easy to master, but because the gunwale acts as a fulcrum, you are actually pushing the canoe down into the water as well as sideways. This considerably reduces the efficiency of the stroke in relation to the amount of energy you expend. Also, since the gunwale fulcrum is much stronger than your grasp can possibly be, it's an easy stroke with which to snap your paddle.

THE BOW RUDDER

A last stroke is the bow rudder, used for swift turns. Again something to be practiced many times in a slow-moving canoe till you get the feel of it and learn how to gauge your strength. As its name implies, this particular maneuver is performed only by the bowman. You thrust the paddle, its blade vertical, into the water *in front* of the canoe. Set it at roughly a 30-degree angle from the keel line, with the blade not dug in fully. Hold it tightly in this position; the flowing water will do its work. The paddle will try to pull out and push back into your chest, or even your face if you're short, so hang on. For extra support, with both the bow rudder and the pry stroke, I wrap the fingers of my lower hand around the gunwale as well as the paddle shaft. Watch so you don't pinch yourself.

TIP A CANOE AND RIGHT IT TOO

If you can, take a few days to practice your strokes and get a general feel for the canoe before setting out on a long trip. To do a really good job of it, put on a bathing suit, find a sizable lake to launch the canoe in, paddle out a ways from shore, and lean and twist in your canoe until it capsizes. You'll find it's a lot harder to upset than you thought. Loaded with gear, the craft will be even steadier. Meanwhile you'll know how your canoe will respond. You'll be confident—hopefully not overconfident, however.

It's often recommended that when a canoe is capsized, you should right it first and then bail it out with your hands while treading water next to it. I'm all for righting it. But unless I was several miles from shore, I'd tow it to the beach rather than try to bail under those conditions. In any event, don't panic and leave your canoe behind if it capsizes. Canoes are either naturally buoyant or equipped with flotation tanks. Either way, they'll keep you afloat.

Bottoming up a canoe, of course, presupposes you know how to swim. Life preservers are one thing, but everyone who goes canoeing should know how to swim. If nothing else, it almost assures you won't capsize.

READING THE WATER

Speaking of capsizing, lakes and meandering streams are one thing to travel on; rapids are something else again. Whether you're running a river with a canoe or with a kayak, you watch for the same signs. White water is increasingly becoming a kayak sport, however, and, on most white water, spray decks are required on canoes to keep the water out, turning them in many respects into kayaks, so let's leave how to read the waters for the chapter on kayaking.

POLING

The canoe—honestly and truly—is not the skittish, difficult craft of its undeserved notoriety. Obviously a broad-beamed rowboat is more stable. But the old maxim about never standing up in a canoe is just so much bilge. Poling, although not used often, is a method of propelling the canoe which definitely has its place. And to pole you have to stand up. Like all other canoeing skills, furthermore, poling is an acquired one, demanding more than a little practice. So get your sea legs in a canoe.

Poling can be done downstream, but its primary use is to ascend rapids too swift for paddling and too deep to wade comfortably while floating the canoe, lightened by your being out of it, along. There's always portaging, of course. But poling may be the easier of the two on a long, not too turbulent haul. Besides, it's a lot more challenging. Start by working shallow rapids with a reasonably slow flow to them.

Ash poles twelve to fourteen feet long and about an inch and a quarter to an inch and three-quarters in diameter are traditional. Tradition also once called for stripping them from an accommodating tree along your way. But followed with a frequency matching the growth in popularity of canoeing today, this practice would decimate many a riverbank. Luckily fiberglass poles are not only good, but better. Some polers use aluminum. However, even the best-quality aluminum doesn't have the spring of fiberglass. It also can get mighty cold. Ordinary hardwood poles may be purchased from logging equipment suppliers. Ask for a pike pole.

To grip the river bottom firmly, a canoeing pole is often shod with a cast iron shoe. On a wooden pole, this serves the added function of keeping the pole end from fraying or brooming out. A pole shoe is either cuplike or spiked at the end to aid in grasping submerged rocks. The bit of extra weight also helps the pole balance and sink.

The top of the pole may or may not have an elongated knob. It's primarily to remind you, when you're intent on the water, that you've reached the end of your pole.

To pole a canoe, trim it—that is, distribute the weight—so that the downstream end, bow or stern depending on which way you're heading, rides a bit lower than the upstream end. This gives the canoe a tendency to align with the current flow. In addition, angle the side of the canoe opposite that from which you're working the pole slightly into the current, to compensate for the side-thrusting of the pole.

Set the pole into the water just behind where you are standing, at your normal paddling place if there are two of you, almost amidships if you are alone. Then push down. The pole will flex and the canoe move forward. Feed the pole back by going up hand over hand until you run out of pole. Finish off the dig by bending into a slight crouch and giving a firm but smooth shove. Then retrieve the pole, without dragging it through the water, and start over. Bracing one calf against the rear seat or thwart will add stability to your thrust.

When you first try to go upriver, you're best off having two people poling. Even standing amidships, it is quite difficult for one person to keep the canoe parallel to the stream flow. And once the current grabs the bow, you'll be heading downstream again.

If tandem paddling requires rhythmic unison, tandem poling requires almost supernatural coordination. Don't despair if your first couple of ventures turn out to be wet ones. And tangled poles should come as no real surprise.

Both parties pole on the same side, usually alternating thrusts so that while one is completing a push, with a momentary halt to hold the canoe in place, the second member digs in and starts pushing before the first man retrieves his pole.

TRACKING

When you reach a set of rapids you aren't sure you can handle—*don't try*. The usual alternative, and the one I opt for, is to portage. Nevertheless, much has been said about tracking. At least in print—I've never seen anyone do it.

Tracking takes two people. Tying a line to the bow and another to the stern of the canoe, each man tending one line, you walk along the shore, or the towering cliffs of the gorge, as the case may be, and guide the floating canoe through. Going upstream, if the bow is kept always slightly further out from shore than the stern, the canoe will keep the lines taut. To maintain control going downstream, the stern should be the most distant point.

It's all sort of fun, I guess—trying to keep the lines from tangling in the brush dotting the shore, or figuring out how to climb the boulders without slacking tension—unless things upset and you soak the gear. But since there has to be a path of sorts to walk along in order to track, I just find it easier to portage.

CANOE SAILING

Although not often used in camping unless one expects to cross long lake after long lake, a sailing rig, available with many models, makes a canoe more versatile for weekend use. It adds a new dimension to the traditional role of the craft, leaving things to the wind rather than the pace of your paddles or the mood and makeup of the waters.

Most canoes rigged for sailing use either a gunter or a lanteen single-rig mast, with leeboards and a tiller arrangement. We've often made a temporary square rig with a tarp for a lazy day's downwind run, and it's a good thing to keep in mind as a break in pace. Our latest improvisation on this theme occurred during Genevieve's initiation voyage in La Véréndrye, when after a week of rain we finally had a sunny day with a good snapping wind. We tied Genevieve's diapers, washed but undried because of the continuous downpour, in a four-to-a-sail pattern and lashed the quartet between two six-foot paddles. With the paddles held upright between my feet and the stern thwart, we gurgled along at five or six knots, averaging four dry diapers to every fifteen minutes.

PORTAGING

When you can't paddle, pole, float, or maybe even track a canoe any further, there's nothing left to do but carry it. The very word "portage" seems for some reason synonymous with hard labor. Yet it's really not that bad. Besides, it gives you a certain feeling of accomplishment. And I never cease to get a kick out of the strange walking-on-the-moon feeling you have after putting down an eighty-pound canoe you've carried for a mile or two. Your muscles have set up an accommodation for all the extra weight. When it disappears suddenly, your feet almost pop off the ground with each step. You're walking on clouds.

Hopefully without sounding like Pollyanna—for it is work, no doubt about that—portaging also tends to break up a long canoe voyage. You get a chance to stretch your legs and move around a bit. And after a couple of days' paddling, hiking can be almost a novel experience.

A portage trail usually begins by a natural mooring spot—some submerged logs, a clearing, a sandbank. In Canada, established canoe routes often have signs at a portage. La Véréndrye, for instance, uses what look like yellow road signs, with a black silhouette of a man carrying a canoe. Rounding a point of land and meeting up with a traffic signal is a bit startling after a week in the wilderness. It's also abundantly clear.

Once you've nosed into the mooring, unload the canoe before beaching it. If there are two of you, traveling light, you can make a portage in one trip. Before Genevieve came along, Susan would take my pack, the tent bag, and the kitchen duffel, and set out ahead of me. I'd don her smaller pack, shoulder the canoe, paddles lashed inside it, and follow. By keeping about twenty feet ahead of me, she could call out a warning about any obstructions in the terrain, low-hanging branches, marshy ground, loose roots—or blueberry bushes. The berry bushes aren't much of a walking impediment, obviously, but they sure do drag out a portage. Once you start picking blueberries, well, let's hope there weren't any rain clouds on the horizon when you left the river.

Over a long portage, or if we ran aground on blueberry bushes, she also kept a sharp lookout for suitably forked trees to park the canoe in. A portage trail is often too narrow and twisting for you to comfortably put the canoe down to rest. Besides, if you put it down, you have to pick it up again. To avoid this, if you find a tree forking out at about the eight- to ten-foot level, all you have to do is approach it slowly, raise the bow of the canoe until it's even with the V, and prop it there, bow in the wedge, stern on the ground. Bend down and walk out from under the canoe. When you're ready to move on, just duck under the canoe, stand up, and back out.

With Genevieve along, we double each portage. We take most of the small gear across first, reconnoitering the trail as we go. Then we head back, I for the canoe, Susan for the pack, Genevieve just for the ride.

Then there was the first time we ever came to a portage. None of this down-pat organization at that one. We didn't know a thing about portaging. Susan and I carried the canoe ashore. Since our gaits are totally unsynchronized, it was obvious we weren't going to get very far with it between us, and any fool could see those shoulder pads were meant to rest on one person's shoulders. But how did that one person—me—get the canoe off the ground and up onto the shoulders?

Finally we rolled the canoe over, belly up. I lifted the bow about four feet, gave it to Susan to hold, scrunched down on my knees and backed in under the canoe. Susan's hands gave out just as I got to the yoke. When they dropped the world on Atlas's shoulders, it couldn't have weighed much more. To the accompaniment of popping tendons, I rose slowly, uttering a string of expletives that probably curled the ears of the local caterpillars, and began walking.

Things got worse, not better. The portage crossed and then followed a highway for about half a mile. I'd expended so much energy picking up the canoe I had to take a break. But there was no room along the side of the road to put down, collapse under, or drop a canoe. With great embarrassment and even more of a Keystone Cop routine than before, I managed to get it off my back at a gas station. Any idea of what it's like to crawl out from under a canoe, drenched in sweat on an 80°F. summer day, at the local Shell station, and have the attendant come sauntering up with a big grin, saying, "You want high test or regular?"

Luckily we ran into someone a few days later who showed us how to pick up a canoe. The basic principle is not to pick it up, but to literally *throw* it onto your shoulders. With a bit of practice, you'll find it takes surprisingly little effort. And I could have modeled for all those Charles Atlas advertisements—as the ninety-seven-pound weakling who gets sand kicked in his face.

There are two ways to properly heft a canoe onto your shoulders. The first, the shoulder hoist, is the easier, but can only be done comfortably if the bow thwart of the canoe is so spaced that when the yoke is resting on your shoulders, your outstretched hands will just reach and be able to grasp the thwart. This happy conjunction of measurements generally occurs on a fifteen- or sixteen-foot canoe if you're roughly between five feet, eight inches tall and six feet two.

To proceed, put the canoe on the ground lying as if it were in the water. Stand beside it slightly behind the bow thwart and facing the stern. Bend down. Take hold of the bow thwart, placing your hands close to the gunwales. Then in one swift, continuous operation, yank up hard, swing the canoe onto its side, over and up, bend your knees

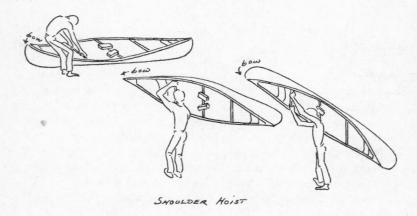

SHOULDER HOIST

and twist so you're now facing the bow. With the aid of the momentum from the original yank, the bow of the canoe has swung over on top of you. Duck your head as it drops down on your shoulders, yoke in place. The stern will now lift off the ground. *Don't stop halfway* through the sequence to think about it. The whole pickup is one fast, smooth movement—culminating the first time in surprise that the canoe is actually sitting on your shoulders and it all happened so quickly. It's much easier than it sounds. Just remember you're literally throwing the canoe around.

A longer canoe, say eighteen feet, will react differently. Instead of the yoke landing neatly on your shoulders, the inside hull will land on your head, that confounded yoke somewhere uselessly behind you. Some people do manage to use the shoulder hoist on the larger model. They'll rest the canoe lightly on their head as it swings over, stern still resting on the ground, switch their handhold from the thwart to the gunwales, and then inch back into the yoke by sliding their hands down the gunwales. It's nowhere near as graceful, but it can be done smoothly.

The other way to hoist a canoe is the knee roll. Standing midway between bow and stern of your beached canoe, roll it onto its side so the keel faces you. Now reach over it for the center thwart, placing the far hand around it by the gunwale, the near hand grasping the near gunwale. The hand grasping the far side should twist your shoulders slightly so your back is turned partially towards the bow. Bend your knees slightly, just enough so they dip under the keel of the canoe,

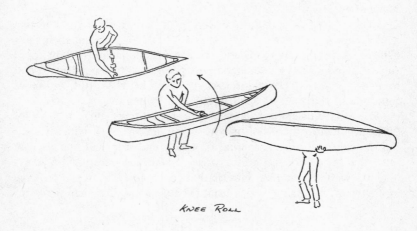

KNEE ROLL

still lying on its side. Roll the canoe onto your knee by pulling up with the far arm and pushing away with the near one, give the canoe a slight shove with the knee and literally throw it upwards and over. Again duck your head under and into the yoke as the canoe swings over your shoulder. Grab the gunwales as it comes to rest on your shoulders, and you're all set. Here again, the procedure sounds much more complicated than it is, and here again, the whole secret is to hoist it in one continuous swift movement.

Oh yes, about putting the canoe down when you get to the end of the portage: just reverse the pickup procedure. Plan to roll it off your knee so the bow lands in the water if you're going downstream, the stern if you're going upstream. The current will swing whichever end hits the water first downstream. Bow first? You're headed in the right direction for going down the river. Stern first? The current will swing it downstream, directing the canoe upstream.

STOWING THE GEAR

Canoe camping allows more flexibility in gear than, say, back-packing or ski touring. There's no reason to set off without a reflector oven, for instance. In fact there may be good reason to have it along if you're going to be out of buying distance of a loaf of bread for a long time. Don't get carried away, however, even though a sturdy seventeen-foot canoe can carry between eight and twelve hundred pounds—remember the portages. Try to keep the cargo down to the point where you can portage everything in one carry, or at least a maximum of two.

Actually there is some justification for making each portage in two trips. Whoever is carrying the canoe doesn't get to see much besides a few feet of trail. Walking the portage unencumbered except for a rucksack and duffels gives him a sneak preview of trail conditions, and a chance to look for woodpeckers or squirrels' nests. But any more rounds, and the route is apt to become a bit tedious.

Once you've assembled the gear you want along, you're faced with the question: to waterproof or not to waterproof? Even without spilling the canoe, a certain amount of splash and drip will find its way into your bilge. Voyageur Enterprises makes a waterproof polyethylene bag with a sliding bar closure that conveniently seals the package at any height. Ranging in size from twenty-two by thirty-six inches to twenty-four by sixty inches, these versatile envelope bags not only keep your equipment dry, but will float should you capsize. However, you have to watch out for tears (easily fixed with enclosed cloth/plastic tape), and they're a bit clumsy to portage.

A common waterproofing procedure is to lay a tarp over the gear and lash it down. I go one step further, laying the tarp out along the bottom of the canoe on a bed of spare paddles spread lengthwise across the ribs as an extra precaution against bilge flooding in heavy rain. The paddles can be pulled out easily enough if needed, as long as the cargo isn't too heavy. After packing in the gear, I fold the sides and corners of the tarp up and over the thwarts like a Christmas package, and batten it down with some rope. Keeps everything dry from all sides.

Always pack the gear so that the center of gravity is kept as low as possible and most of it is amidships. Never pack a canoe that is not floating. It won't break the back of an aluminum or fiberglass canoe, but it's a poor habit to get into.

If you're expecting to run into white water, the load should be tied down securely once everything is in place. Lashing it all to the canoe may be cumbersome and time-consuming. On the other hand, trying to find a soggy sleeping bag somewhere along shore downriver is much worse.

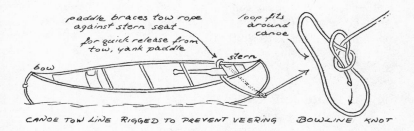

A COUPLE OF WORTHY EXTRA ITEMS

Who would ever take a sponge canoeing? Well, it doesn't take up much space and weighs nothing. Mighty handy for mopping up the bilge. Being more or less flat, the bottom of a canoe is hard to scoop up water from unless it's ankle deep.

Outside of this one homely little item and some extra quarter-inch nylon rope for a painter, towing, and such—about a hundred feet should do—there's no special equipment needed beyond a good canoe, spare paddles, and a repair kit.

REPAIRS ON THE RIVER

Neither aluminum nor fiberglass canoes are indestructible. Aluminum ones will acquire small dents while banging into rocks and boulders. The larger ones can be pounded out by a hard rubber hammer or wooden mallet methodically wielded. If you don't carry either, put a heavy rock inside your shoe and pound with the heel. Tap—firmly but gently, as they say—on the inboard side of the hull, using a sock or similar sack filled with sand to cushion and spread the load on the outside. Most small dents are best left till you get home.

To mend a break in an aluminum hull, first pound out the dent that accompanied it. Then apply some epoxy and an aluminum patch over the break till you can rivet a patch on permanently. If you don't carry a patch kit—and there's really no need to unless you're going to slop around in some mighty rough white water—an unexpected crack can be filled quite satisfactorily with a gob of pine sap and some needles from the same tree.

Fiberglass boats usually come supplied with a small cloth and epoxy repair kit able to solve most of the problems you'll encounter. If you somehow manage to stove in the whole side, repairs will have to wait till you get home.

ON THE RACK FOR THE WINTER

Your chances of damaging an aluminum or fiberglass canoe while on the water are slim. The chances of damaging it at home are great. Probably more canoes are ruined by careless storage than by any other factor.

A canoe is designed to distribute its load admirably when afloat. On land it's like a fish out of water. Lying on its side in the garage, it inevitably gets something set down on it temporarily. There's one dent. Or the kids decide to play house in it. There's a grand total of sixteen dents. Or it's stored out of the way at the back of the garage, and one evening you pull the car in too far. Cracked fiberglass all over the bumper.

The best place for a canoe is upside down on the rafters, if you have rafters in your garage. The second best place is upside down on sawhorses in your basement. The elements at large won't affect fiberglass or aluminum canoes, but inside storage protects them from other accidents.

If you live in an apartment with neither garage nor basement at your disposal, rent your canoes. Or buy a kayak of the folding variety. It just might fit in that extra closet you don't have. But in any case, do explore the waterways of the wilds.

WEARING A KAYAK

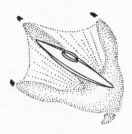

Canoes were designed to transport freight, food, and passengers across the watery web of North America. Kayaks were designed to carry one hunter out to sea in search of game—whale and seal and polar bear. As a hunting craft on turbulent, ice-choked oceans, it had to be as agile and fast as its target. And so it became a craft one literally wears. A kayak will turn you into a mermaid of the waves, taking you down remote rivers inaccessible to any other craft.

You will probably want to start your inland nautical career in a canoe. But after a while, no matter how fond you are of it, you will begin thinking about switching to a kayak. It's not as stable as a canoe, generally speaking. You'll have to cut down on the bulk of your camping equipment. And although there are two-man models, it is primarily a one-passenger craft, which usually means each man for himself. On the other hand, a kayak is swift, incredibly maneuverable, and seaworthy. (Dr. Hans Lindemann sailed a Klepper across the Atlantic in 1956.) And since you're wearing it instead of sitting in it, a kayak gives you a feel for the water no other craft does.

RACING AND TOURING MODELS

Kayaks come either in fiberglass or with folding rubberized hulls. Fiberglass models are designed primarily for white water racing, a sport of such increasing popularity as to have recently become a competitive event at the Olympics. For camping and touring, the folding model is the roomiest, with the added advantage of being the only boat a city dweller can dock in his closet.

The selection of a folding kayak usually means a Klepper. It's the oldest and best-made of the folding boats; it's also the only one available in many regions. Klepper's flagship model is the two-passenger Aerius. With an overall length of seventeen feet, one inch, and a thirty-four-inch beam, it weighs in at sixty-four pounds. The dismantleable frame is made of ash and cross-laminated Finnish birch. It is decked over by waterproofed long-staple cotton and hemp, and the lower hull is five-layer vulcanized Hypalon (a rubber and hemp fabric familiar to you if you happen to have been around industrial conveyor belts). Built-in air-filled sponsons make the craft much more stable than most kayaks, and thus ideal for the beginner. Packs into three bags. Assembles in less than half an hour, no tools needed.

I must admit I had my doubts about rubber hulls and thin wooden frames—it all sounds so fragile. Then one day in Moosonee on James Bay while I was helping pound the lumps out of an aluminum canoe that had come down the Mattagami River, a Klepper sidled up to the dock. We went down for a look. To our amazement the rubber hull had come down the same route with nary a scratch. Part of that was due to the kayak's superior maneuverability, part no doubt to superior paddling technique, but one could easily see that the hull could really take roughing it.

THE PADDLE

A kayak paddle is double-bladed and usually feathered; that is, the blades on both ends of the shaft are set at a right angle to each other. If they were set parallel, when one was in the water, the other would be exposing its flat side to the wind, causing a not inconsiderable amount of wind drag as well as steering difficulty. A few paddlers use parallel blades, in spite of the disadvantages, to avoid the asymmetrical grip required with feathered ones. But it would be to your advantage to develop the proper wrist action instead.

The blades themselves may be either flat or slightly spooned. The spooned blades look racier and are a bit faster. On the other hand, it's more difficult to brace with them. Also reverse paddling with spooned blades is more complex, less effective.

Paddles range in length from about eighty-two inches for white water up to a hundred and two inches for cruising. Sometimes the paddles are jointed in the middle of the shaft so they can be disassembled for storage and transportation. However, this joint is a potential weak spot. A happy combination is to use a one-piece paddle and carry an easily-stored jointed one as your spare.

PUTTING ON THE KAYAK

The first time I climbed into a kayak, a slim blue racing model on the Danube, I wasn't wearing a watch, but I would estimate I was on my own in less than ten seconds, with the inverted boat floating rapidly downriver. The second time it was still well under thirty seconds. About an hour later we had become friends, if not exactly partners. By then I had acquired the sense to practice in a bathing suit. The Klepper Aerius, with its sponsons, is considerably more stable than the nervous racing kayaks. Still, you don't hop around in it the way you do in a canoe.

To make sure you get into a kayak dry, squat down beside the cockpit, facing the bow, the long double paddle horizontally across the deck of the kayak behind you. Grasp the paddle shaft and cockpit rim together in one hand. Now lean the kayak and the paddle slightly towards shore so the paddle touches ground, making a brace. Shift one leg over the gunwale into the boat, making sure you keep the weight distributed slightly towards the shore side so the bracing effect of the paddle remains. Shift in your second leg, followed by your seat. You're in.

PADDLING

Since the kayak's double-bladed paddle is a two-cycle engine, so to speak, the stroking pattern used for canoe propulsion is inapplicable.

The basic kayaking stroke uses a considerable amount of wrist action because of the feathered blades. And much the way canoeists tend to favor one side for stroking, kayak paddlers favor one wrist. Usually the right if they're right-handed, the left if they're southpaws. Whichever the case, the favored is the fixed hand. It's the one that keeps a firm grip on the shaft, setting the angle of the blades for each stroke.

Starting on your fixed-hand side, as you dip the blade into the water, the wrist is bent slightly upwards. When the stroke is completed, as you're switching to the alternate side, the wrist drops down, rotating the paddle ninety degrees so the opposing blade will now dig cleanly into the water. Meanwhile the other hand holds the shaft, but loosely enough to let the paddle twist freely. Watch out for blisters your first couple of times out. The shaft should be roughly forty-five degrees to the horizon during a power stroke, the blade fully submerged.

Backpaddling is the reverse of forward. There is no need to reverse the blades. Practicing backpaddling is important, not only to master the maneuver itself, but to help you develop a feel for setting the blades quickly.

The strokes used primarily for white water include such advanced strokes as the Duffek besides modifications on the draw, the sweep, and others. However, white water kayaking really must be learned visually. You can work on it yourself once you've watched it, but the best thing to do is search out one of the numerous clubs founded by river runners and learn from them. Pass your swimming test before you go.

MANEUVERING

The simplest way to change directions in a kayak when all that's needed is a broad arc is to drag the paddle as a rudder, at the completion of a stroke, on the side you want to turn towards. For an abrupt change in course, use the forward stroke on one side and the backward one on the other. With practice you'll just about be able to make a right-angle turn.

THE BACK BRACE

It may not be walking on water, but it's as close as you'll get. With the back brace you're actually leaning on the water. It can be used

BACK BRACE

as a maneuvering stroke. But its primary function is to enable you to brace yourself against capsizing—particularly in turbulent waters where an eddy will suddenly sweep towards you sidelong. Its secondary function is to get you cutting straight into the eddy.

Hold the paddle shaft at waist level directly in front of and close to you. The blade on your leaning side should be slightly behind you, *flat* on the surface of the water with its leading edge slightly higher than the trailing edge. What you have then is essentially a water ski as an outrigger. And as a water ski can support your weight, so can the paddle blade.

There are two variables that dictate how much the back brace can bear: the speed of the water and the distance of the paddle blade from the hull. The further out the blade planes, the greater the leverage action. The faster the water speed, the more support it offers.

Back bracing will help you keep your balance when you first start out kayaking. Any time you feel yourself tipping, just push yourself upright again against the brace. Once you're whizzing along with real momentum, even on a quiet lake, because of the aquadynamic properties of your hull the back brace can also be used for turning while at the same time giving you something of a feel for the rakish angles of a white water run. As the blade planes across the water—or slides just below the surface—and you lean with it, the kayak hull cantles out of the water so it rides asymmetrically on the water surface. Now the current pulls at the hull on the side opposite that on which the paddle is braced. You swivel around the paddle almost as if it were nailed to one spot in the water.

THE ESKIMO ROLL

It may sound like an Arctic breakfast bun but the Eskimo roll is a vital part of kayaking—one that puts you underwater and out again.

It is very difficult to perform in the sponson-supported Aerius; on the other hand, the stability of this craft practically eliminates the need for it. Should you feel yourself tipping in the Klepper boat, a simple back brace will set things aright. Still, if you get a chance to practice the roll in a racing kayak, not only is it fun, but it's a challenge that will give you an immense amount of satisfaction and boost your kayaking confidence as well.

Before you begin practicing the maneuver—we're certainly pre-supposing you can swim by now—capsize your kayak a few times, as you would a canoe, to get a feel for its stability. These upsets will also relieve you of the nagging suspicion that you could get trapped in the snug-fitting boat if it overturned. So automatic is it to fall out of a kayak when it spills, you'll have to work at staying in long enough to practice your Eskimo roll.

In an Eskimo roll, as the kayak tips over, say to the left, instead of struggling to restore your craft's balance, you help it along until you've turned all the way upside down. Then, with the aid of the momentum gained in going that far around, and with the flat of a paddle blade extended out perpendicular to the kayak for maximum leverage, you pull yourself—with what almost amounts to an upside-down brace—the rest of the way around on the right side until you're upright again.

If at all possible, learn the roll from someone experienced in the maneuver. It is difficult to figure out from a book; more importantly, it is very difficult to analyze your own moves as you go around under-water. A pair of snugly fitting goggles, which offer less water resist-ance than a snorkel mask, and a nose clip will help a bit too, making you more comfortable and permitting more careful study of your underwater antics.

But first, to visualize the maneuver, picture a large clock in front of you. Sailing into the clock as if it were a sunset is a kayak and its paddler.

Let's say he's rolling over to the left, or port side. His kayak's tip-ping toward the horizon—call it nine o'clock. Now he leans from the waist in the opposite direction, to the right, as he goes over. Once he submerges, he starts straightening out his back. By the time he reaches six o'clock, the completely upside-down stage, his back should be straight. Now he begins to lean to the left. As his torso begins to reemerge fom the water, he leans to the right again—if he's leaning properly, from the waist, his hip motion is pushing the kayak further upright.

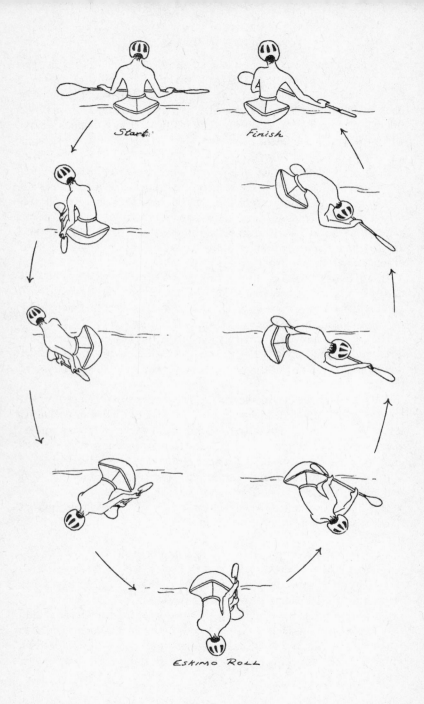

Start

Finish

ESKIMO ROLL

That takes care of swinging his torso around. Now about his head. For maximum momentum and smooth rolling, it's important that the head be the last thing to leave the water—not the first, as is instinctive. The paddler waits till his body is almost clear of the water to snap his head up, straightening his back and returning to an upright position.

Now *you* do it. As you perform the stroke, relate all movements to your own body—not up or down.

While you're performing this double sideways jackknife with your body, you will be using the paddle to pull yourself around with. As you capsize, let's say to port again, slide your left hand along the shaft till it reaches the left blade. Twist the shaft so the right blade is feathered, ready to slice through the water rather than fight it, by the time your head is at six o'clock. Now reach out with the right blade till it lies horizontally on the surface of the water somewhat towards the bow of the kayak. In effect this gives you an upside-down brace. Pull the extended paddle towards you as quickly as you can. It should make a wide arc from three to four o'clock, and from somewhat in front of you to slightly behind you. By the time the paddle has completed this arc, your body will be out of the water, only your head still submerged. Keep the back braced and, using hip action, pull your head out.

Resume normal paddling position. Your circular momentum may be surprisingly strong, however. Be prepared to brace on the port side to keep from rolling over again, and again, and again. . . .

Verbal description makes the Eskimo roll sound much more difficult than it is, not to mention agonizingly slow—which is why, although you can learn to do it yourself, it's best to see it in action and to have some help around the first few times you try it. Fifty years ago the roll was considered a feat almost impossible to perform unless you were an Eskimo and your survival depended on it. Today it's a stroke every kayak racer can perform—strenuous but not impossibly difficult.

STRAIGHT ON

The prime rule in river running is always to remain relatively aligned with the current. In a one-man kayak you're on your own; keeping your bow-to-stern line paralleling the water movement is thus easier. In a two-man kayak or canoe, the paddlers must operate in unison. Good communication, good rapport, and experience as a team are essential. It's particularly important for the bowman to remember that he has a whole long canoe following him. Under the pressures of trying to read and follow a swift-flowing river, it's all too easy for him to think in terms of the boat's bow, and maybe a couple of feet behind him, clearing an obstruction, forgetting about the rest.

All rules have an exception. When running over the haystacks, or big standing waves, that form when large amounts of water drop over a ledge or boulder, don't head straight into the waves. Take them at a slight angle, to keep the bow from burying itself in each successive wave flooding the boat.

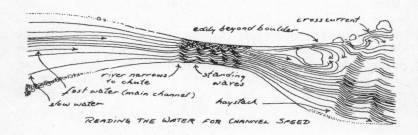

READING THE WATER FOR CHANNEL SPEED

READING THE WATER

The only way to learn how to run a river is to run one. Obviously you start with the easiest rivers, sometimes going over them time and time again to gain confidence and skill, until the roaring sirens of spray lure you on to ever more difficult waters. There are, however, several basics to take into account before you set out—things to watch for, to learn from.

First, know your canoe or kayak. Secondly, know your river. It's sound practice to walk the banks before you shoot wild rapids, mapping out which route you intend to take. You can always change your mind once you're on the water if for some reason you need to. But by having your actions planned in advance, you have something specific to deviate from. This makes it much simpler to respond. Grade I and II rivers, classified by local clubs and usually marked on canoeing maps, need not be inspected before your descent. However, if it's your first run, you may want to pull over to shore occasionally to give yourself time to think. Running rapids calls for a lot of split-second decisions.

Remember that water flowing in a channel is slowed by friction at the sides and bottom. That means your fastest current is at surface center. However, obstructions such as boulders, drops, and ledges introduce hydraulic phenomena which vary this center flow from spot to spot. Also there's the fact that when the channel narrows, the water speeds up; when the channel fans out, the current becomes more sluggish.

There is an old maxim that in order to stay on course your boat must be traveling faster than the current. It isn't even necessary to paddle to maintain this speed, though you'll probably be doing so. Merely by floating on the fast center of the stream, you are already exceeding the speed of the remaining flow of water, and thus have some control. To fully utilize this differential in maintaining direction and stability, you should leave a paddle in the water between strokes that are spaced out, to act as a brace leeboard or rudder in the slower current.

CHANNELS

The strongest current usually leads to the most open channel, and the best. If a river fingers out, the channel that begins to drop the soonest is generally the least violent. Those that look smoother and seem to have less of a drop to them are apt to end in one large, abrupt plunge. Remember, they all have to reach the same level. The one that starts first has the smallest gradient.

Water in a channel will run faster as the banks narrow. The main chute is usually marked by a tongue of relatively smooth, swift surface water rippled by small standing waves. Those are the ones that seem to remain in the same spot relative to the riverbank. The more even the pattern of standing waves, the more clearance your hull will have.

Since the widening out at the end of a channel reduces the water's velocity, the fast-flowing channel water itself runs smack dab into a much slower current below it. This causes large standing waves, or haystacks. Fierce in appearance, they are an indication of good depth. Small, broken waves are not.

The same principle holds true when a river fans out into shoals. The largest waves are produced in the deepest channels.

MODIFIED STANDARD INTERNATIONAL
RIVER CLASSIFICATION SYSTEM

Beginners

GRADE I   Very easy. Clear passages. Small regular waves.
Obstructions include sand banks and bridge piers.

GRADE II   Easy. Clear if somewhat narrow passages. Small
ledges. Enough spray to ship some water.

Experienced Only—Crash Helmet Necessary

GRADE III   Medium. Passages clear if sometimes only one
canoe's width. High degree of maneuvering skill
and teamwork needed. Backwash eddies, rocks,
high waves. Spray shield recommended for canoes. Visual inspection necessary.

GRADE IV   Difficult. Extended rapids. Waves boiling, high,
and irregular. Rocks obstructing passage. Preshooting inspection and spray shield essential.

GRADE V   Very difficult. A ladder of violent rapids. Sharp
drops, whirlpools, obstructions like those of a
pinball machine. Powerful crosscurrents. Steep
gradient. Preshooting inspection essential and
often dissuading.

GRADE VI   Good luck, Charlie Brown.

ROUND THE BEND

The deepest channel is always on the outside of a bend in the river,
but that's also where erosion is quickest. And crosscurrents and water
rolls flowing under the weakened banks can cause many a quirky
current with fast flow. Often these crosscurrents together with cen-
trifugal force can suck your craft up against the outer bank. To avoid
ramming, you have to keep the boat as close to the inside of the bend
as possible.

There are two ways to handle the curve itself. There's the hell-bent-
for-leather paddling forward approach where you swing the bow in
the direction of the curve, your craft's trajectory being similar to that
of a racing car. This method is exciting, flashy, and gives you no time
for mistakes. Hold off on it till you become more experienced.

What might be called the Bank of England turn is more sedate, gives you time to rectify mistakes. Sober but safe. Paddle backwards with enough force to keep the stern always angled slightly towards the inside of the curve. Your hull will then be more or less parallel with the current—it doesn't go around the curve the way a car would either.

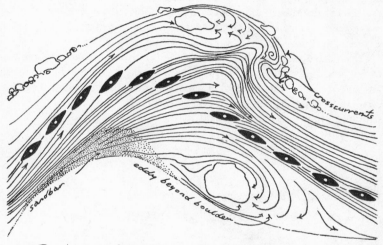

READING THE WATER FOR BANK OF ENGLAND TURN

OBSTACLE COURSES

Solid obstructions like rocks and water-permeable ones like trees have very different effects on the current. A boulder will deflect enough water to form a cushion between your boat and itself. This deflected water also helps you skirt the obstruction. A fallen tree will stop your canoe as effectively as a rock. However, water ducks under it and flows through branches as if they were sieves, so there's no water bed to land in. Because of this you must take evasive action much sooner than with a solid object.

If you do run into a tree, once you're broadside, the canoe will almost certainly be capsized by the undertow along the tree's trunk. Grasping at a branch only aggravates the problem. Bracing well out on the side away from the tree will sometimes offer relief. But the best solution is to avoid the problem by giving it wide berth.

SETTING

So there's a huge boulder or a tree right in your path and you've been told to stay away from it. What do you do, stop and get out of the canoe? Not quite, but almost. You stop the canoe's forward movement by backpaddling. Then you cross the river, canoe or kayak set at a fractional angle away from the stream flow, till you get in a line that clears the obstruction. After all that hurried backpaddling, however, you may need a brief rest. In rough water, it may not be possible to reach shore. So you find a nice little eddy to park in for a while.

Any obstruction that breaks the water's surface has an eddy behind it. Very roughly, the eddy is twice as long as the obstruction is wide. And in the eddy the water flows *upstream* at a mild speed. Set your canoe into it stern first—or you'll spin around—executing a maneuver similar to that you used to avoid an obstruction dead ahead.

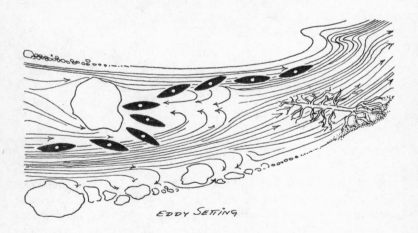

EDDY SETTING

Besides serving as rest spots, eddies have another very practical use. They are equivalent to the old locomotive roundhouse turntables. The occasion may come when during a maneuver your stern swings out of line far enough so you can't keep control. The current sweeps it around till you're descending the river broadside in a suicidal fashion. In this case it's easier to continue the swing by paddling forward until your bow is facing upstream. It's embarrassing to shoot a river backwards but it can be done. Broadside, it cannot. Once you've realigned your reversed canoe or kayak with the current, find a large eddy to pull into if you can. Then nose your bow into the current upstream, keeping the stern in the quiet eddy. Just as the bow enters the current, which will head it downstream, lean and brace to the inside of the turn to avoid capsizing. Several maneuvers like this and you'll eat hearty and sleep well, come evening.

THE SELF-PROPELLED BIPED

The concept of walking any distance has almost vanished from urban man's existence. Even the evening stroll has been largely replaced by the six o'clock news roundup. But in the wilderness you'll do a lot of walking. It's primarily a matter of putting one foot in front of the other, the same as when you walk from the house to the car. There are a few tricks to this means of locomotion, however, particularly handy if you're carrying your home on your back. So a few words on walking might be in order.

YOU GOTTA HAVE RHYTHM

There you are walking down the street. The traffic light turns red. You stop. No cars are coming. You're in a rush so you cross against the red light. Suddenly a car sweeps down out of nowhere at twice the speed limit. You break into a run and jump up on the curb on the other side. Then you bump into somebody who stopped short to look at a window display of ties on sale. With a quick dodge to the left, you regain your course, only to shift gears again when assaulted by a baby carriage. That's walking? No, it's more like a ricocheting billiard ball.

When you plan to get away from it all, take a bit of time beforehand to regain that natural walking rhythm and pace you had when you were a kid swinging your books home from school. This can only be achieved by walking uninterrupted for a while when you're consciously relaxed. Half a mile of daydreaming and you're back in stride.

But half a mile of daydreaming isn't enough to get you into shape if you're planning to do any extensive backpacking. You need something more.

Swimming, tennis, even Ping-Pong will help. Still, when it comes to training—and I really don't mean the word to sound awfully intensive—for walking, nothing beats walking. A dozen or so weekend hikes, preferably with a rucksack or pack on your back, will do wonders in building up your stride and endurance for that three-week excursion into the Sierras. Besides, they'll just make you feel great. Start out with a light pack load—just a fine picnic lunch, a tarp, and a sweater. Graduate to heavier gear each time.

Forget about the charts that say so and so many miles an hour is good for desert country, and x number if you've had a double serving of breakfast. Like anything else, walking can be turned into a fetish, with scheduled ten-minute breaks exactly every fifty minutes for 150 calories' worth of gorp to recharge the old batteries. You're out there to enjoy yourself, not to become an automaton. In a like vein, I've seen people trying to maintain their stride going up a hill like a bulldozer with a broken governor, and then collapsing for a two-hour break at the top. I've got nothing against the two-hour tea break, but it's more pleasurable when you're not exhausted. Taking a break a few minutes after you think you need one is about the right pace.

REMEMBER THE TORTOISE AND THE HARE

Although I'm convinced everyone has a natural walking rhythm that comes to the fore given half a chance, the same can't be said for speed. Revved up by urban living as we are, and eager as we are to get away from it through camping, we have a tendency to start out too fast. A dashing charge for the first mile or so of a backpacking trip can destroy most of what follows. Start out at your normal pace, consciously reminding yourself that you have all day, so what's the rush?

And by all means slow down when the ascent begins. The classic concept here is to try not to expend much more energy on the upgrade than on flat ground, which means slowing your pace in direct proportion to the gradient. If the climb gets really steep, of course, this may make it mathematically impossible to go on at all. Still, it's a good idea to bear in mind.

For the really rough spots, a theorem often put forth to help you last a little longer is the "lure yourself along" formula. When you've really had it—you're exhausted, your feet hurt, you're fed up with the whole thing—you set up some easy goal and mentally dangle a reward from it. "Another hundred yards and I'll have a candy bar," for instance. After you've chewed up the sweet at that stop, you induce yourself to go on with the promise of a drink of water after another hundred yards. Et cetera. It's a common school of thought among backpackers. All I can say about it is, hogwash. I'm all for a real challenge. But when backpacking starts becoming nothing but grueling work and Pavlovian food pellets, that's where we take separate paths. Mine leads to a nice quiet campsite where I can look around at my surroundings—and enjoy them.

LIMPING ALONG

When you see a backpacker limping down the lane, it usually doesn't mean he's sprained his ankle. Chances are he's just doing the limp step, variously known as the Sierra Shuffle, Lumbago Limp, or Doggie Drag. Designed to relieve the knee—the joint that takes most of the strain and vibration of walking—of some of its pressure, it consists, for all its more alliterative names, simply of limping. As you put your forward foot down and just before you shift your weight onto it, you relax the leg completely for a second or two. Relaxing the trailing leg instead for a second before carrying it forward is just as effective, and for some people an easier habit to acquire. Half a dozen limps does a lot to relax your knees.

THE INDIAN STEP

If you want to take the trouble of learning to walk all over again from scratch, like a baby, you can switch to the Indian step. I would recommend it more highly than I do except for the fact that it really does mean developing a whole new walking habit, one that comes hard at that. Still, it deserves mention because it is so much more efficient than our usual stride. Step forward with one foot, at the same time swivel that hip forward from the waist, and lean into the step. Now do the same with the other foot. And so on. The feet should come down one in front of the other as if you were walking on a log.

The Indian step tends to develop a longer stride, but more importantly, when you're using it, that bounce often associated with walking disappears, which means a lot of energy saved lifting your pack up and down.

SLOSHING ALONG

Water is vital when you're exerting yourself. Any appreciable activity, including walking with a heavy pack, will cause you to perspire much more than in your everyday humdrum existence. You can only compensate for this by drinking proportionately more. Since you will surely get thirsty, my bringing up the point is just a reminder to take advantage of that urge, and a caution to do it slowly. Sip your water, don't chug it, particularly if it's from a cold mountain stream. Ditto for ice and snow in the wintertime. Salt tablets are usually recommended for extended trips involving continuous strenuous activity.

END OF THE TRAIL

Falling into the sack after a day's hiking with a pack is no different from any other camping bedtime—except that you have to be more careful how you do it. No one would take a racehorse directly from a long run on the track and put him in his stable. First, he would be walked to bring down the sweat and keep the muscles from stiffening. Maybe you couldn't care less about the perspiration, but watch those muscles. Walk about packless for at least an hour—it's a good idea to have along a light pair of camp moccasins to cool your heels in—before you go to bed your first day out. Otherwise you may decide to skip the second day.

UP AND DOWN

The old "because it's there" syndrome seems to be pretty deep-rooted in man. Just about anyone, from the age of two on, when faced with a mountain on his wanderings, wants to go over rather than around it. Hill-walking is easy enough, it's merely a somewhat vertical extension of our ordinary day-to-day means of self-propulsion.

As long as a mountain can be walked up, all that is required is commonsensical caution, stamina, and an awareness that in many cases it will be more difficult to come down than it is to go up. Knowing that, you will want to conserve your strength as best you can. One way to do so when you must constantly take large climbing steps is to use your hands for extra body leverage. After raising one foot, place your hands on the forward knee and push, thus helping your second foot to lift the weight of your body and pack. At all times watch your balance and remember the principal rule of hill-climbing: keep as vertical as possible. The force from your feet will then be *straight* down. If, instead, you scramble uphill, your weight is distributed back and out, down the face of the hill. On loose soil or talus, this can mean starting a slide. On firm rock face, as long as your shoes are gripping the surface, everything is all right; should they slip, you may well end up with some nasty abrasions.

Technical rock climbing is what we all think of as real mountain climbing. Walking up somehow doesn't count. If you enter the world of technical rock climbing, you'll become acquainted with such equipment as swami belts, ascenders, wedge nuts, pitons, and carabiners, not to mention the all-essential rope. However, you cannot enter this world alone, or with a book. Personal teaching is the only passport. In many areas there are professional climbers who will give you lessons. Such climbers usually post their notices on the bulletin boards maintained by most mountaineering and camping equipment shops. Eastern Mountain Sports has one of the best-known climbing schools in the country, offering courses for the beginner as well as intermediate and advanced climbers. Their outdoors curriculum includes winter mountaineering, rock and ice climbing, as well as mountain rescue seminars.

The other end from up, of course, is down, into the mountain, or more accurately, the upper layer of the earth's crust. I suppose it's a toss-up—which direction, up or down, is the more dangerous. But neither needs to be that perilous, given the proper equipment and training.

For spelunking you need first of all a cave, which is a little harder to come by than a mountain. The techniques and equipment parallel those for rock climbing, but with the addition of a carbide lamp, usually mounted on your hard hat. Finding an instructor for caving will be considerably harder than finding one for technical rock climbing, simply because it's a much smaller area of outdoor—or indoor, if you prefer—activity. But again, to set off on your own would be foolhardy, verging on suicidal. The usual minimum party for a spelunking venture is four people.

To locate spelunking groups in your area, write to the National Speleological Society, Cave Avenue, Huntsville, Alabama 35810. They will be able to inform you about local grottoes or spelunking clubs.

If the sport intrigues you, and its popularity is growing, I'd suggest taking the simple "Langer Spelunking Test" to see how you'd like it before you set out in search of a guru. I failed the test, incidentally, and will therefore remain aboveground. Find someone to help you. Then pack a lunch and two quarts of water. Have your helper lock you in a dark, empty closet not big enough for you to stretch out on the floor. You should take with you no means of telling time, and your friend should be instructed to let you out anytime he decides, between five minutes and two days after he locks the door. Outside of the range given, you should have no inkling of how long your confinement may be. And remember—to sow a little seed of doubt—after two days he may have forgotten about you entirely. Several factors will be missing; for instance, the cold (caves usually hover around 50°F.) and the dampness. Still, if you don't try to break down the door or holler to be let out before your indefinite time is up, chances are that caving's right for you.

IF THE SNOWSHOE FITS . . .

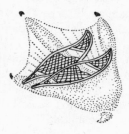

The snowshoe is as American as, well, say, the canoe. Both were developed and perfected by the Indians, and neither one is indigenous to any other part of the world. Foot extenders, a cross between skis and snowshoes, were found in Central Asia eons ago. But snowshoes as we know them were first fashioned by Indians living in the eastern and western interior coastland areas of North America. And whereas skis, their Continental counterpart, devised by the Europeans for fast travel through their undergrowth-free, almost parklike forests, have gained great popularity in the United States and Canada during recent decades, snowshoes remain about as common in Europe as palm trees in the Alps. Which is a shame. Snowshoes can carry one over much ground inaccessible to the skier because of underbrush or rough terrain. It's an invigorating, yet not too strenuous, mode of transportation offering the winter camper one of the best ways to visit the white wilderness.

SHOE STYLES

When it comes to picking out a pair of snowshoes, you'll find that ten people will have ten different opinions about them. The only point

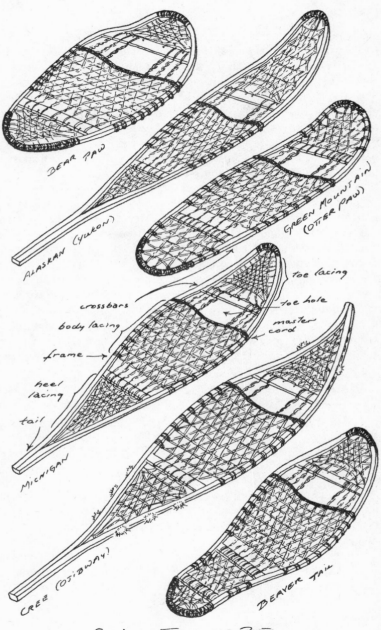

BEAR PAW

ALASKAN (YUKON)

GREEN MOUNTAIN (OTTER PAW)

crossbars

body lacing

frame

heel lacing

tail

MICHIGAN

toe lacing

toe hole

master cord

CREE (OJIBWAY)

BEAVER TAIL

SNOWSHOE TYPES AND PARTS

they're apt to be unanimous on will be that white ash is the best of all frame woods. No doubt even this point of agreement will soon disappear; more and more plastic snowshoes are coming on the market, and it can't be long before someone champions their cause. Personally I agree with the old Cree Indian who, over a roast goose dinner, replied to my question about plastic snowshoes by spitting some shot lodged in his bit of goose over his shoulder and saying with definitive disdain, "Plastic is for children." Besides being of poor utilitarian quality, I find them esthetically displeasing. Suppose we just dispose of plastic snowshoes for now, and settle on white ash.

A good snowshoe is a good snowshoe, and although one type may be better than another under certain conditions, one can't help but pick a favorite. Mine is the Cree. Now I have friends who swear by the Bear Paw. I find it all right for short hauls, poor, on the other hand, for covering a lot of ground. First of all, it's too wide for hill climbing. It tilts downslope readily when you're traversing, straining the ankles. Also it tracks poorly, since it has no tail. (You'll learn about tracking—the shoe's tendency to stay aimed in the direction you're trying to go—with your first snowshoeing steps.) And in deep soft snow, since it is tailless and therefore has nothing to drag down the rear, the tip tends to dig in more easily. This adds insult to injury, since the short rear tends to kick up snow against the back of your leg as you walk.

Bear Paws were designed for areas of very heavy underbrush. There, the same qualities that make them unsuitable as a general-purpose snowshoe are, of course, pluses. One can turn more quickly, and within a shorter radius. And they have no tail to foul in the brush. Unless you plan to spend your winters checking trap lines, however, you'll probably want something more versatile.

At the other extreme from the Bear Paw's tailless form is that of the Alaskan, also known as the Yukon. This snowshoe is quite long and narrow, with the toe turning up earlier than in other models, which makes it particularly good for extra-deep snow or trail-breaking for dog sleds.

If you don't have a dog sled, well, the Alaskan is still a good trail shoe, but so is the Michigan. And the Michigan has a slightly shorter tail and a more pointed toe, making for easier handling as the brush gets tighter. Besides, it looks exactly the way you always imagined a snowshoe would.

A shoe of growing popularity, particularly on the East Coast, is the

Green Mountain Bear Paw, occasionally known as the Otter Paw. It's an elongated, slimmer version of the original Bear Paw, with the toe pitched slightly steeper. These modifications have eliminated some of the negative properties of the Bear Paw.

While we're on the subject of paws, there is yet another modification, called the Beaver Tail, which I saw once around James Bay, but never used. It looks like a Bear Paw with a webbed beaver tail stuck on the end. I'd have thought the extra bends would tend to weaken the frame, but the owner said he'd swear by it as the world's most nearly perfect snowshoe.

All these models aside, my own choice is the Cree—in some places referred to as the Ojibway, although I've also seen this name applied to the Michigan. Unlike most snowshoes, the Cree frame is made of two joined pieces of wood rather than one. The effect is to make it stronger, since the weakest point of a shoe is at its sharpest bend, the toe. Also, in very deep, soft snow, the Cree's sharp tip acts like a knife, cutting into the snow instead of letting the toe load up. All in all, except for in exceptionally tight underbrush, a great snowshoe. Besides which, Crees look classy with their fluted toes and red pompons where the toe and heel webbing loop through the frame.

SIZING UP THE SHOE

The bigger the snowshoe, the more weight it can support—and, of course, the more it weighs itself. This is no minor matter. Carrying weight on your feet consumes considerably more energy than does the same weight on your back or even in your hands. So the tendency is to get a snowshoe of the smallest size possible. Theoretically this makes sense, but in practice it often causes difficulty, for the smaller shoe which supports you readily on corn snow may suddenly give way on freshly fallen snow.

The weight you yourself expect to carry is an important differential in choosing your snowshoes. Going out on a day's hike is one thing. Add a thirty-pound rucksack and it's quite another. Here's a rough set of rules of thumb on snowshoe size/weight of load. For the oval type of shoe (Bear Paw, Green Mountain, etc.), the length and width added together should equal 44 to 45 inches if you and your pack weigh less than 175 pounds, 46 to 48 inches if you're over 175 but under 200 pounds, and 50 inches or more if you're over 200 pounds total. In the case of medium-width shoes (the Cree, Michigan, or others), the figures would be 60 to 62 inches for 175 pounds or less, 62 to 63 inches for 175 to 200 pounds, 65 inches or better for over 200 pounds. The very narrow models (the Alaskan or Yukon, for instance) call for 65 to 67 inches of shoe to carry 175 pounds or less, 71 to 73 inches to bear 175 to 200 pounds, and 77 inches or more for over 200 pounds.

As for the weight of the shoes themselves, there is relatively little variation among the different models for a given size. However, what you can and should do before you go out on your first long snowshoe walk is take some weights about as heavy as your snowshoes (you can get belted weights at many sporting goods stores) and wear them around your ankles at home. Keep them on for half an hour to an hour a day the week before you set off. Otherwise, if you do any extensive wandering, you may well come down with that delightfully named, if unpleasant, malady the French Canadian *voyageur* called *mal de raquette*. Basically this is just cramps in calf and thigh muscles subjected to carrying the unaccustomed extra weight on the feet below them. Another way to avoid *mal de raquette* is that old but often forgotten refrain, "Don't overdo your first time out." With snowshoeing in the wilds this admonishment has the added urgency that you have to be able to make it back whence you've come, and on your own two padded feet.

CONSTRUCTION

If after all this discussion you've managed to decide on a model of snowshoes to suit you, check out the construction of the shoes before you buy. We've already settled on white ash. Old-timers will tell you that the wood should first be air-dried and then split along the grain for maximum strength, rather than sawed from planks. They're probably right, but as far as I know no actual stress comparisons have been made between cut and split frames. The question is also becoming somewhat academic, since only a small group of hand craftsmen take the time to split their own frame stock. Mass-manufactured shoes are all made from kiln-dried sawn stock.

So what do you do? Unless you want to make your own, you check each frame to make sure there are no knotholes or growth cracks and the grain of the wood runs straight. Incidentally, should you be fortunate enough to find a pair of handcrafted snowshoes that have been split-cut instead of sawed, the frame will probably appear a little irregular in shape as compared with manufactured shoes. This is because the splitting process follows the grain much more closely.

Other things to check: Both frame and crossbars should be smooth and slightly beveled. The mortised joint where they meet should be neat and tight. All webbing holes should be splinter-free and slightly countersunk for maximum web tension and minimum wear. Small details such as the varnish being unevenly applied or the webbing slack, particularly on the heel or toe segments, are signs of poor and rushed craftsmanship.

A frame alone does not a snowshoe make. What's stretched between it is just as important. It is also almost as controversial. Snowshoe webbing is sometimes described as being made of gut, which it is not. It is rawhide—or used to be. Synthetics, particularly Neoprene, are making deep inroads into the webbing field. I still like the rawhide myself. But I'm not such an entrenched traditionalist as to insist that only beaver or caribou hide are worth talking about. Cowhide, the most commonly used, is fine, and most people, including me, wouldn't be able to distinguish its capabilities from those of the other hides— except moose, which in wet spring snow would stretch to such a degree you'd think you were walking a soggy trampoline. One manufacturer, Tubbs of Vermont, has switched almost exclusively to Neoprene, and another, Snowcraft, is well on the way, so apparently Neoprene has found its devotees and is here to stay. Tubbs, incidentally, makes a very nice Cree snowshoe (listed as an Ojibway).

Whichever *babiche,* or lacing, you select, it must be even in diameter and tightly strung. That used for the center, body section will usually be thicker than that for the toe and heel segments. What is important is that there be no thin points along the individual lacings.

There is a new form of webbing in which the cross lacings are threaded through die-punched holes in each other instead of being woven. I'd let someone else wear these for a long time before I'd consider them.

At the front of the body lacing of a snowshoe is the master cord. In front of it is an open, unwebbed area. This is the toe hole. The ball of your foot rests on the master cord, and your boot or moccasin must be able to dip into the toe hole freely without catching on the front crossbar or rubbing against the sides. If the boot toe snags, you'll risk tripping with every step. Make sure the toe hole is large enough for the boot you wear. It should not be much larger, however, since it has no supportive function.

The master cord is the weakest link in your snowshoe. It takes the most wear. In addition, it is the point of attachment for your bindings. Be sure there are no flaws here.

BINDINGS

In the same way that there is no agreement on which is the best shoe, there is no consensus on the best binding, harness, or lashing to keep it on. So, for maximum flexibility in choice, bindings are sold separately. The standard ones are the Howe, the H type, the Army plate, and to a lesser extent the squaw hitch and the Alaskan 8.

The Howe, H, and Army plate are particularly popular with mountaineers because of their heel control. The firm heel straps, even more so the heel cups, keep the foot from shifting laterally when traversing

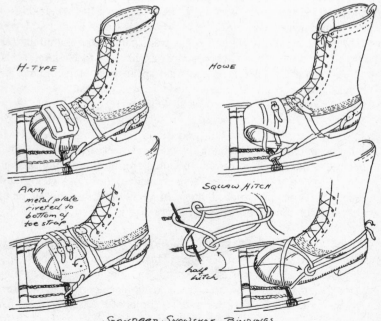

STANDARD SNOWSHOE BINDINGS

slopes. In the case of the Howe binding, a wide forward support comes over the toe, which keeps the foot from sliding forward when you're coming down a mountain. Any of these is suitable for the beginner who wants an easy-to-put-on binding.

The squaw hitch is a simple, efficient, and trouble-free lashing, without buckles or other weak points. It can be made from any handy length of rawhide or, as in the old days, lampwick. Lampwick has the advantage of being easy to handle and tie in cold weather. It is still recommended by many, but try to find it at your local hardware store sometime.

The unfortunate demise of lampwick has not decreased the popularity of the squaw hitch, however. Used with rawhide, it is probably the most popular of the bindings among Canadian trappers who are snowshoers by trade. It would be my first choice as well if I hadn't seen the Aleuts using the Alaskan 8.

The Alaskan 8 is a lashing even simpler than the squaw hitch, with the added benefit that you can take your snowshoes on or off without undoing the hitch, in fact without even bending over if you're so inclined. This feature isn't just a matter of laziness and wanting to keep one's hands in their warm gloves. It's deucedly difficult to swim with snowshoes on, or crawl onto the ice from a hole you've fallen through. The Alaskan 8 can be kicked off in seconds—a nice safety feature even if you never have to use it. The flexibility of the binding also means there is less likelihood of breaking your leg in case of an accident.

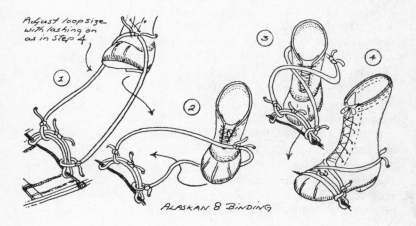

Adjust loop size with lashing on as in step 4

ALASKAN 8 BINDING

On steep slopes there is some lateral shifting of the heel with the Alaskan 8, and it takes more practice to develop the proper snow-shoeing stride with this binding. But once you've mastered it—and it takes a fair amount of skill—you'll be able to jump and run along with the rest.

THE OTHER SHOE

You can't wear shoes with snowshoes. The footgear must be heel-less, for a heel will rapidly wear through the webbing. The ideal foot-gear for snowshoeing is either the Alaskan mukluk, a kind of high boot moccasin, or the Scandinavian Laplander's shorter, curled-toe version. The Lapp boot, incidentally, is perfect for cross-country skiing as well. Its reverse hook on the top of the toe slides under a loop on the ski, which is about as simple a binding as you can get. I've tried this hook and loop binding on snowshoes, but unfortunately it doesn't work. With the toe dipping into the toe hole instead of holding in place on a solid ski, the boot slides out.

Having said that the mukluk type of footgear is the ideal for snow-shoes, sadly I have to add that if you're not heading towards Alaska or Lapland, you'll probably be unable to find such boots. Even if you do find them, you'll discover that they cost upwards of three to four times what your snowshoes did. A not inconsiderable investment.

Going barefoot is not recommended. But skipping the boot entirely is not at all a bad idea as long as the temperature holds below 20°F. Two pairs of extra-heavy wool socks work fine. Just make sure they are wool, and if you use the squaw hitch or Alaskan 8, make sure the rawhide is not so tight as to cut off your circulation. Lest you think going around in stockinged feet in midwinter is a personal aberration of mine, in Sweden when I was a kid a lot of us wore sock slippers out in the winter snow, saving our *pjäxor,* the standard heavy winter shoes, for the rough stuff. It has to be cold, dry snow, of course, to warrant leaving the boots home.

Probably the best all-weather compromise, if you can't get high moccasins, is wool socks with either rubber boots or hunting, or snow, pacs—boots consisting of a rubber shoe topped by a leather sleeve. This gives you both warmth and water protection. However, rubber can't breathe, which could mean a perspiration problem on a long hike. And if you use a combination of buckled galoshes and one of the rawhide lashings, you have to be careful that they don't interact. Rawhide has been known to unbuckle the bottom buckle of the boot it's harnessing with almost every step.

EXTRAS

Maybe you thought ski poles were just for skiing. Actually most snowshoers going out into the wilds carry a set as well, or at least an ice ax with an extra-long handle and an attached ski pole basket. The reason they do will become obvious the first time you walk yourself into a spot too tight to maneuver in. You can't turn around. You can't back out, because as soon as you lift a foot the back of the snowshoe digs in. What do you do? Take off the shoes and walk out? Obviously not, since if you could do that you wouldn't have to be wearing them in the first place.

With the poles you press down lightly on the tips of your shoes as you lift them and step back. This keeps the tails from digging in. If you have no poles, but are carrying some extra rawhide to use as emergency bindings (a very sound idea), tie the rawhide to the tails of your snowshoes and pull them up clear of the snow with each backward step. A bit clumsy, but it will do in a pinch.

Poles or an ice ax are also good for keeping your balance on steep climbs. By preference I use a single pole with an old-fashioned, oversized basket that holds against the snow well. An ice ax has more uses, but it is much heavier and the additional weight militates against it. While I'm all for the multiple-use principle in camp gear, I find I rarely need an ice ax anyway except in very high country. And if you're not familiar with them, they can be quite dangerous in a spill. Poles should fit snugly under your armpits when the tips are level with your feet.

Packed snow and/or a steep walking gradient may call for crampons or snow cleats. Cleats, sawtoothed and about one inch deep, are usually fastened permanently to the snowshoe cross frame with screws. They do not add much drag in soft snow and do give good additional traction on crust. However, for really slippery conditions you will have to take your snowshoes off and put crampons on your boots. You can attach crampons directly to snowshoes, but if it's so slippery and the ice so solid you need the crampons, you shouldn't need the snowshoes.

A last item well worth considering, particularly if you're using an

ankle-high boot and it's snowing, or you're in close enough to the
brush to be showered with tree snow, is gaiters. These are usually made
of two layers of coated nylon, with instep straps to keep them down
over the boot. Either zippers or Velcrotape is used for the closure.
Velcrotape can't jam in cold weather. Then again, try to brush packed
snow out of Velcro. Personally I'll take a nylon or Delrin zipper.

YOUR FIRST STEPS

So you've bought your gear and are ready to head for the white,
trackless hills. Now how do you actually go about snowshoeing? Well,
first, you don't head for those hills right away. You concentrate on
achieving just one step. If you step on one snowshoe with the other,
as is likely the first time, don't try to move both feet at once. Stop
everything. Then extricate yourself. Bearing that sequence in mind,
you're ready to take your first step.

Stick your left pole in the snow ahead of you. Slightly out from
your body. Now pick up your *right* shoe, just high enough to lift the
front two-thirds clear of snow. The tail will—and should—drag,
except on the Bear Paw model. There are two things to watch for as
you bring your right foot forward. It must be out far enough so that
the frame of the moving right shoe does not hit your left ankle. By no
means should this be overdone. You don't want to walk straddle-
legged. Secondly, you must place the shoe forward far enough so its
tail doesn't sit on the toe of your other shoe. Well, you think, if the
tail is going to get in the way, maybe I should pick the tailless Bear
Paw after all. Wait. As you put your foot down you'll notice that there
is a gentle thrust forward on your shoe. The tail actually pushes your
shoe ahead slightly as you step down, making for faster, easier travel.
You'll find a tailed snowshoe makes for considerably less fatigue on
long walks.

Having taken your first careful step, you now place the right pole
ahead of you and move the left shoe up. That's it, you're off and
running. (At least you will be running, after some practice. Snowshoe
races are great fun.)

I'm reminded of the overall rhythm of walking in snowshoes every
time I see Genevieve sliding along in her mother's sandals—which
should give you some idea of how it works. Your gait should be some-

what rolling, but a little more definitive than if you were just shuffling along. This ensures that the snowshoe settles in, steadying your balance.

Before you set off on any long treks, there's one more thing to learn —edging. Edging on snowshoes is the same as edging in skiing, except that, of course, the snowshoes are wider, so it must be done a bit more carefully. When walking across a slope, the object is to keep your feet level rather than tilted down the side of the hill. To accomplish this, you concentrate your weight on the uphill side of each foot as you put it down. If you are wearing squaw hitch or Alaskan 8 bindings, it's very easy to shift your whole heel a bit towards the hillside as you put your foot down. This makes edging much simpler. Use your poles for balancing. Without them you're apt to take a spill.

FALLING

Speaking of spills—and we might as well—take a few steps and fall. That was easy enough and rather fun. Now about getting up with a pair of size 72 Quadruple E shoes on. The principle of snowshoes is that their flatness distributes your weight over a large surface area to support you. So in order to get up again, particularly in very soft, deep snow, you have to keep your shoes sitting flat on the ground while you rise above them. A not insurmountable problem, but still, easier said than done. It may be possible to pull yourself up on your poles. More likely they will just sink, unable to support your weight. Or you can drag yourself over to a tree and pull yourself up. But why struggle? Quite often it's the better part of valor to simply unfasten the shoes, set them out properly on the snow, pull yourself up on the "platform" and start over again. A companion, of course, can help you up. (Watch that you don't tangle in his shoes.) All the same, practice solo a couple of times, just to be prepared for those occasions when you're on your own.

HITTING THE TRAIL

You know how to walk and how to fall. Now practice turning, moving your feet one at a time a little to the left or right until you've circled the desired number of degrees. Then do a kick turn. That is, pick up one foot and with a kicking motion turn it a complete 180 degrees so that the toe settles down by the heel of the other shoe. Now pick up the second foot and bring it around a full 180 degrees so you're completely turned around. Okay, you're ready to set off on your first hike. Preferably with a couple of experienced companions. If you must go alone, stick close to home base the first half dozen times out.

Groups moving on snowshoes usually go Indian file, taking turns breaking trail. Breaking trail means simply going first, leaving a packed track for the others to follow. Still, the difference in energy consumed between breaking trail and following is considerable, so take turns—and munch some gorp when you switch to lead position.

When you get to your first steep hill, you'll notice it is quite difficult, if not impossible, to walk straight up. So you zigzag, or traverse, always keeping your shoes well edged. A bit difficult at first, but you master it and get to the top.

Now you remember the old maxim about its always being easier to climb up than down. The slope is too steep to walk down. You begin to slide and are struck with a great idea. Why not sit down and make like a sled? Well, there are two good reasons. First of all, it wears out the webbing of your snowshoes very quickly. Secondly, that little twig sticking up halfway down the hill may be the branch of a buried tree on which your snowshoe is going to snag, bringing you to a very abrupt halt, perhaps even breaking an ankle or two in the process. So instead you zigzag your way down again.

At the bottom of the valley you notice a crystal palace of icicles hanging from the spruce boughs by the edge of the creek. Across the valley you see some movement. It's a deer heading for shelter, steam blowing from its nostrils. Why not follow it? The hillside ahead of it is heavily wooded, rough hewn and uneven beneath its hood of white— impassable with skis. There's plenty of snow, but no way to go straight for more than four or five feet at a time. The wind sends clumps of snow sailing to the ground from the rustling spruces.

Why not indeed follow the deer? The soft swish of your shoes joins that of the wind and the trees. Those are the only sounds in the valley as you head for where the deer is probably yarding up. You've just been hooked on snowshoeing.

END OF THE SEASON

All good things come to an end, and when the spring melt comes, it's time to stash away your snowshoes till next year. Wipe the dirt off and clean them thoroughly with a damp cloth. Check the condition of the webbing and bindings. Give the whole shoe—including the lacings —a couple of light coats of marine-grade spar varnish. The finish will keep the tension high during humid summers. Epoxy resin is increasingly replacing spar varnish. It is an excellent waterproofer and far more durable than varnish in resisting abrasion. The side effects, if any, it may have on rawhide aren't fully known yet, since it's only been used for a couple of seasons. But it looks like a good bet to outdo varnish altogether.

When your snowshoes are thoroughly dry, tie them together tightly, bottom to bottom. Better yet, if you're handy with small tools, make a press for them, like that for a tennis racket. They can then be hung by the press instead of their frames. At the same time the vise will prevent warping.

Snowshoes should be hung, whether by their tails or by the press, in a dark corner of your attic. Use a fine strong wire for suspension. Mice and other rodents find snowshoe webs a delightful midsummer snack, so don't hang the shoes with twine or rope which small creatures can readily climb.

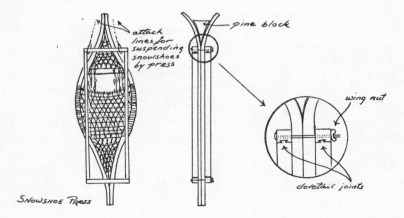

attach lines for suspending snowshoes by press

pine block

wing nut

dovetail joints

SNOWSHOE PRESS

CROSS-COUNTRY SKIING

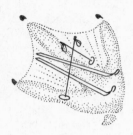

Going to school in winter was one of the greatest times I had as a kid. The going was so great, in fact, I often kept right on past school and into the snow-covered woods for the day. The location of our house was particularly fortunate, since between it and the school lay two ski routes, a very steep, speedy, short morning special, and a much longer western path with a gradient suitable for a leisurely run home after a hard day chasing foxes across the farmers' fields and into the forest. Both routes gave the appearance of going to and coming from the proper educational direction. Not many people get to ski to work or school these days, but it's still a great way to get around the wilderness in wintertime.

My skis—we didn't differentiate between cross-country, or x-c, as some write it, and alpine in those days—were a narrow, battered old wooden pair complete with gnarled tips after the fashion of the Lapps, toe loops, and buckled leather heel straps for bindings. Needless to say, the skis didn't always stay on foot. They were particularly devious when used on our jerry-built, six-foot shipping-crate-and-packed-snow ski jumps.

Skis and bindings have come a long way since then. But one of the beauties of cross-country skiing is that it doesn't require much newfangled stuff. In order not to sound too much like a querulous old codger asittin' in front of his mountain hut shakin' his head over all them fancy fittin's, let me explain. To get started ski touring, you'll spend maybe a third as much money as you would to outfit for alpine skiing. Perhaps even more of an inducement, anyone who can walk can ski cross country.

The other beauties of cross-country skiing—well, go discover them. You'll find them over the white rim of the easy-going hill with nary a human footprint on it. But first you need a pair of skis.

SKIS FOR TOURING

Cross-country skis come in two models: touring and racing. The racing ski, with an under-the-binding width of less than two inches, is an ultralight, maneuverable, fragile sliver designed not only for skiing fast, but for doing so on a well-prepared track. Taking a pair of racing skis out in the woods for winter camping is like racing a low-slung McClaren Ford on a country lane. It can be done, but then you'll probably need some other form of transportation to get back.

The touring ski is wider, from about two and a half inches at the binding down to two inches for a lightweight model. Here it may sound like I'm quibbling over the proverbial fraction of an inch, but the difference is quite significant. For deep powdered snow, or for touring with a rucksack loaded for a week's outing, you almost always need the two-and-a-half-inch ski in order not to sink in too deeply. Since most of the good cross-country skis are manufactured in Europe, this means a ski in the range of fifty-eight to sixty-four millimeters wide. For mountain touring, look for widths up to sixty-five milli- meters or more.

These wider skis will also be heavier, somewhere between five and seven pounds a pair, as compared with a lightweight touring/racing ski like the excellent Langrenn Blå, weighing in at only three pounds, thirteen ounces. Made of five layers of laminated birch and balsa for maximum strength, with a hickory bottom, or sole, and lignostone edges, which prevent the ski from fraying or splintering, the Langrenn Blå is very narrow (forty-six millimeters), limber, and swift as the wind. By the way, if the word "balsa" stands out, from your model- airplane-building days, as the soft little sticks you could snap with your fingers—yes, it's one and the same wood. But although balsa is indeed soft and light, its strength-to-weight ratio is much higher than that of steel. In lamination with other materials it makes for a sinewy, superlightweight ski. The same holds true for the lignostone edge, which is compressed beechwood impregnated with a phenolic resin; although it's not quite as strong as steel for the same purpose, it's quite strong enough, and weighs much less.

For all their seeming toughness, skis of the narrow, lightweight type are designed for zipping across meadows or on packed tracks. They simply can't take the rough abuse of touring in the wilds. So if you're counting on your skis to put you well out of reach of civilization for a week or two at a time, stay with a relatively wide model.

Again, look for a high-quality lamination. The best among the heavier-duty cross-country skis, such as the fine Bonna Turski 2400 or the EMS Asnes Turlangrenn, have hickory soles, with lignostone edges. Hickory is tough, giving you durability and good handling. Birch-soled skis with hickory edging are faster and hold wax better, but for winter ski camping they are not as durable. All laminated wood skis should have tail protectors to help prevent splitting.

Synthetics have not swept the cross-country ski scene yet. Nevertheless, they are trickling onto the market. Fiberglass shows promise for the future, although the glass skis now available don't have the spring of the wood ones, nor do they permit wax to bond as well. Then there are the plastic soles with fish scales. Someone had the idea of mimicking nature's nautical pattern on the bottom of skis in the hope of developing a surface that would maximize both glide and thrust—all without the use of wax. But the efficiency of the no-wax plastic skis, even with fish scales, is questionable. Although a beginner eager to get started might be tempted by their no-wax claims, I think it would be better to slow down and enjoy the waxing instead. It's a rather pleasant task, as tasks go, and the waxes, especially base wax when it's being burned on, smell great.

A last plus for wooden skis: Should you gouge a hole in the sole too deep to sand smooth, it can be filled with plastic wood. Mending nonwood skis is much more difficult.

Some skiers like a plastic-impregnated lamination for the sole. This eliminates the need for base-waxing with pine-tar compounds, used primarily as a wood preservative. However, base wax when burned on, which is the only way it lasts, need usually be applied only once or twice a year. If you don't want to be bothered with the job, most equippers will do it for you at a reasonable fee. And base-waxed wood skis hold their running waxes better than the plastic-impregnated ones currently on the market.

LENGTH AND CAMBER IN A CROSS-COUNTRY SKI

A lot of things have changed in cross-country skiing over the years, but the old rule that the skis should reach from the floor to the bottom of your palm with your arm extended overhead still holds. If you expect to do extensive winter camping, carrying a well-filled rucksack, however, it's a good idea to get a pair that reaches to the base of your fingers, or even the top.

The weight-carrying ability of your skis is a function of both surface area and camber. The camber refers to the bow in an unloaded ski laid flat on the ground. When you buy yours, you'll notice that only the tip and tail touch the floor. The middle is suspended in air. Fine. But check to make sure the camber of both skis is the same, or their performance characteristics will not be. In an extreme case of unequal camber, it's like skiing with a limp.

To check if the flex is right for you, put the skis on and let them flatten out under your weight. On a smooth floor, you should still be able to slip a piece of paper under the skis at the point of the bindings. If you can't, they have too much give, or are too soft. The paper should go underneath smoothly but with a slight grip. If the paper just sails through without any resistance whatsoever, the skis are too stiff. Again, take into account whether you're buying skis primarily for day touring or for extended winter camping: if you're planning long tours, wear a pack of your average carrying weight while trying them on. This might be a good time to look at one of those touring rucksacks with slots for carrying your skis as well.

The built-in camber of the ski distributes your weight along its full length. Were it not there, your weight would be much more centered, considerably reducing the handling qualities of the ski. The camber also adds flexibility and spring, enabling you to cope with rough terrain better.

BINDINGS HEEL AND TOE

In bindings you have a choice of heel or toe. The variety available in both categories is ample, in some cases maybe even getting out of hand.

For winter touring, over any terrain that's very hilly, heel bindings are best. For mountain skiing they are a necessity. Heel bindings, using a cable to keep the shoe firmly in the toe lug while allowing the heel to move freely up and down, weigh more than toe bindings; they compensate for the extra weight, on the other hand, by offering more lateral support and being sturdier. Their most important plus, however, is the extra side hitches mounted on the skis near the heel, available with the best cable bindings, like Jofa and Tempo. The side hitches permit the down pull necessary for alpine skiing. For really rugged mountain skiing, a safety release is a wise precautionary feature. Silvretta offers a good front-throw cable binding with front hinge and variable safety release that also allows heel lift even with your rigid-soled climbing boots.

Speaking of boots, decide on these before you get the bindings. Most heel cable bindings have adjustable toe lugs to accommodate soles of various thickness. Boots for toe bindings, however, must match the bindings exactly.

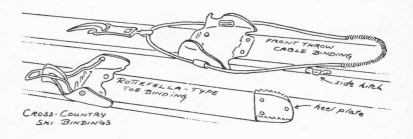

For cross-country skiing where rough or hilly terrain will not be a major factor, toe bindings are lighter, easier and quicker to get into, and require no adjustments to fit the boots, since they are matched to begin with. Most toe-clamp bindings use the standard Scandinavian three-pin layout. The pins stick up from the bottom of the binding. The sole of the shoe has a matching set of pinholes in front of the ball of the foot. Once these are mated, a clamp locks the sole down at the toe. The three-pin setup will probably become the standard of the future. Meanwhile some toe bindings use a sole hook. These step-in bindings, such as ones made by Eie and Troll, interlock a specially constructed metal boot toe and the binding. Remember, though, in each of these cases, you can use only a boot designed for the specific binding in question.

Whichever type of binding you decide on, heel plates or popups, screwed directly on to the ski, should be used with it, to keep snow from balling up as well as to add lateral stability to the driving foot and control to your turns. Unlike in downhill skiing, the heel for cross-country is free to move up and down at all times. Heel plates are usually of serrated metal. Popups are currently made of rubber, although I wouldn't be surprised to see Teflon or similar ones coming on the market.

SKI BOOTS CAN BE COMFY

If you're used to those cement block boots associated with alpine skiing, relief is just a cross-country ski away. A light touring boot, made of soft flexible leather, weighs between two and three pounds. Usually available in above- and below-the-ankle-bone cut. The higher ones are warmer, keep out the snow better, and, some feel, give added support. The low-cut are, of course, lighter. The differences are minimal and mostly a matter of individual comfort and taste. Mine lean towards the over-the-ankle.

You can skip buying a pair of touring boots entirely if you plan ahead when getting your hiking or mountaineering boots. A heel cable binding requires a deep groove around the back of a boot's heel. For the stiff-soled climbing boots a front hinge on the ski binding is needed as well. But that's all. Nobody says you have to get ski boots. Several hiking and mountaineering models come with the heel groove for four-season use.

As with all footwear, the most important test here is fit. Your boots should be snug, but *not* tight. If you plan to use double socks when skiing, make sure you wear both pairs when you go to try boots on. Also, in cross-country skiing your foot moves around more than in almost any other activity short of tap-dancing, so be particularly wary of loose heels—or you'll be popping blisters all night—and watch out for shortness when you try the next size smaller to get a heel that fits—or you'll have toenails jammed into your toe knuckles.

POLES

If everything about cross-country skiing sounds fairly simple and straightforward so far, it's probably because manufacturers are just beginning to think of it as a big growth field. The diversity and complexity of equipment that hits a recreation activity or, as it's now named, the leisure industry when mass-marketing techniques come to the fore are as yet mostly absent. As an extra lure to the would-be cross-country skier, this makes the sport one in which quality is still relatively inexpensive.

Most cross-country ski poles are even today made of bamboo, sometimes called Tonkin—after the region where the bamboo stands are best, even if the skiing is nonexistent. Bamboo poles are light-weight, flexible, and shock-absorbing. Although poles made of alumi-num—the Scott make has earned an "in" reputation as the premier pole among aluminum fanciers—fiberglass, and even steel ones are in-creasing in popularity, I'll stick with the bamboo. They are every bit as good for all but the most grueling workouts, not as cold to the touch, and inexpensive. Besides, I have a sentimental attachment to them.

To select the right pole length for you, stand in your boots and skis. Tuck the poles straight up under your armpits. They should fit snugly. Using shorter alpine poles for cross-country skiing is not only in-efficient, it will give you a backache as well. Also, unlike the straight-tipped alpine poles, the tips of cross-country poles should be curved *forward* in order to break free of the snow cleanly.

Ski pole baskets most often used to be wood hoops with two leather crosspieces. Nothing beats this combination. Yet nowadays more and more poles are made with plastic baskets, some even a stamped one-piece unit, which never manages to level with the snow and is an abomination. The wider the basket, the better it handles in deep snow. Remember your poles are one of your major sources of propulsion. You don't have to get six-inch-diameter baskets, but they should be at least four inches across, and probably four and a half.

Grips are usually of leather or cork. Cork feels nice, but leather wears better and doesn't hold cold moisture as long. Again there's plastic, but let's not go into that.

The straps on your poles should be adjustable, so you can compen-sate for snow conditions and depth. The deeper the pole sinks, the looser you will want the strap.

SEALSKINS, SKI TIPS, AND AVALANCHE CORD

Climbers for skis—that's where I really used to wish synthetics would make some inroads on the natural material, simply from the ecological point of view. And at last they have. Eastern Mountain Sports now offers "imitation sealskin" climbers in the 180 to 215 centimeter lengths. Like the natural fur, these climbers have directional hairs, which stay firmly and evenly in line.

Climbers strap onto the bottoms of your skis from tip to tail. As you go down a hill, the synthetic sealskin is smooth and offers a good slide. Going uphill, the hairs literally stand on end, keeping you from backsliding. They aren't needed for plain and simple cross-country day skiing, but on extended trips through frequently hilly country, with a pack on your back, sealskins come in mighty handy.

Also essential for any extended cross-country trip is a spare tip for your skis. Made of either aluminum or plastic, it slips over your ski to carry you home if you end up snapping off the original tip. Remember skis can carry you to areas from which returning on foot could be quite difficult, or at the very least tedious. If there are several of you, one ski tip for every three persons should be quite sufficient. Certainly a good idea in rough country. An alternative would be to pack along your snowshoes. They'll not only get you out in an emergency, but— a thought on the happier side—can take you off the trail where skis cannot.

Speaking of emergencies, it's also a good idea, for extended ski camping, to carry a small screwdriver to tighten binding screws should they need it. Spare cables come under the same category of fix-it gear.

For mountain skiing, even if you're staying close to a base camp, should it be in an area of known or suspected avalanche tendencies, take along an avalanche cord. This is a light, strong, usually red-colored line around fifty feet long with marks every meter or two. It isn't to pull yourself out with if you are buried by an avalanche, but so your partners can find you. When skiing across an area likely to have avalanches, do so one at a time trailing your cord. Safest of all is to avoid these spots.

DRESSING FOR THE OCCASION

There's no need to get fancy with ski clothes for cross-country touring. In pants, the best thing you can wear is the wool knickers you got for autumn hiking. They allow freedom of movement, and the pants cuffs, being nonexistent, won't rub against each other. As to the rest of your attire, anything goes, but keep two things in mind. First, all clothes must be loose enough not to chafe. That means no tight stretch garments. Binding around the shoulders or crotch is particularly annoying. Secondly, avoid the nonbreathing materials, like nylon, often associated with alpine skiing. Cross-country skiing, with its variety of terrain and altitude, will involve the use of almost every muscle in your body. You're going to be warm as long as you keep going. Lots of enthusiasts wear shorts and short-sleeved shirts. Although this may be overdoing things, it indicates what's in store. You will need a warm sweater. But only for your rest stops. Make sure you don't get chilled then, after working up a sweat. A wool cap, gloves or mittens, and gaiters, if you want them, round out your windproof ski wardrobe.

THE SKI REPORT

The object of all this outfitting is to move with pleasure and perhaps with grace across fields and through forests when they're wearing their white winter mantle. To do so most easily, it helps to know something about the material on which you intend to travel. Snowshoes carry you over the vast expanses of snow a step at a time— one step down, then another, firm and sure, no matter what kind of snow it is. Skis *ride* the snow, and what kind of snow it is can make a big difference.

Volumes have been written about snow, its crystalline structure, the interrelations of air temperature and humidity during crystal formation, all the technical factors that make such volumes not exactly best sellers. There are even two major systems of classification, the International Snow Classification and the Magono and Lee, for typing the various snowflake crystals.

NEW SNOW

FINE·GRAINED SNOW

CORN SNOW
(FROZEN GRANULAR)

For skiing, your knowledge of snow need not be that extensive. It's sufficient to start out knowing that, thermodynamically, the intricately branched crystals of newly fallen snow are highly unstable. There's a continuous tendency for metamorphism to occur, converting the soft, delicate snowflakes that make up a powdery ski surface into hard round granules of ice, which make for a totally different surface. This can occur not merely when the temperature hovers around 32°F. or above and thawing is present, but even with the temperature down around zero. A process much more complex than simple melting is behind the change. But what is important here is just the fact that such a change from long-tentacled crystals to small ice balls will occur.

In determining skiing conditions, snow is usually divided into three primary categories: new snow, loose, with a distinct crystalline structure; fine-grained snow, the second stage of metamorphism, where most of the intricate branches have disappeared, leaving smoother crystals which permit faster skiing; and a last stage in which these crystals melt into each other, forming tiny pellets of ice usually called corn snow when still moist from melting, frozen granular when refrozen. What stage the snow is in will determine what running wax you use on your skis.

BASE AND RUNNING WAXES

One of the mysteries of cross-country skiing to the uninitiated is why the ski glides forward at one moment and grips the snow at the next. Well, it's all a matter of the wax on the bottom. A ski does not really slide on the snow, but on a fine layer of water—actually moisture would probably be a better word since the film is thin indeed. The pressure of your weight on the ski combines with the friction of its movement to melt the snow ever so little. However, to continue your forward movement, the ski must also be able to grasp the snow so you can push against it. This is where those variously shaped snow crystals come into the picture.

Fresh snow, with its many feathery needles, digs into the wax of your ski readily when you shift your weight onto it preparatory to a forward thrust. This is all, of course, on a microscopic level. As the snow gets older and the weather warmer, the snow crystals' needles round off, which means they are not as efficient in grasping the wax. To compensate for this, you use a softer wax. At the extreme end of the line—wet snow or particle ice—moisture, which acts as a lubricant, is present to such an extent that it effectively blocks the snow crystals' grasping ability. Then you have to use an ultrasoft, sticky liquid wax called klister. Klister is the Swedish word for glue, which will give you some idea of what it's all about.

Although ski waxes have been refined considerably since we were kids using paraffin on our skis, choosing the right one for the right snow conditions is nothing to be intimidated by. There are two basic types of wax: base and running, or surface, waxes. Base wax, going under brand names such as Röde Grunvalla, Swix Grunnsmöring, and Holmenkol, is usually a pine-tar derivative. It seals the bottom of your skis so they don't get waterlogged. Not necessary for plastic-soled skis, of course.

Under many conditions, it's quite possible to ski, and well, with just a base wax. I'm sure I'll be accused of being back in the seventeenth century when I suggest that if you're planning on ski camping, you consider doing so with just tar-waxed skis. Assuming you're not in a fiery rush, you don't really need the racer's edge of the surface waxes. And with all the changes in temperature and moisture conditions you will encounter during a week's worth of full-day runs, you could spend most of your time waxing, outdoors, at that, in a vain attempt to prepare for every different condition you meet.

If you're ski-touring at latitudes or at times when melt is likely to set in, however, take along a can of red wax and a tube of violet or silver klister (the color is the manufacturer's coding for hardness). Although tarred skis will carry you satisfactorily over any snow when it's below 30°F., once you hit moist snow, you will need extra grip. And when it comes to speed and flexibility on track or day runs, surface, or running, waxes become a decided plus. Currently the most popular running waxes are put out by Ex-Elit, Holmenkol, Rex, Röde, and Swix. The differences among them are fine-drawn, and you'll do a lot of skiing before you settle on one brand—if you ever do.

Running waxes come as hard waxes, packed in tins, or klisters, packed in tubes. The basic rule for choosing which running wax to use is: If it's new snow, use a hard wax; if the snow has melted and refrozen, use one of the klisters. The waxes come in a whole palette of colors—green, blue, violet, turquoise, silver, and so on—the color coding being an indication of the wax's hardness, to be coordinated with both temperature and snow conditions. Each manufacturer prints a key recommending which wax to use when. Another rule of thumb: When in doubt, use a harder rather than a softer wax.

Learning to choose the right running wax for each of the intricate variety of conditions offered by nature in winter is an art best learned from other skiers. Ask what wax they're using on a particular day. Think about it, try it out, observe how it meets the snow. But don't wait till you become an expert on waxing to head into the long, low, untouched hills. That important it's not.

PUTTING ON, BURNING ON, AND IRONING WAX

Base waxes come in burn-ons, rub-ons, and aerosol sprays. Only the burn-on tars really last, however. The tarring job's a bit on the messy side, but you'll love the smell.

For tar waxing, you'll need a blowtorch. If the very word "blow-torch" sends a small shiver of trepidation up your spine, relax. Primus makes a compact little unit, working off disposable butane cartridges, which looks more like a side-firing camp stove than one of those old brass monster blowtorches of yore. It's easy for the beginner to use and adjust. In addition to this and the wax, you'll need a good-quality paintbrush and rags, plenty of rags. Plenty of newspapers as well if you're trying to keep the floors clean—waxing is best done indoors.

To steady and protect skis while you're working on the soles, lay them sole side up across a couple of two-by-fours. Sawhorses are great if you have them; they'll save you from stooping. If you prop the skis with their tails against a wall, you won't have to clamp them down.

Should you be working with new skis, before waxing you must first remove the manufacturer's varnish from the soles. The varnish is put on to minimize moisture absorption during storage. To take it off, use liquid paint remover and a scraper specifically designed for skis. Such a scraper will have a rounded edge for easy access to the groove. Once you've removed all the varnish, sand down the soles, then give them a super smoothing with steel wool. When using a flammable liquid solvent, let the skis rest a day before waxing; it's essential that they be very dry.

Tar wax is best spread over the soles of the skis with a good paint-brush. A rag will do a better job than a cheap brush that loses hair. Once you have the soles completely covered with wax, give them a torch job. Starting at the tip of each ski, heat the tar with a slow-swinging movement of the blowtorch flame until the tar begins to bubble. Move further and further along the ski till you've boiled the whole thing. Keep the flame sweeping back and forth, to avoid charring the wood. If the tar catches fire, just move the flame quickly along; the fire will go right out.

After you've gone over the skis once with the blowtorch, go over them again. This time, stop when you've got a couple of inches bubbling and wipe off the excess wax with your rags. If there's no excess you haven't used enough wax. Watch so you don't torch your hand in the process—direct the flame away from the ski while you're wiping it.

When you're finished base waxing, the skis should be left at room temperature for three to six hours before any running wax you may plan to use is applied. Press your thumb gently against the wax surface. Barely tacky? Fine, there's just the right amount of base wax on your ski.

Your running wax, if you use one, will probably be selected, in the beginning at least, by consulting the chart put out by the wax manufacturer. There's been a series of attempts to make the color coding of the different brands compatible. They are not identical yet, however, so don't pick up a Swix chart if you're using, say, Ex-Elit or Ostbye wax. Besides the wax itself, you'll need a ski cork (now often made of synthetics) for rubbing the wax smooth or an ironing head for your blowtorch.

Surface waxing is best done at room temperature. The hard waxes themselves should be chilled outside for half an hour or so to firm them, before use. Klisters, on the other hand, are very difficult to apply cold, so if you have to work outdoors, you'll need a blowtorch to get any results at all.

Be sure your skis are free of any trace of water before you start waxing. Apply hard wax with short, smooth, front-to-back strokes as evenly as possible over the entire surface of the sole, leaving free only the groove. Next you want to smooth out the wax, again working from front to back, until you have a thin, shiny layer. The wax can be smoothed with a blowtorch, but it takes a lot of experience. A wax-ironing head that fits over the blowtorch flame, however, is inexpensive and permits even amateurs to torch-smooth their wax. The simplest device for smoothing wax is a ski cork.

Let the wax set fifteen minutes or so outdoors before you use your skis. Then test them out. If the skis slip going up a slope, the wax is too hard. If they seem to drag on the snow, the wax is too soft. Try another wax. In preparation for prolonged touring, you may want to apply several thin layers of your running wax, allowing each to cool outside before the next application. Several thin coats are better than one thick one when it comes to wear and tear on surface wax. Applying a hard wax in a chevron pattern, with the points towards the ski tip, and then not smoothing it completely, is something I haven't seen done often. Yet it will give your skis considerably improved grip for touring, without cutting down their slide.

Klister, as opposed to the hard waxes, is best applied when it's at room temperature or warmer. With tube in hand, go down the ski on one side of the groove and up on the other, squeezing out small streaks of klister in a zigzag pattern every inch or so. Then smooth out the wax with torch or cork. A shortcut method is to melt the klister in a pot and simply paint it on. Again use a high-quality brush that doesn't shed, make your strokes even, and avoid the groove.

You don't want to get either a hard running wax or klister in the groove because it's hard to get out; and should a wax too soft for later conditions chance to remain, it will ball up snow like a magnet with iron filings. The groove is to your skis what the keel is to your canoe. Stay with good old-fashioned paraffin for the groove. And while you've got a pot of paraffin going, put some on the lower part of your poles and the baskets as well, to keep snow from clinging.

A last thought on waxing: You can apply a soft wax over a harder one, but you can't apply a hard wax on a softer one. So eventually you have to remove all the running wax and start over. Just melt it off with a blowtorch and wipe down with rags.

CROSS COUNTRY WITH A SINGLE STRIDE

Remember, anyone who can walk can cross-country ski. Find a level spot. Put on your skis. Slip your hands through the pole loops and set the poles in the snow about a foot out from your skis and two feet in front of your boots. Lean forward slightly, feel your balance just standing there. Then slide one ski back and forth a couple of times. Do the same with the other ski. Feel smooth and comfortable? All right, that's sliding in place. You're halfway to walking in place. Now how about picking up your feet?

Place your poles the same distance away from the skis as before, only this time a couple of inches behind the heels of your boots. Bend your knees slightly, but keep your back straight and your head up. That's what I'd call the hesitation sit. You were about to sit down but stopped short before you got very far, wondering all of a sudden if someone had perchance put a tack on your chair. You're about 20 percent of the way to sitting. Sit a little further. Stand, sit, stand. All the while feel how much support the poles are giving you and how much you need. Now, in the same semisitting position, shift your weight onto one foot and lift up the other ski six inches or so. Put it down, shift your weight, and lift the other ski. Keep relaxed. Fine, you're walking in place.

Practice a couple of times. Then, while you've got a ski up in the air, bend your ankle and touch ground with just the tip of the ski. Then just the tail. Repeat with the second ski. The interaction of poles, skis, arms, and legs is as natural as walking. So why not set off?

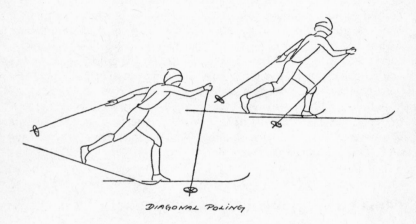

DIAGONAL POLING

Line up the skis. Set the poles on either side about even with your boots. Now shuffle forward, starting with, say, your left foot. To do that you push on your right ski, gradually transferring your weight to the gliding left ski. Where do you put the poles? you ask. Well, where did you just naturally put them? You moved the left foot forward and pushed with the right pole to keep your balance. Then you slid the right foot forward, pushing on the left ski and with the left pole. As you came forward you brought the poles with you, placing them where needed for balance without thinking about it. When you walk, the swing of your arms counterpoints that of your legs. And cross-country skiing at its simplest is merely walking with a pair of straightened barrel staves on your feet. That's the beauty of it.

So let's go someplace. Push with opposite legs and arms till you've covered a couple of hundred feet. Hang loose and feel the rhythm of the movements you make. Then start hopping *forward* slightly with each step, as if you were jogging, but with the difference that each stride is followed by a short glide. The power is all in the knees; lean forward but don't bob up and down. As you hop with the left leg you also push with the right pole, and so on. Carry the pole forward on each glide. Don't flourish it with a swing. There you are— diagonal-poling, or doing the single stride, or the diagonal stride. Whatever you call it, it's 90 percent of cross-country skiing.

Gliding smoothly and well, extending your stride into racing form,

DOUBLE POLING

takes practice, practice, and more practice. Which means skiing, skiing, skiing. But how painless can learning be?

DOUBLE-POLING

For gradual downhill terrain or flat terrain covered with icy snow, or preceding a step turn, double-poling comes naturally. At the same time that you bring your trailing ski forward, bring both poles forward simultaneously. Then, when your feet reach the next-to-each-other position, dig in with both poles. Put your body weight into the poling as much as you can. When your arms bend, sink down on your poles while you push. Reaching forward with your whole body adds leverage. But don't overextend the first time. Work up to it.

You can start double-poling from a standing-still position, with your skis parallel and side by side. It's good practice. But when you're touring, double-poling is usually interspersed with diagonal-poling, either to vary your pace, compensate for changing snow conditions, or increase speed when running downhill.

STEP TURN

THE STEP TURN

There's a grove of trees ahead. Time to turn. Slow down a minute and practice a step turn. You'll use exactly the same step under way later, but a bit of stationary practice is all to the good. Get into that semisitting position again. Move, say, your right foot forward till its instep is roughly even with the toe of your left. At the same time lift the ski tip off the ground half a foot or so. Let the tail drag as you set the ski over at an angle towards the right. Lift the other ski and place it parallel with the first. If you haven't changed directions enough, step out again. And again. You'll turn a little farther with each step. Now ski off and do just one step turn while under way. See by how much you changed directions. Try a few more. Keep practicing till you get a feel for the continuous uninterrupted motion of the turn. Although in the beginning it will be easier to do the turn in several slow steps, once you get used to it you'll just pick up a ski, aim it all the way round in the direction you wish to go, then bring the second ski over parallel.

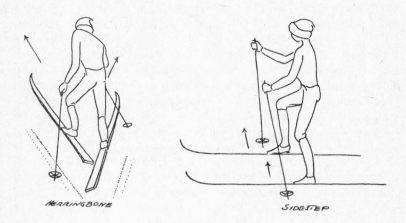

HERRINGBONE

SIDESTEP

GOING UP

Small hills you can just ski up, using the diagonal stride the same way you've been using it on flat ground. If the hill's too steep for that, you traverse, the same zigzag way you would on snowshoes. Ski diagonally and up the hill as far as you can go without running into the trees or other obstructions, then turn and make another diagonal upwards in the opposite direction. The track you make is just like the roadway going up a steep incline.

The two other principal ways of heading uphill are the sidestep and the herringbone. To sidestep, place yourself sideways to the hill. Lift the uphill ski upwards a foot or so, digging its upper edge in for a good grip. Then bring the downhill ski alongside. Follow the same procedure to the top of the hill. The herringbone, which is much quicker but also more tiring, involves spreading your ski tips so they form a V facing uphill. Dig the inside of each ski in well as you move the sides of the V upwards, one ski at a time. The steeper the hill, the wider you need to make the V. Don't lean forward or your weight will push the skis downhill. Stand straight. Look back. Behind you there'll be a nice pattern resembling a herring's backbone.

COASTING FOR A CHANGE

All right, enough work. Let's coast awhile. Pick a slope. Not a big hill—this is cross-country, not alpine skiing. The slope should have an outrun. "Outrun" means just what it sounds like—a clear place where you can keep going till you slow down, run out of speed, or stop. The fastest way down a hill, and the easiest as well, is straight. Relax, stay limber at the knees, go with your feet flat on the skis. Put your hands in front of you at thigh level, poles pointed back or dragging slightly like outriggers to help you steer. A crouch position, in which you rest your forearms on your knees, poles straight out behind, cuts down the wind as well as giving you a bit of a rest. It's an unstable position, though, so watch the bumps. Keeping one ski half a foot in front of the other will add stability to help you over the rough spots.

If the hill is wide open, you may want to traverse down. That way you'll get more downhill mileage for your uphill struggle. Make your angles as slow as possible until you get used to handling the step turn on a downhill slope. After a while you may even help revive the classic Telemark.

SITTING DOWN AND PICKING YOURSELF UP

For everyone striving to learn a physical act of coordination like skiing there comes a time when he oversteps his skills in an attempt to progress—that is, he goofs. When that time comes, sit down. You're shooting down a hill, for instance, and you suddenly discover it's too late to turn. You've got nowhere to go. Don't just fall; sit down. Better still, time permitting, ease down till you can drag your hands as balancing outriggers in the snow, and then plop.

Once you've fallen, intentionally or otherwise, the next problem is how to get up again. Bring the skis parallel to each other and at right angles to the fall line. If you rolled a snowball down the hill, it would go the fastest route—that's the fall line. If your skis aren't at right angles to it, you'll start sliding as soon as you get part of the way up. Take your wrists out of the pole straps. Hold the poles together on the uphill side. Now use the poles to pull yourself into a standing position.

THE FIRST SKI TOUR

There are faster ways of poling, other ways of turning. To help your style along, if you get a chance ski next to someone who's good and fluid, and copy his every move. In the meantime the techniques mentioned in these pages should see you through the beginnings of your cross-country adventures.

Don't plan to make skis your primary form of winter transportation until you're really comfortable with them on your feet and a pack on your back. Certainly take a couple of overnighters before you set off on any extended jaunts. And on those long tours it is highly advisable not to go alone. Many ways of the wilderness are for the solitary, but extended winter ski camping, like snowshoeing, is mostly a team activity.

END OF THE SEASON

For me it's always easier to put things away shipshape at the end of a season than to fix them at the beginning of the next. Then I'm ready to go when the wanderlust hits. On the other hand, lots of people like the anticipatory feeling of puttering with their equipment before they set out, and that's fine too. Whichever end of the season you choose, you should scrutinize your equipment for potential problems and keep it in repair.

Ski pole straps and baskets should be checked for any weak spots or loosening. Replace worn parts. Check your bindings, particularly the screws and cables if you have them.

Give your boots a thorough cleaning with saddle soap. Wax them well, but don't waterproof before storage. Let the leather breathe. If you don't have boot trees, stuff the boots with wadded newspaper.

Check the ski soles for gouges and holes. Deep ones should be filled with plastic wood. Then scrape the soles. If you've done any really rough ski camping, the center of your ski may have worn down some, leaving the harder edges protruding like railings. These can seriously impede your maneuverability. Take them down with your scraper till they are level with the center of the ski.

Before putting your skis away give them a good last-of-the-season hard wax job. This will keep moisture out while they're stored. Since the top surfaces of your skis are coated with varnish, plastic, or some other moisture-impenetrable material, were you to leave the soles exposed serious warping could develop.

Skis should be stored upright in a cool dry place, strapped together sole to sole with blocks, just thick enough to keep the camber, wedged between them. Don't bother to try putting more camber into them with extra-large blocks. It's almost impossible.

After the chores are done, go hunt up that article you saw in *Sports Illustrated* on cross-country skiing in Kashmir, sit down with the faint reminiscent smell of wax still on your fingers, and map out that just-perfect winter vacation's run for the next time out in the still, quiet places of winter.

Discovering the Way
of the Wilderness

GETTING LOST AND UNLOST

Any camper who tells you he's never been lost is either lying or hasn't ever been off the beaten track. The great art, of course, is finding your way again. And the only real danger is panicking and not being able to think what to do. A little preparation will go a long way towards ensuring your safety in the wilds.

The same guy who tells you he's never been lost also usually scoffs at compasses as "Boy Scout stuff." Now I've done plenty of camping without a compass—in areas that I know well, not only geographically, but sensually. I'm primarily a northern fir and spruce woods man. I know the Adirondacks, for instance. I feel at home there, where the trees close off the sky and the old rounded mountains meld into each other. Take me out West to the edgy, sharp-canyoned, open terrain, and I'll pick the dead-end double-back ascent half the time if I don't have a map and compass.

It's a common occurrence, this kind of displacement, so I don't feel I'm alone in it. No one should. There's an old man of my acquaintance who probably knows more about getting around the mud slides and head-high undergrowth of the northern Thailand and eastern Burma jungles than anyone alive except perhaps his son. Yet while we were talking about jungle pathfinding one afternoon at his game farm north of Chiengmai, he admitted that were he let loose on the spruce and fir stands of the glacial shield in Canada, he'd probably have trouble finding his way back to camp from the latrine without a map.

Which brings up the subject of that mysterious sense of direction that some people seem to have. A sense of direction doesn't really exist—even in those who think they have it. Tests have demonstrated time and time again that the most experienced guide will walk around in an ever-tightening spiral when blindfolded and let loose on a flat field on a cloudy windless day offering no external clues as to his direction of progress. The phenomenon of circle-walking has never been explained. Personally I wonder if it's not induced by the slow spinning of the earth. The same spin that causes the water in your sink to whirlpool out when you pull the plug.

Even animals let loose on terrain far different from that to which they are accustomed will bump into objects and stumble in a bewildered fashion long after they've calmed their fright. Obstacles that would be nothing on their native grounds are confusing barriers because of their strange shapes, smell, and even sound-reflective and absorptive variations.

What people with the so-called sense of direction have are powers of observation honed far beyond the average individual's and a certain familiar feeling for the terrain, that's all. This means you too can have a sense of direction.

DEVELOPING A SENSE OF DIRECTION

At home you have a subconscious monitor that keeps you aware of what's happening around you. When you cross a street going home from the store, you know the traffic moves on the right. You know you have to step down off the curb before you cross, and up again once you do. Without your really looking at it, a red light registers in your mind. When you jaywalk, you know (or think you do) that the car barreling down the street is not moving fast enough to hit you, as long as you dash. On a sunny day, the shady side of the street is usually crowded; you head for it if you want to stay cool, for the sunny side if you're in a rush. Push the elevator button and the elevator comes. Put your key in the lock and turn the doorknob, the door will open. But watch the loose corner of the carpet or you'll trip, you remind yourself.

Chances are you made no really conscious decisions the whole way home. The answer to "How'd you get there?" would be simply "I walked." Set up the same type of subconscious patterned responses in the wild. That's your sense of direction.

The first thing to do when trying to get the feel of an area is to stop, look, and listen. Look at how the vegetation changes as it goes up or down a valley, becoming sparser or lusher, the trees taller or shorter, which species grow where, and so on. Observe which way the fallen trees lie (usually the direction of prevailing winds). Check how a stream has cut its gorge, to see the thickness of the soil layer, the direction of rock outcroppings, and variations in plant life. The moss growing on the bark of that tree over there, is it really on the north side as legend has it? Well, yes and no. If the tree is blocked from the sun by others, there will be more moss on the northern side. Then again it may well be all the way around the trunk. And there's a lichen that looks almost like the moss in question, but which grows on the sunniest side—which may or may not be the southern side. Find a trail, look for animal tracks, figure out why the animal chose the run that way, where it was going, where it was coming from.

Now listen. Close your eyes, so you focus your hearing more. What does the stream sound like when your back's to it? When it's at your side? Rub your feet across gravel, sand, a mossy surface, leaves. When you can tell the difference in the sounds immediately, you're well onto the way of laying down some rudimentary sensory paths in your mind. Listen to the rustling of the birches. Strange, it's louder when the wind blows up the valley than when down. Cup your hands behind your ears to simulate an animal's way of hearing, and you'll be surprised how many more sounds you pick up.

Touch a boulder on the sunny side. On the shady side. Of course there's a difference in temperature, but you want to be so intimately aware of it that when you're climbing up a hill hand over hand, passing from shade to sun to shade, your fingers register it as automatically as your eyes, or the back of your neck. Feel the bark of a pine, of a birch, of a maple, of anything you can get your hands on. Register as much texture, temperature, shape, and size as you can.

Take a series of short sniffy breaths. Gracious, it's really smelly out. There's a musky scent from the river, a dry, acrid one from the oaks by your side, that familiar pine fragrance from the evergreens on the promontory. And could that be? Yes, definitely something burning. The campfire way on the other side of the ridge. You hadn't thought it possible to smell it all the way over here. And so it goes. Soak and saturate the senses till the wilderness, at least the part of it where you are, becomes second nature to you.

Pick a path running from your camp to a landmark a couple of thousand feet away—a large boulder, a lone tree, a bend in the creek, or a rotting log. Walk slowly towards your object. Look behind you frequently to see how landscape features change as you approach, pass, and go on. Get rid of that urban tunnel vision. Look up into the trees, down at the path, to the side, but not just at eye level. Check things out from ground to sky. What's that growing over there? And is that a bird's nest up by where that fluttering sound comes from?

Walk the same trail in the morning, on an afternoon, and at night without a light. Approach your goal from different directions, fanning out in an arc from left to right. Soon that little patch of ground will be as familiar to you as a walk down your own street. In all probability even more so. Fine, you're well on the way to developing a sense of direction for that type of terrain. Now as time passes and you camp elsewhere, do the same thing again and again. *Observe! Focus!* Forget everything but your five senses in relation to where you are at the moment—slowly you will build up your sixth sense.

YOUR FATHER THE INSTRUMENT

A feeling for the wilds is best communicated from father to son, companion to companion. But how many of today's campers have an intrepid Indian guide or trapper for a father? Technology, usually the antithesis of nature, can come to your rescue here.

It's possible to get a feel for what the temperature is by checking a simple camping thermometer whenever you are curious. And "How cold do you think it is?" is probably one of the most frequently asked questions in the woods, any season but summer. A metal-cased Taylor pocket thermometer measuring from $-30°$ to $+120°$F. is only five and a half inches long, weighs an ounce and a half, and clips onto your shirt pocket like a pencil. Bigger maximum-minimum thermometers will give a fixed high-low reading from the time they were last set.

You can always count cricket chirps too, of course, if they're around. Take the number of chirps to one minute. Subtract forty from that number. Divide what's left by four. Now add fifty, and that's the temperature almost to the degree.

You probably will never be quite as accurate as a cricket in estimating the temperature by feel. Still, checking a thermometer will sharpen your temperature sense and make you aware of variations within even a small area. It's surprising to find it's a full ten degrees cooler down by that tiny creek than up on the hillock only a hundred yards away.

Speaking of hills, altimeters aren't limited to airplanes in this gadget-oriented world of ours. While a pocket altimeter is about the last piece of camping equipment I'd get unless I camped primarily in the mountains, there, where it's most useful in conjunction with a geodetic map, its couple of extra ounces might be worthwhile—certainly fun.

Most altimeters register in from twenty- to hundred-foot intervals on a scale calibrated up to twelve thousand, sixteen thousand, or twenty-one thousand feet. The more expensive models, such as the German Lufft or the Swiss-made Thommens, are temperature-compensated.

Basically an altimeter is a barometer that's calibrated in feet instead of inches of mercury. So you can use it to sharpen your sense of weather forecasting as well as for determining altitude. If you're sitting around camp mapping out the next day's hike and you notice the altimeter taking a nose dive, it's not your mountain collapsing, merely the barometer rising, indicating a fine day ahead.

An altimeter will tell you how high you are, a sense that is almost impossible to develop to any degree of accuracy whatsoever; it will also do much for your weather wisdom, which is easier to improve. But what about distance? Travel is, after all, a combination of time and distance. Our time sense, although by now pretty dependent on watches and clocks, at least still exists; for most children of the age of technology, a distance sense does not. How could it be otherwise when your mode of transportation may fluctuate between a leisurely stroll to a sixty-mile-an-hour drive in the car and a five-hundred-mile-an-hour flight enclosed in an airplane with no outside reference points whatsoever, all in a day? Consider taking both a watch and a pedometer.

A pedometer, weighing about two ounces, is calibrated to your normal walking stride on a couple of test walks over a measured flat distance. Therein lies the catch. Your stride climbing a steep grade, or bounding over a rock-strewn field, is quite different from over flat terrain. Which brings up another point to consider. All these instruments can teach you something. But that doesn't mean you have to descend on the wilderness equipped like the sensor of an analog computer. It takes years to get to know nature. If you're going in for instrumentation, take along those suitable for the terrain. A pedometer is fine in flat and rolling country, worthless when you're mountain climbing. An altimeter in a flat region of relatively constant barometric pressures like the desert will not give you many bits of information.

Your watch, if you wear one, and I admit to not doing so, will help you get a feel for the time of day as told by the sun and stars. But only if when you check the time, you check nature as well. Knowing that it's 6:00 P.M. on May 31st will do nothing to sharpen your senses. Knowing from where and how high the sun shines, what the shadows look like, which flowers are beginning to close, if the fish are biting, and that bats are just beginning to dart jerkily across the sky at 6:00 P.M. on May 31st wherever you happen to be—will teach you a lot. Don't forget about daylight saving time. Most campers leave their watches set on standard time when in the woods so as not to confuse their senses.

EYE EXTENDERS

Binoculars can be a real help in mapping out a route visually from a high vantage point to avoid dead-end canyons and difficult fordings and to pinpoint helpful landmarks. As a pleasure tool, they add even more to your stay in the great outdoors. They're not just for getting yourself up into that formation of wild geese or checking if the moose across the lake has whiskers below his lip, but for closer details as well. Have you ever been eyeball-to-eyeball with a frog six feet away that appears as large as a dinosaur? Or almost joined a squirrel in his nest for afternoon acorns? You can even go one step further and turn the binoculars backwards, using the objective or large lens as your eyepiece and putting the small end half an inch or so away from a mushroom cap with a snail on it, or an ant, or just about anything you wished you'd had a good magnifying glass along for.

For camping purposes, a lightweight pair of binoculars is best. That doesn't mean opera glasses, however. You need both fairly decent magnification and a respectable light-gathering lens. When you look for a pair of binoculars, you'll see some numbers, like 6 x 25, 7 x 35, or even 10 x 45, stamped on the casing. The first number indicates the magnifying power, the second is the diameter in millimeters of the larger or light-gathering lens. Usually, except for naval night glasses, the ratio of the two figures is between 4 and 6. In 6 x 25 binoculars, for example, it's a little over 4.

You can get binoculars with a magnification considerably higher than the 6 or 7 commonly seen, but these require a bulky tripod, or at least propping them up very steadily against something solid like a boulder. It's hard to keep your point of observation within the field of vision once magnification goes above 8, simply because it magnifies your tiniest movement, including such necessities as breathing, as much as it does everything else.

A diameter number exceeding 35 also can be found readily. But again you don't need it unless you expect to use the binoculars frequently under adverse light conditions such as dawn, dusk, or night.

Look for an established brand—Leitz, Zeiss, Bushnell, or Krombach, for example. The first two are pretty prohibitively priced, but they're good for comparison shopping even if you don't want to spend all that money. As an example of what to look for, the Bushnell 6 x 25, selected by NASA for the Gemini missions, weighs only eleven ounces and is small enough to fit into your jacket pocket. If you're burdened with eyeglasses, as I am, the extendable eyecups make things easier. All good binoculars come with a comprehensive parts and service warranty. The Bushnell one, for instance, runs twenty years.

THE COMPASS

All the preceding instruments add to your enjoyment and knowledge while camping. All are also dispensable if you must travel ultralight or simply don't want to buy them just yet. The same cannot be said for the compass. It's a rare trip away from civilization on which a compass need not be carried. You may never have to use it, but it's a friend of whom you always can ask the question "How do I get out of here?" and be properly enlightened.

I've had an old Silva, now complete with air bubble, for more years than I can remember. I was about to switch to the Suunto KB-14, which received the highest hand-held rating for both maximum error and standard deviation in *Wilderness Camping*'s testing of the more popular compasses. Some critics might object that for truly accurate readings, a compass should not be hand-held. However, I never seem to be able to find that flat rock or perfectly level stump the books always tell you to lay your compass down on before you take a reading. So the hand-held test was just what I was looking for. Unfortunately, I found the Suunto KB-14 difficult to use wearing glasses. One sights the desired landmark through a small magnifying lens in the compass, lining up both it and the scale on the floating dial, by means of an optical illusion, with a hairline. A bit of a feat for us quadreyeds. So it's a Silva 15T Ranger for me.

Compasses come with either a free-swinging needle or disc that indicates north. A needle compass does not settle into its point as readily as the floating dial variety. Even the dial tends to move around while you're taking a sighting, so better compasses of both kinds are liquid-filled to dampen the swing, making the pointer come to a rest both more quickly and more steadily.

Then there's the matter of keeping your eye on two things at once: the compass and the object on which you are trying to get a reading. Just holding the compass in your hand, looking at the needle, then at your goal, then back at the needle, and so on, is not only bound to induce errors, it'll drive you batty.

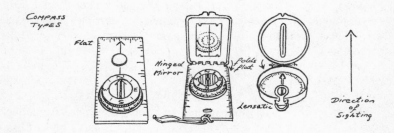

The problem of sighting is solved by one of two means. The lensatic compass has a small lens on a hinged arm that opens vertically, while the compass itself remains flat. As you look through the lens, you sight the distant object through a slit opposite the lens; the lens permits you to read your compass dial at the same time. The second method, and the one I find most comfortable, employs a hinged mirror for the same purpose. This is the way the Silva Ranger works. Silva's experimental floating dial compass promises even better results, since most people find it easier to take a reading from a floating disc than a needle.

USING THE COMPASS TO GET THERE

Before you start taking bearings, make sure you are well away—six to ten feet at least—from any magnetic objects, like the ax head, for instance, that would cause the compass to deviate. Way in the distance is Raintree Mountain, where you want to go. To find your bearing, sight your compass on whatever side of the mountain you want to head for. Let the needle come to a complete rest pointing to magnetic north. Now twist the compass housing on which the degree scale is engraved till the housing's north marking lines up exactly with the north point of the needle. On the Silva compass the housing has a north arrow outlined on it; all you do is line it up so the needle and arrow point together. Now read the degrees where the dial crosses your sighting line. This is your bearing. Say it turns out to be 265°. Pick a good landmark in line with your mountain—tall twin trees, a rock formation, maybe a creek bend—and walk to it. You're descending into a valley and can no longer see old Raintree, but you get to your first goal. Find another one with a bearing of 265°. . . .

Well, after you've walked awhile, stopped for lunch, cooled your feet in a stream and gone looking for that rabbit you thought you saw in the bush, you suddenly discover you don't know which way you're wandering anymore. Just take out your compass. Line up the two norths again, and you'll know which way 265° is. Look for a new landmark at 265°. Go that way. When you get there, take out the compass once more, find another 265° landmark. And so on, till you've crossed the valley and find yourself on the side of the mountain you were looking at when you started out.

Orienteering races were a great thing when I was a kid back in Sweden. The entrants would start off, compass and map case in hand, at fifteen-minute intervals, to see who could make the best time over a complicated ten- or fifteen-mile course of dense forest, with swamps, lakes, and brooks as obstacles along the way, and mandatory check-ins at control points every mile or so. It was great sport, and I wouldn't be surprised to see it someday come into popularity in this country.

THE COMPASS AND THE MAP

Hand in hand with a compass goes a map. Even if you don't need a compass to show you the way, it will show you how to orient your map.

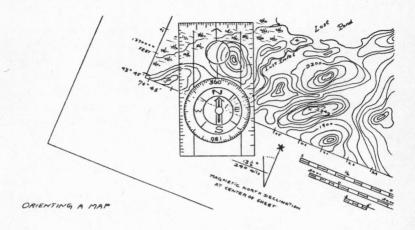

ORIENTING A MAP

When you unfold your map in the middle of the woods, which way do you lay it out so it conforms to the actual terrain? Well, the top of the map is always north. So you just take out the trusty old compass and set the map so the north needle of the compass points to the top. Right? Wrong. Remember being told back in high school that there was a difference between the true north and the magnetic north? Well, here's where the dichotomy comes into play. At the bottom of a topographic map you'll see a small V, composed of a half-arrow and a line running true north-south, usually labeled "magnetic north declination at center of sheet." If you lay your compass down and turn the map so that the half-arrow of this V lines up parallel with your compass needle, the map will be in tune with the terrain. Proceed from there.

The compass can also be used for triangulation. If you don't recognize where on the map you are, pick out two distant landmarks in the terrain that you can also locate on the map. Orient the map as usual to compensate for magnetic deviation. With your compass, take a reading on the two landmarks, and jot down the figures. Through each of the landmarks on the map, draw a line running at the same degree, or angle, from the magnetic north direction line indicated at the bottom of the map as the visual reading you got. Where the two lines intersect is your location. That's triangulation, using two known points to fix the position of a third, but unknown, one.

How to take your bearings with the compass, how to use it to make your map conform to reality, and how to locate where you are on the

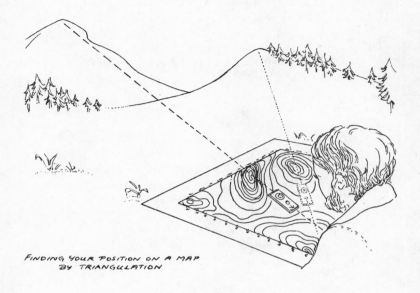

FINDING YOUR POSITION ON A MAP
BY TRIANGULATION

map by triangulation, are all you will probably need to know for most general camping purposes. If you plan to do a lot of hiking in new country or are interested in orienteering races, the standard manual on the subject is Kjellström's *Be Expert with Map and Compass.*

STEPPING INTO YOUR MAP

The best maps for camping in this country are those made by the U.S. Geological Survey, and in Canada the Department of Mines and Technical Surveys. Unlike the planimetric maps you get at gas stations, which show everything in a flat two-dimensional perspective— you know where the roads and rivers are but you can't tell about the hills and valleys—the Geological and Technical Survey maps are topographical. They may be printed on flat paper, but they do show the terrain very much in three dimensions. And as with 3-D movies projected on a flat screen, you can learn to step into a topo map— visually, that is.

At the bottom of each map is a heading "Contour Interval," followed by the specific interval for that map. Say it's twenty feet. That means every one of those countless brown lines on the map are in

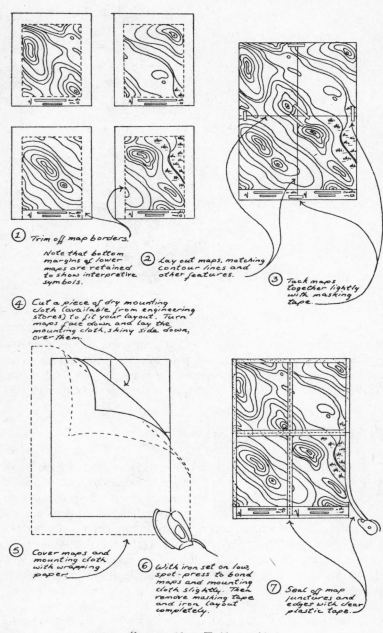

① Trim off map borders.

Note that bottom margins of lower maps are retained to show interpretive symbols.

② Lay out maps, matching contour lines and other features.

③ Tack maps together lightly with masking tape.

④ Cut a piece of dry mounting cloth (available from engineering stores) to fit your layout. Turn maps face down and lay the mounting cloth, shiny side down, over them.

⑤ Cover maps and mounting cloth with wrapping paper.

⑥ With iron set on low, spot-press to bond maps and mounting cloth slightly. Then remove masking tape and iron layout completely.

⑦ Seal off map junctures and edges with clear plastic tape.

HOW TO MOUNT YOUR MAPS

reality twenty feet apart. If the lines are very close together, this means a steep rise; far apart, a shallow rise.

You can mentally walk down a steep mountain, watch the lines widen out in front of you as you approach a lake, which of course has no contour lines because the top of the water is flat. Instead it will have a number like 1528 which indicates the height of the lake from sea level. If an adjoining lake has an elevation of 1922, and they are, say, two miles apart, the river connecting them is almost a waterfall the whole way. If the second lake has an elevation of 1534, well, then, the connecting river is probably as smooth and soft as a cat's back. Unless you see a marking for marshes along its bed, in which case it may be impenetrable even by canoe.

The U.S. topographic maps usually come in a scale of 1:62,500 or 1:24,000. That is, one inch on the map equals either 62,500 or 24,000 inches in the real world it represents. (You won't have to measure that with a ruler. There are also equivalents for feet, meters, kilometers, and miles at the bottom of the map.) The choice of scale isn't up to you; the decision as to which map is made depends on the terrain. You gets what they got, as the saying goes. The same thing holds true for the year when the map was made. Our Adirondack ones, for instance, were made from aerial photos in 1953 and field-checked in 1955. The place has changed a bit since then. Even so, the maps can't be beat.

If you've never done any map work on topos before, the best way to familiarize yourself with them is to get one of some local area you know well. Map in hand, go over it inch by inch—that's inches on the map I'm referring to, of course. You'll be surprised how quickly you learn to step into a map with both eyes. And while you're sending away for maps, get the quadrangle for the area in which you live as well. It's always fun to find your house on the map.

HELP, AND HOW TO AVOID CALLING FOR IT

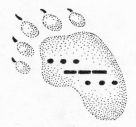

On one of the out-islands of Fiji not too long ago we met a young Canadian couple on their honeymoon. Because he worked for an airline they had come almost free all the way to the South Pacific. Which was about as idyllic and romantic a situation as one could hope to find —except that they'd spent practically the entire week since their arrival on opposite sides of the bed in their darkened room. The first day they had frolicked wildly in the surf and sun. However, even the most liberal application of suntan lotion was not enough to counteract the rapid change of environments; and their sunburn was so bad they could hardly move, much less embrace. If you go bush on a once-a-year vacation—approach things gently.

Wherever you're going camping, familiarize yourself with the area beforehand, either by talking to people who've been there or by writing ahead for information. There isn't a campworthy area in North America that doesn't have a Chamber of Commerce, state, provincial, or national government plugging it in one way or another.

Not only can advance information make your trip safer and you more self-sufficient, it can make it more comfortable. You can avoid the May-June black fly season, or the September rains, or whatever other yearly phenomenon plagues the area. You aren't trying to learn all about the place where you're going, just enough to gear up properly for it and avoid any seasonal drawbacks it may have.

Second to knowing something about where you're going is making ready for it. Particularly for any sudden adjustments it may involve for your body. The old Boy Scout motto "Be prepared" might be in for a lot of derision these days, for being, well, you know, boy-scoutish. Nevertheless, it's still the single most important difference between a camper who goes out into the wilds, enjoys it, and comes back enriched, and the one that gets hauled out. This doesn't mean you should burden yourself down with a lot of fancy equipment you don't need; it simply means taking the commonsensical essentials. Take water into arid land, sweaters and maybe a space blanket into cold; be sure you've got your snakebite kit with you when you're heading for poisonous-snake country; know the simple basics of artificial respiration before you take the kids out on Hudson Bay; by all means add calamine lotion to your first aid kit if you happen to be allergic to poison ivy; and have a tetanus booster shot if you hadn't gotten around to it somehow in the routine of the last couple of years. And so on.

"CHICKEN!"

Probably more accidents are caused by campers—and not just beginners, but even experienced ones who should know better—forcing themselves into situations they know are questionable, but feel they must conquer anyway in order to prove themselves. It's part of the romantic explorer spirit that causes manufacturers to advertise their equipment as "expedition" gear. Well, sad to say, the world's been pretty well conquered these days. Even professional explorers have run out of places to explore. This doesn't make the wilderness Times Square, but conquering it is passé. Live with it, know it, respect its ways, and your chances of ever needing rescue or survival techniques are about as good as they are for needing rescue from a burning building.

Before you get into trouble, admit you can't balance across that slippery log. If the trail is steep and dangerous, don't call it duck soup. If a storm is brewing, make camp rather than pressing on. As veteran wildland backpacker Harvey Manning says, "Beginners die on trails because they do not have the guts to be cowards."

Together with not sticking your neck out goes knowing yourself and your capabilities. Does altitude bother you? Do you chill easily? When you go for a walk in a dense forest, do the trees or some animal seem to be constantly reaching out for you? Do you have any idea under what circumstances you would panic? Tackle your fears gradually, a day or a weekend at a time. If heights make you nervous, start with molehills before you tackle the mountains. Molehills can be darned interesting.

FIRST AID

Somehow too many people have gotten the idea that camping is a constant rigorous workout where broken bones, bear bites, and semi-starvation are the order of the day. Now accidents do happen in camp, but most of them are no different from those occurring anywhere you may live—a burn because you forgot to use the potholder, a finger cut while cleaning fish, numerous scraped knees and elbows on the kids, and maybe an occasional good-sized gash—any one of which the average individual handles as a matter of course from his store of elementary first aid knowledge.

Should a serious accident occur, and that's a possibility anywhere, someone is going to have to get help—which is something to take into consideration before setting off solo into the wilderness. I could go on to describe the basic treatments for shock, severe bleeding, fractures, concussion, and third-degree burns. But to the best of my knowledge everybody gives that kind of material in a book a sideways glance rather as if it had the plague or halitosis. In any case, and much more to the point, the Red Cross *First Aid* manual (latest edition) and/or *Medicine for Mountaineering* can't be beat. My recommendation is that if you haven't already, long before this, learned the basic principles of first aid, as well as the general safety rules that help prevent accidents even at home, you certainly do so before you go out of reach of the telephone. Beyond the so-called common emergencies, however, there are four very specific outdoor dangers which, although not frequent—or perhaps for that very reason—you should be aware of and know what to do about if trouble threatens.

AVALANCHES

Predominantly an occurrence on young, sharp mountains exposed to severe weathering, avalanches come in two varieties: rock and snow. Any slope with a gradient of over twenty-five or thirty degrees is susceptible to slides. Whether they will actually occur or not, and particularly when, would be hard to predict. Probably the majority of fatal avalanches are triggered by people crossing a slope that is ready to run. If you stay away from these, your problems should be minimized.

A rock slide that is ready to let loose usually looks like it. Boulders, stones, those small stone piles called scree, and talus flowing down a mountainside in what looks like a frozen river are obviously potentially a flowing river—of stone. Don't walk across it. The word "scree" is a derivative of the Icelandic word for "landslide." Any sloping surface with a layer of loose rocks, large or pebble-sized, should be considered a hazard, not fun to try sliding down on. Screeing down, as this is referred to, is an awful lot of fun—till you find out you can't stop. I have both the laughter and the broken ankle from my brash youth to prove it.

The cardinal rule when crossing such a layer is to keep a vertical posture. If you can't, don't cross. By bending over and using your hands to steady your walk, you automatically force the weight concentrated on your feet back and out down the hillside. It may be just the extra push a hillside of talus in exact balance with gravity needs to start it sliding.

If you do get caught in a rock slide, your one hope is to outrun it. If that's impossible, and there is a ledge or outcropping you can reach and duck beneath, the slide may pass over you. Then again, it may bury you. Prevention is, as usual, much easier than the cure. Admire possible rock slide areas from the distance.

Potential snow avalanches may be harder to spot. Treeless streaks running down a steep mountainside are usually indications of past disasters, as are piles of uprooted trees at the bottom of a clear run. Avalanches tend to occur on slopes exposed to wide temperature fluctuation. They are particularly likely when old snow has frozen into a solid crust of slippery ice, upon which new snow settles. The double layer then shears easily when triggered by a loud noise, wind, or just a sudden rise or drop in temperature.

If you are skiing or snowshoeing across a slope and you notice cracks running ahead of you or making semicircles up a hill, a slide may well be imminent. Get back to safety if you're less than a third of the way across the slope. If you're more than a third across, it's usually faster to go on than to turn around. Don't stop to look at the view.

Should the slide already be descending on you, drop your poles, kick off your skis or snowshoes, and try to get the rucksack off as well before it hits. As it hits, try to literally swim up the wave of snow, keeping your face as high as possible. If you get buried, try to cover your face and mouth as well as you can with your hands and arms. Should you not be too deeply buried to move, you might be able to dig yourself out. But which way is up? If you can't tell, spit. Remember, spit doesn't fall up.

FALLING THROUGH THE ICE

The safety of walking across unknown ice, even in the middle of wintertime, is questionable. However, sometimes it must be done. If so, it's not a bad idea to carry an opened knife in your hand. Should you fall through, it can be used as an ice pick to help pull you out.

Gauging ice thickness can be difficult, since it rarely freezes evenly. One telltale sign of potential trouble ahead is dark ice interspersed with lighter-colored ice.

Dark ice is dangerous ice anywhere in the world. Dark ice means that something—thawing, a rapid current, or a subsurface obstruction, for instance—has thinned the ice layer, usually to the point where you are actually seeing the dark water beneath it. If it's that thin there is a risk of you or your equipment falling through.

This is an important point to remember if you are covering slough or swampy territory. Even with the temperature hovering around zero and the surrounding lake frozen to a depth of several feet, the slough ice can be paper-thin in spots. What happens is that decaying organic matter on the shallow bottom generates heat, which rises to the ice, melting and thinning it. Within five yards, you can go from firm ice to ice-cold water.

Should you fall through the ice, the sudden cold could be enough to make your heart stop—literally, if it isn't in good shape. If you feel yourself falling, go spread-eagled at once. Hopefully your arms will strike the ice around the edges of the crack, keeping you from going under. Then, although your first reaction will be to struggle out, take a few seconds to break off the surrounding thin ice of the hole. Flutter your feet and literally swim out and onto the ice. The knife will be very handy for hooking into the ice and pulling yourself along with. Stay low and crawl till you get well back along the path you came on and know to be solid enough to support your weight.

If you're close to a soft snowbank on shore, roll in it quickly. Should your clothes be at all water-repellent, the snow will sponge a great deal of moisture off. Get a fire going and soup warming. Change your clothes as quickly as possible and drink plenty of hot liquids.

HYPOTHERMIA AND FROSTBITE

Much in discussion these days when the subject of winter ventures comes up is hypothermia—or what used to be known as exposure, or just plain freezing to death—a condition that develops when external circumstances are such that the body cannot maintain its normal temperature, even in the central cavity where the vital organs are located. When your core temperature drops fifteen to twenty degrees below normal, you are dead.

The reason the term "freezing to death" has been replaced is that it is possible to develop hypothermia in above-freezing temperatures, taking into account the wind, particularly if your clothes are wet. Now I'd be the last one to want to minimize the dangers of exposure. It just seems to me sometimes that the discussions lately are beginning to verge on the hypochondriacal. Percentage-wise, the number of people who die from hypothermia as compared to those killed crossing the street is small.

Someone who has fallen through the ice or been otherwise exposed to such a degree as to hazard hypothermia should be watched for the symptoms of it: fatigue, lack of coordination in speech and movement, loss of memory and rationality, dilated pupils, slow pulse and breathing. In extreme cases foam will form around the mouth. Keep the victim as warm as possible, particularly internally with warm liquids. Don't let him assure you through his shivering that he's all right—a common false reaction on his part.

In below-freezing weather, before you get a good case of hypothermia, you'll get frostbite, which is much more common. Hard-pressed to keep your temperature up to normal, your body is willing to forgo heating your outer extremities in an attempt to keep its central core warm.

If you should get frostbite, don't rub it with snow. The snow rub is classified as an old wives' tale, one definitely not true. Warning against it is mandatory when one is discussing winter camping. Frostbitten areas should not be rubbed at all. They should be warmed up slowly by wrapping gently in a blanket, wool scarves, or something else warm and soft, or by immersing in tepid water. The water should be about body-temperature, no warmer. But by all means try to avoid getting frostbitten. It's not only that severe cases lead to gangrene—thawing out is excruciatingly slow and painful.

QUICKSAND

When I was a kid, there was a small patch of quicksand on the drainage side of the lake where we lived. The horrors of being sucked into quicksand, reinforced with assorted stories of trolls and snakes, were used in a vain attempt to keep us out of what was deemed to be the more dangerous areas of the wood. The reverse, of course, resulted. We spent many a summer day trying to fill the quicksand. Countless logs and rocks—luckily none of us—vanished in the mire over the passing years. We never did fill it: our theory was that the "hole" descended into the bowels of the earth, where all our offerings were consumed by fire.

Scientifically, of course, we were wrong about its depth. But we did develop an awesome respect for that particular mystery of nature. More importantly, perhaps, we learned how to cope with it. And you should too. For quicksand is not a phenomenon confined to *The African Queen* and other tales of adventure. Areas of quicksand large or small crop up in the most unexpected places, like New York City or Cincinnati, Ohio, where quicksand was discovered partway down the foundation excavations for tall office buildings, whose substructure had to be redesigned. And although the majority of quicksand areas are small, some are impressive enough to swallow a train locomotive— or so the story goes about the disappearance of a Kansas Pacific Railroad engine in the late 1800s after a washout on the Kiowa Creek in Colorado.

As a wilderness hiker your chances of running into quicksand are probably better than you realize. If you frequent flat low-lying areas with a high degree of soil moisture, they're in fact quite good. However, your chances of getting sucked down into it are almost non-existent, particularly if you have a basic knowledge of the phenomenon and know how to react.

Quicksand is ordinary sand. And what may be firm one time may be Jell-O at another. What makes it "quick" is a combination of its water content and how the water got there. For some strange reason when water seeps into a sandbank from the top or sides, as groundwater, the mixture remains stable; but when it is forced up from underneath by artesian pressure, it develops a strong "swallowing" ability. So if there's a patch of likely looking quagmire that you've crossed many a time during the fall with firm footing, come your first spring hike there, be prepared. Just in case.

Should you come across quicksand, if you're just beginning to sink ankle deep, you can usually still move quickly back the way you came. In most cases the quagmire or quicksand only goes down a couple of feet and can support this kind of movement briefly. Shout a warning to your companion if you are with one.

If you're shin- or knee-deep, freeze. The less you move at this stage, the slower you'll sink. Should you be carrying a pack, remove it slowly and with as little shifting of weight as possible. If you're sinking fast, drop the pack at once. If, as is much more likely, you've only sunk another inch or two in taking off the pack, throw it as lightly as you can towards firm ground. Best of all is to have a length of all-purpose rope along. Shirts, sweaters, and other such articles of gear can also be knotted together to make a line. By attaching it to the frame or one of the accessory or shoulder straps before you throw the pack, you can usually pull yourself to solid ground alone.

If everything else fails, or if you're sinking very quickly, lie down flat. Quicksand is basically a hydraulic system. The larger the surface area over which your weight is distributed, the less the sinking. Spread your arms out ninety degrees from your body for extra support and lie there. If there's any possibility of rescue, stay motionless and wait. Should you be alone, remember that although quicksand has been described as "too thin to walk on and too thick to swim in," swimming is your key to getting out. Propel yourself *slowly* forward on your stomach with a shallow breast stroke.

EMERGENCY SIGNALS

If in your wanderings you should become trapped or injured and be unable to go on, and if people know your whereabouts and expected date of return—as somebody should whenever you venture into the real wilds; that's another of those commonsensible precautionary measures to take, just in case—prepare to aid the search party. First, stay calm, take stock of your situation, make yourself as comfortable as possible, and *wait* to be rescued. Secondly, three of anything is the standard distress signal: three blasts on a whistle, three fires forming a triangle, three shots from a gun if you carry one, and so on. However, noise, no matter how loud it is, will not attract a plane if an aerial search is made; and fires are best seen at night unless they are very smoky. If you spot a plane, and you're lucky enough to have a sunny day, try to bounce sunlight at it with a mirror, real or improvised. An old two-sided Army signaling mirror is best for this, since it has a sight through which you can aim. However, eyeglasses, tin cans, aluminum foil, or any other highly reflective material may be used. Keep it up till the plane wriggles its wings to indicate that the pilot has seen you.

Tuck this information away in your memory. The chances of your ever having to use these signals are slim. But it's comforting to know what to do, all the same.

THE SKY ABOVE AND
YOU BELOW

When was the last time you looked up at the ceiling? Not very recently, probably, unless you fall asleep on your back. Out in the wilderness, however, things are different. The sky becomes very much a part of your existence, an integral piece of your life offering not only beauty, but warmth, warnings, and wonder. It is with you always, day and night, your companion and informant.

CLOUDY SKIES

Before our technical age swept in new terminology and modern myths, nature's movement in the heavens was described in evocative, picturesque terms, often in rhymes and couplets. To me it's still easier, for that matter more pleasant, to remember the old sailor's chant

> Mackerel scales and mares' tails
> Make tall ships carry low sails

than to think of cirrocumulus and cirrus clouds as indications of

CIRRUS CLOUDS

CIRROCUMULUS CLOUDS

stormy weather ahead. Cirrocumulus do indeed look like the sky's been covered with mackerel scales, and only someone who's never seen a horse on a meadow swatting flies with its tail—or can't imagine one —could fail to make the association with the elongated flaring cirrus clouds. Whichever way you choose to remember them, if the sky is full of both, rain within twenty-four hours or less is almost certain.

CUMULUS CLOUDS

Sheep, or fleece, clouds, those white picture-calendar puffballs scientifically known as cumulus, on the other hand, are a camper's delight, fairly guaranteeing a beautiful day ahead. Except—and what good are rules if they don't have exceptions?—when they decide to merge, forming bigger and bigger tall, top-heavy clouds, or thunderheads, sinking visibly under their own weight. When they start pressing down from the sky, they'll bring with them rain, lightning, and possibly hail. Usually they will darken at the bottom as they build up, and the rain they bring will be scattered in localized summer showers or squalls under the dark areas. The faster they change from white to black sheep, the shorter the storm. Conversely, if it's all day a-coming, it will be around for a while.

Stratus clouds, long plowed furrows of white that go from horizon to horizon, bring either rain or snow if they build up enough. If not,

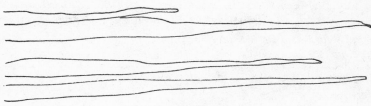

STRATUS CLOUDS

why, it'll still be clear the next day. The only way you'll know which to expect is to have watched them, and the results that followed, many times. Keep your eye on them, and you'll learn to gauge the future of the weather.

Nimbus clouds are a sure bet it will rain or snow. Unfortunately, by the time they have arrived on the scene it's usually already in-

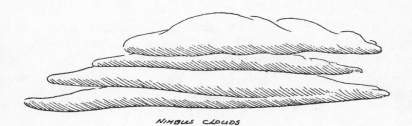

NIMBUS CLOUDS

clement weather. They are a low-hanging, gray, shapeless mass, a misty dark overcast. The trick is to be able to spot the beginnings of this low mist. The first sign of its pulling itself together usually means prolonged drizzly weather ahead. Low clouds in general portend bad weather.

THE WINDS THAT BLOW

Wind brings the clouds, and the weather. In many regions it's the best indication that a change is imminent. If there's no wind, there'll be no change in the weather. Before we go any further, which way does a west wind blow? It blows *from* the west.

Although there will be local variations produced by canyons fun-

ESTIMATING WIND SPEED

Wind Velocity (mph)	Beaufort Scale	Air Movement	Indicators
0–1	0	Still	Smoke and steam rise straight up
2–3	1	Light air	Wind affects smoke direction, but not waves
4–7	2	Slight breeze	You feel wind on face, leaves rustle, waves affected lightly, fresh snow eddies
8–12	3	Gentle breeze	Leaves and twigs move continuously
13–18	4	Moderate breeze	Small branches wave continuously, dust and snow stir
19–24	5	Fresh breeze	Whole small deciduous trees sway, tents flap
25–31	6	Strong breeze	Large branches wave, whitecaps on most waves
32–38	7	Moderate gale	Whole large trees sway
39–46	8	Fresh gale	Twigs break off, you have to lean into the wind in order to walk
47–54	9	Strong gale	Whole branches break off, high waves
55–63	10	Full gale	Poorly rooted trees topple, branches fly
64–72	11	Storm	Extensive wind damage of all types

neling the wind and mountain ranges blocking it, Izaak Walton's
rhyme gives you a basic idea of the weather-calling the wind does:

> When the wind is in the North
> The skillful fisher goes not forth;
>
> When the wind is in the East,
> 'Tis good for neither man nor beast;
>
> When the wind is in the South,
> It blows the bait in the fish's mouth;
>
> When the wind is in the West,
> There it is the very best.

Although there are other rhymes and sayings that claim to portend
what the wind will bring, they all suffer from one acute problem. They
don't work. About all that can be said is that a west wind is indeed the
very best. From any other direction, the wind can spell trouble, particularly when it shifts back and forth ninety degrees from one direction to the other.

FOLK SIGNS

One of the classic folk weather signs is a ring around the moon
at night or around the sun during the day, at which times they are said
to be in their "house." This means it will always rain or snow the
next day. Well, almost always. To be more exact about it, there's a
very good chance it will. Although none of the old rules are that
accurate, I've found they're usually as good as, if not better than, the
radio weatherman's.

Probably the most consistently correct verse forecast, particularly
in ocean, lake, and river regions, is:

> Red sun in the morning,
> Sailors take warning.
> Red sun at night,
> Sailors delight.

Another old saying with high reliability is:

> When the dew is on the grass,
> Rain will never come to pass.

For it's true that humidity at ground level has a strong relationship to that higher up in the atmosphere. When you see a heavy dew or frost in the morning, you can usually count on a good day. If it's dry in the morning, you can almost always count on the sky feeling the ground needs to be moistened a bit.

While you're sitting by a campfire, watch the smoke. If the smoke rises straight, the weather will stay clear; if the smoke just spills over and hangs heavily around the ground, rain is almost certain.

You may doubt it after some camping trips, but the weather, in any given region, is good far more often than it is bad. The prevailing wind in the region is, therefore, a good omen. Look at the leaves on the trees around you. They naturally lie so they won't be ruffled by the wind. Wind from a different direction than usual, however, blows the leaves' undersides up. Bad weather ahead.

When you're outdoors away from the artificial stimuli of an urban environment, there are many ways you can feel a storm coming, using your own senses. I don't mean your rheumatism either, although it too can be used with some accuracy. No, what I had in mind was sensing the dropping air pressure. Smells are stronger and carry further. So do sounds, particularly distant ones that travel then with a faint reverberation.

ANIMAL SIGNS

Wild things are much more sensitive than we to the changes in atmospheric pressure, and their behavior reflects it, in many cases turning them into living barometers. Although you probably won't see enough animals on a regular basis to test them out on this, it's fun to know what their actions have to tell you when they do happen to be around.

Probably the best long-range weather forecaster is the elk. Out West, come fall, when the elk decide to descend from their mountain pastures, you know winter's only a couple of days away. Deer in the

Northeast do the same, although they don't object as violently to spending the winter aloft, and thus aren't as consistently reliable.

Migrating birds are another sign that you should get your winter camping gear ready. And if the geese come early, be prepared for a long cold season.

If the ducks overhead are high, the weather will be good; if they are low, they'll be taking shelter soon. In general, birds will snuggle up close to a tree trunk rather than sit far out or high up if rain is coming. They will also stop singing, rain not being much to sing about when you're living in a tree.

CATCH A FALLING STAR

One of the most impressive sights is surely the Milky Way on a clear, crisp autumn or winter night. It's amazing, when one is used to a sky seen from areas of urban light, to notice that the Milky Way is actually an almost solid, glittering band of white. So many stars with so many planets, and in all likelihood so many civilizations staring back at us wondering if there really is any intelligent life in the universe besides themselves.

The key constellation in the northern hemisphere is Ursa Major, or the Great Bear, more commonly known as the Big Dipper. Actually the Big Dipper represents only the bear's tail and hocks, but you need a pretty good imagination to put a bear together using the rest of the stars, so a dipper it remains in modern times.

The Big Dipper is easy to find, and important for two reasons. The first is that the two outer stars of the dipper point to the handle of the Little Dipper, thirty degrees away, which is much harder to locate by itself. The star at the tail end of the Little Dipper is Polaris, the north star—your evening compass. But how far away is thirty degrees when you're not used to the perspective of the wide open sky? Well, the distance between the two pointing stars of the Big Dipper happens to be a convenient five degrees, which is the second reason the Big Dipper is important—as a convenient yardstick for the sky. So to find Polaris, just sweep your eyes over a distance six times that of the five degrees and you've got it. Once you have Polaris in front of you, due north is in the same direction.

Shooting, or falling, stars, which in reality are meteors, sometimes make spectacular evening shows. Once during the Perseids showers, I saw so many shooting stars I couldn't make wishes fast enough. The secret to catching a falling star, visually at least, is knowing when they are coming. And although it might seem like asking a bit much from the heavens to put on a display with the predictability of the midnight movie, meteor showers do come with calendric regularity.

ANNUAL METEOR SHOWERS

Name	Date	Orbital Pattern
Quadrantids	January 3	Low long paths
*Lyrids	April 21	Swift streaks
Aquarids	May 4	Swift long paths
Delta Aquarids	July 28	Slow long paths
*Perseids	August 11	Swift streaks
Draconids	October 9	Swift streaks
*Orionids	October 19	Swift streaks
Taurids	November 9	Slow and short
Leonids	November 15	Swift bluish streaks
*Geminids	December 12–13	Swift short paths

* Indicates exceptionally good displays

Designated meteor showers are named after the constellations from which they appear to be coming. In reality, the light of a shooting star is generated as the meteor burns up entering the earth's atmosphere. However, if you know the name of the shower, say the Perseids, you know which part of the sky to look at, namely, the constellation Perseus. You also know what time of night you can expect to see the shower; since Perseus rises late in the evening during late summer, you won't get your best display till midnight or so. In general, meteor showers are at their most spectacular after midnight.

To help you locate the constellations and stars, planispheres of the night sky are available. Like perpetual calendars, they can be used for any month of the year almost forever. The stars are projected on a flat round card. A second card with an oval cut out of it and the hours of day and night marked on its edge fits over the star card. By setting the hours at which you're watching the sky against the date on which you're doing the observing on the star card, the planisphere will match the sky exactly. Now all you do is lie down and enjoy the stars.

There are several different stellar planispheres on the market. Most of them are cardboard, which means they don't last long in the rough-and-tumble of your pack. A plastic one called the Philips' Planisphere, weighing hardly an ounce, is available from the Hayden Planetarium in New York.

AURORA BOREALIS AND ZODIAC LIGHTS

Besides meteors, the most spectacular night sky display is without a doubt the aurora. In northern latitudes and the Arctic, the night sky often lights up in an incredible fashion. Curtains, streamers, arcs, and rays, in all the shades of yellow, pink, green, white, red, reach towards the zenith in eerie silence. It's something that has to be seen. It simply can't be described, except prosaically, in terms of what's happening. Solar rays bombard the almost perfect vacuum of the upper atmosphere around the sixty- to six-hundred-mile level, exciting the rarefied gases that exist there. The principle is very much like that of the neon tube. But Broadway never looked so good.

Although one can never be sure when the aurora will decide to put on her show, it is positively related to the same radiation activity that causes sunspots. So if you know that during a certain year sunspots are expected to be plentiful—and that's usually written up in the newspapers—it may be the year to go camping up north in Canada or Alaska.

The zodiac lights are primarily a tropical phenomenon, although they are often seen as well in the northern latitudes early on a March or April evening, or before dawn, if you get up that early, in September and October. They're nowhere near as colorful or spectacular as the aurora. Still, on a clear, moonless night the zodiac lights will outshine the Milky Way. The first time I saw them was in Canada. I had thought I was out in the middle of nowhere. Yet when dusk came, there was the obvious glow of a big city, say the size of Los Angeles, lighting up the sky. I knew it wasn't possible, and yet. . . . The really strange thing was that the distant city seemed to roll up its sidewalk around 10:30, which seemed a trifle early for a metropolis of that size to turn down the lights. It was only later I learned I'd been watching reflected sunlight on pinhead-sized meteorites circling the earth, which is what causes zodiac lights.

WINTER'S OWN WILDERNESS

One of the best times to visit the great outdoors is wintertime. Just the mention of winter camping may bring to mind those Polar Bear Clubs, whose members go swimming in holes chopped through the ice, but there's no need for it to be like that. With today's camping equipment, much of it designed for below-freezing or even subzero weather, winter camping can be a pleasure, and an uncrowded one at that. Nearby recreational areas open to the overnight visitor and national parks alike are deserted the day after Labor Day weekend—compared with the weekend before.

You can always find a spot of nature to explore in, say, January without going in for snow camping, of course. Large parts of the United States never see much of the icy temperatures and long dark nights that come with the coldest season of the year. You can follow the ducks south to warmer climes instead of venturing out into the white wilds.

But it's up in snow country that you will discover the real beauty of camping in winter. One of the best times to learn the ways of the wilderness and the wildlife is when the pale mantle drops over the dark woods. And there are no insects about to distract you—a small point, but a sometimes significant one from the standpoint of comfort. In snow country, animal tracks are easily seen. The animals themselves are generally less frightened and more curious than at any other season of the year. Some of them will be hibernating, some will have migrated, but those that remain will have little ground cover to shelter them when they're on the move, so even when they aren't right alongside your camp, you'll be able to spot them relatively easily. Hang your food high, though; curiosity isn't the only thing bringing them around.

Sometime, sooner or later, you'll probably want to give winter camping a try. When you do, add the following few details to your store of camping knowledge, for nature is not always gentle in winter, and its dramatic ways demand a little more notice, a little more care than needed in the mellower seasons.

MAKING CAMP IN WINTERTIME

Cold is one thing, wind another. Everyone knows that when you're walking around on a chilly day, the wind is what really bites into you. In wintertime, make your camp in a spot as shielded from the wind as possible. Alpine conditions may not afford much in the way of a windbreak, but every bit will help. Nature sometimes lends a hand overlooked at first glance. If you pile enough snow up on the weather side of your tent site, for instance, it will break the wind very nicely. Don't pile it against the tent itself, however.

As long as you stay below the tree line, you should be able to find a grove of trees in which to set up camp. Make sure you check to see how heavily laden with snow the trees are, however, before you start unpacking the gear. Large quantities of snow and rime bumbling down unexpectedly could flatten your tent. Camping in groves of shorter, younger trees usually enables you to avoid much of this problem.

Along the same lines, don't make camp in front of a potential avalanche. To be really safe, that would have to include any hill with a gradient of over twenty-five degrees. Although serious avalanche slopes have usually been denuded by past slides, there's always the first one, besides which, powdered snow with sufficient force and mass to bury a camper or skier can slide through a stand of trees without knocking them down.

Snow somehow manages to get tracked into a tent no matter what

The Wind-Chill Factor

Wind Speed (mph)	Actual Temperature (°F)											
	50	40	30	20	10	0	—10	—20	—30	—40	—50	—60
	Equivalent Temperature (°F)											
0	50	40	30	20	10	0	—10	—20	—30	—40	—50	—60
5	48	37	27	16	6	—5	—15	—26	—36	—47	—57	—68
10	40	28	16	4	—9	—21	—33	—46	—58	—70	—83	—95
15	36	22	9	—5	—18	—36	—45	—58	—72	—85	—99	—112
20	32	18	4	—10	—25	—39	—53	—67	—82	—96	—110	—124
25	30	16	0	—15	—29	—44	—59	—74	—88	—104	—118	—133
30	28	13	—2	—18	—33	—48	—63	—79	—94	—109	—125	—140
35	27	11	—4	—20	—35	—49	—67	—82	—98	—113	—129	—145
40	26	10	—6	—21	—37	—53	—69	—85	—100	—116	—132	—148

you do. A tunnel entrance is your best defense against it. But even if your tent is so equipped, in setting up a snow camp, flatten a platform of snow for your tent that is big enough to give you plenty of walking-around room on the outside and a big porch in front. It will save a lot of mopping up with the sponge. Keep pushing back any drifts that encroach.

An evergreen forest offers you, free for the finding, winter's own brand of insulation. If you can locate the beds of needles that collect beneath the trees, they will make a good ground cloth to keep your tent off the snow. Often it's not possible to find a spot level enough on the beds of needles themselves. Still, if you can get at them, it's worth mining and scattering them over the tent site, not only because of their insulating qualities, but because they will help keep the tent floor from freezing to the snow as well. Should such freezing occur, incidentally, don't try to rip your tent free; it will do just that—rip. The only safe way to detach the tent is to steam it free with boiling water.

Real winter weather is where the self-supporting tents like the Eureka, Bishop, or Bauer Draw-Tites come into their own. Sometimes it's almost impossible to drive in tent stakes. The ground is frozen solid, for instance, or you're sitting on five feet of snow and thus need six-foot stakes to get anywhere.

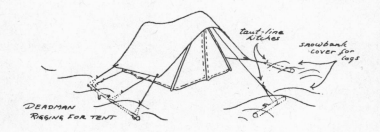

DEADMAN RIGGING FOR TENT

Actually, rigging a line-supported tent isn't all that grim. It does take more time and a bit of forethought when picking your site, however. In deep snow you can use deadmen—long, fallen branches or logs to which you attach your lines so that log and line, viewed from above, form a T. Then you bury the log well in snow and stomp it down. Pour some cold water over the deadman to freeze it in place.

Tighten up the lines and you're set. Rigging to well-anchored bushes and trees is easier and advisable wherever possible.

Once your tent is up, pile snow all along its bottom edge, on top of the snow valances if you have them, to a height of half a foot or so. Don't cover any fabric that's not waterproofed. If you're using a full fly, and you should, this won't be a problem. If you're not, pile the snow only to half the height of your tub floor. If you've come in on snowshoes, you'll soon discover they make excellent snow shovels as well. If you're skiing in, which is faster but requires a little more skill, especially with a heavy pack, it's a good idea to have along a light-weight aluminum snow shovel. One with a demountable wooden handle weighs barely over a pound. The snow around your tent should be packed down well. But down—don't press too hard against the tent itself or you may strain it. In the mountains, lacking snow, pile boulders on what you now call "sod cloths" instead of "snow valances," to help keep the tent in place and prevent cold winds from rushing in under the floor.

TO HEAT OR NOT TO HEAT

There are various tent heaters on the market. Before you decide one of them is going to make your tent cozy as a rug, take into account that when a death occurs in winter camping, it's more apt to be due to asphyxiation than to freezing. This is why when you look at alpine or mountain tents you'll find them so chock-full of ventilation openings. Fueled equipment, be it for cooking, lighting, or heating, requires plenty of air circulation.

Warm clothes, a good sleeping bag, and a closed-cell pad underneath it should do away with the need for a heater. We've always found wool clothing and good down bags stand up to even zero-degree weather well enough. Mind you, we're not exactly sweating while snoozing, but our teeth aren't chattering either.

If you feel you must have a heater—and they are useful in case a camper somehow gets drenched and needs to dry his clothes—make it one of the catalytic type. These come in white gas, butane, and propane models. They are flameless and do not generate very much carbon monoxide. Being highly efficient, they do not use much oxygen either. Still, cross-ventilation is a must, as it is when you are cooking in the tent. And *never* go to sleep with a heater on, no matter how safe the model you have is supposed to be. You may not wake up to dispute the fact.

INSIDE AND OUTSIDE

A gale may be blowing outside, the snow may be flying, ice may be crackling from the trees. The difference in temperature inside your tent, compared with that outside, will be perhaps only ten or twenty degrees. Still, you'd be surprised how much heat just your own body will give off even through those well-layered clothes. Then there may be heat from the stove if you're cooking in a vestibule or cookhole, and that from a lantern if you're using one on those long winter nights the north country has. Make full use of the heat you have. Bring saws and axes inside the tent. Steel becomes more brittle with a drop in temperature. You should also bring in some wood, tinder, and kindling, even if you don't expect to use wood fires. Put it on a piece of plastic and let it dry out. If you never use it, you can throw it out again. But for any emergency, you know you have the makings of a small fire, enough to warm you up and dry out logs for a larger one.

You don't want to bring everything inside your tent automatically, however. Certain things are best left outside. Snowshoes and skis, for instance. The webbing on snowshoes will stretch if warmed up. Even if it doesn't get warm enough for that in the tent, a lot of snow will stick to it when you start out the next morning, and there's no need to carry that extra weight. Snow stuck to your ski soles really impedes your progress.

Although you can just prop skis up in the snow, don't forget to hang your snowshoes at night. All those intriguing tracks around them come morning could no doubt broaden your knowledge, but you won't be interested in studying them if the webbing's been chewed through.

As for boots, we take ours off, feet dangling out the door, knock most of the snow out of the soles, and mop up the rest with the sponge. In the tent we wear extra pairs of wool socks instead of shoes. Leather stiffens up in the cold. To keep it from getting too stiff, wrap shoes and boots in a plastic bag and put them in the foot of your sleeping bag. If you're going to do this, however, make sure they are as dry as you can get them first. That means wiping them off thoroughly with a rag or sponge.

THE ICEBOX GALLEY

Cookbooks sometimes have a section on high-altitude cooking. They don't usually have anything to say about cooking in an icebox. But that's what you'll be doing winter camping. Put a piece of Ensolite underneath the stove if it is a pressurized type. The cold ground will otherwise cut down its efficiency considerably. Also you'll need a lot more fuel than for a comparable summer trip. Your stove will be working much harder and longer, not only in cooking, but also in melting snow. And it bears repeating that melting snow isn't all that easy. Remember the old saying: it takes a bushel of snow to make a pint of water—and add almost fifteen minutes to that as well. Remember, too, that you can avoid scorching the pot by melting only a little bit of snow at a time until you get a quarter of an inch or so of water in the pot. When you add more snow, pack it down to keep what's already melted from evaporating. If you just fill the pan with snow and stick the whole thing over a flame, you'll have a mess on your hands. Melting ice is quicker, so if there's any around, reach for it.

Even provisioning becomes quite a different matter when you camp in continuously below-freezing weather. Since you are effectively living in a freezer, you have to think in terms of frozen foods. Fresh eggs, for instance, can be peeled like hard-boiled ones when frozen solid, but cooking them is a small horror. Bread, on the other hand, is no problem; it stores well frozen. Meat should be cut to portion size before you set out, unless you want to do your cutting with an ax later. The dehydrated and freeze-dried foods are a real boon here, since they can't freeze.

Winter campers tend to drink less than they should. When you're not perspiring much because of cold weather, the purification function of your kidneys becomes primary—and you should drink more, rather than less. So take along lots of soup and hot drink mixes.

Hot liquids, incidentally, will warm you up better than hot food. Stated in baldly unscientific terms, there's more heat in them. Leave a cup of soup and a cup of rice standing sometime, and see which one stays warm longer.

SUNGLASSES, LIP BALM, AND CHEWING GUM

In winter camping especially, you want to be aware of the situations you might meet and be prepared for them and their contingencies with good equipment well maintained, warm clothing, and certainly at least one change of clothing. Don't overextend yourself, stay dry, and keep in shape. In other words, try to avoid trouble.

Every winter camper should have sunglasses along. Snow blindness caused by the white glare is painful, can be permanent, and yet is simple enough to avoid with sunglasses. Don't get the yellow-tinted ones, however; since they are designed to cut haze, they will only aggravate the glare conditions. Polarized lenses are best. And take a tip from an old eyeglasses wearer: those earpieces and the nose bridge get mighty cold in freezing weather. Put a bit of moleskin on the inside of them for comfort.

Lip balm is a self-explanatory item of winter gear. Anyone who's ever had chapped lips will want to take some along.

In below-freezing weather, check your face and hands and those of your companions occasionally for telltale white spots of frostbite, especially on your cheeks, chin, ears, nose, or forehead. If any of your limbs begin to feel numb even while you're moving around and active, warm up by a fire and get some hot soup into you. Chewing gum, as long as you chew with your mouth closed, keeps the circulation up around your face, reducing the chances of frostbite.

CHESS, CHECKERS, BOOKS

Although I have a phenomenal capacity for sleep when I'm away from the city and trying to catch up on lost Zs, ten hours is about the most sleep I can handle at a time, even with all that fresh air and exercise. Yet without going too far north, you'll find yourself down to eight or even six hours of daylight. Now on a clear moonlit night this is no particular impediment. It's great to wander around that mysterious icy landscape glittering like a billion diamonds had been scattered over it from the sky. Lakes crack and cannonade through the wilderness. The ground below you crunches, and sounds are amplified so in the cold silence that you sound like an elephant walking across a vat of popcorn. Even trees, swishing softly in other seasons, bang around to the accompaniment of sharp reports like dynamiting in the distance when the mercury hangs below zero. When the aurora comes out, nature truly outdoes itself.

So you return to your tent after an evening's tramp on your snow-shoes or a run on your skis. Make yourself a hot cup—in our case it's usually several—of coffee, cocoa, or soup. Sip it slowly and feel the warmth fill your body. Crawl into the bag, zip up, and thrash around for a minute. Not enough to build up a sweat. But a little kicking in place as you lie down warms up the sleeping bag quickly. Then you pull the hood around your face and fall asleep while steam rises from your nose, the only thing projecting from the bundle of down.

But when it's storming out, the night so dark and howling fierce you wisely don't want to venture away from the tent, what do you do after you've slept yourself silly? You talk. For a while. A long while even. But then, sooner or later, cabin fever sets in, that strange psycho-logical malady of confined quarters that has turned genteel trappers into murderers, peaceful, loving couples into fighting minks, and solitary campers into strangers to themselves who, convinced they're on a tropical island, shed their clothes in the snow and decide to go for a stroll on the beach.

Normally I would never take a chess set camping. There's just too much to see and hear and smell and touch in the wilderness to spend time on games brought along from civilization. But for lengthy winter camping, if there's any chance you'll be weathered in, by all means take chess or checker set, some cards, and a book or two. It's a great time for going through the pocket guides memorizing tracks, bits and pieces of information about local fauna, rocks, animal life, and even history to help you put together the great jigsaw puzzle of the region you're in. If you're in the habit of reading a lot, even these may not be enough. After a few days, should the storm still be raging, you'll find yourself expending flashlight batteries checking for the hundred and twelfth time, on the back of the instant onion soup package, how to make sour cream dip when you don't have any sour cream along. Take a novel. A thick one. Leave the quick Agatha Christies and Rex Stouts at home. Blizzards require something more substantial—*Moby Dick* or *War and Peace* is what you need. I remember one time think-ing I had *Crime and Punishment* along, only to discover it was a pocket dictionary. Amazing, how long it can take to read Webster's.

TRAILERING A TOBOGGAN

When you're packing it in on snowshoes, a toboggan is a great idea, particularly if you're planning to set up a base camp and are hauling a lot of gear. Trappers and Indians traditionally used these to draw heavy loads in winter. Often, of course, they had those romantic dog sleds. But just as often, particularly where the brush was dense and the trails really not fit for a dog, man did his own pulling.

A party of two, or even better, three, can take turns pulling the load, while those free of the burden break trail. If there are three of you, the two breaking trail should overlap each other's steps, rather than following in the tracks, which is easier. The overlap makes a smoother runway for the sled. Once you get to camp, you'll find plenty of other uses for your toboggan, from windbreak to table on snow pillars. The real delight, of course, is to find a good hill and. . . .

WILDLIFE AND NOT SO

When you're visiting a foreign country, you want to meet the people and learn how they live. These encounters are often the most memorable of any trip. Visiting the wilderness is no different, except there's no main street or neighborhood restaurant in the great outdoors where you can strike up an acquaintance. Or is there? Well, actually, in a sense, yes. All the denizens of the wild come to the watering spots to drink, and many of them follow game trails regularly. Some of those small trails you see through the woods are primarily the animals', not man's. They too are creatures of habit.

STALKING THE DEER AND OTHER FOREST CREATURES

While log sitting by a likely spot is one of the best ways to see the animals, sometimes it takes more patience than you've got on a particular day. You're restless, perhaps, and feel like *doing* something. Learning to stalk may be just the thing to satisfy that craving for activity.

There are many animals that can be trailed and stalked, but let's assume you want to meet up with something reasonably big, not just a squirrel or a cottontail rabbit. Moose or elk would be interesting, but their geographic range is somewhat limited, so let's settle for a whitetail deer. They inhabit a large part of the United States and most of southern Canada.

The whitetail deer's name comes from the characteristic tail, which is white and held erect while running. Called a flag, that white is usually all you see bobbing off in the distance. A whitetail's antlers branch several times, but these branches do not in turn rebranch. Only the bucks have the antlers, and only in the latter part of the year.

What an animal eats is very important to the stalker, since it gives him clues as to where to look. Whitetail deer will browse on grass, young shrub and tree leaves, and aquatic plants in the summer. Come fall, the diet is much more fruit-oriented, with a distinct preference for apples, particularly fallen ones that have begun to ferment. Acorns and corn from farmers' fields, when available, are choice dishes too. In winter, depending on how severe the weather is, the deer are forced to turn to evergreens such as spruce, balsam, and cedar for their sustenance. When things really get tough, it's dead-grass-and-greens time. If you're winter camping and can afford the extra weight, haul along some apples gone by and place them in a good observable spot some thousand yards away from camp. They'll usually draw deer the way honey does flies. But don't bait deer in bear country, or you may end up with the wrong visitors.

Let's assume you're down by a creek and you notice some deer tracks in the mud by the water's edge, and there's a good chance you will if you're in deer country. As an aside, deer tracks often look like those of a pig, and vice versa, but we'll consider you too far away from civilization for stray porkers. The tracks show the cloven hoof distinctly, and since it's mud, the hoofs sank deep enough to show the dewclaws, or small pseudo hoofs above and on the inside of the real hoofs, as well. They show up as two small indentations behind the regular hoofprint.

The ground is quite heavily trampled by what appears to have been just one deer, so it must have been at ease and relaxed. That's as close as a deer will get to being caught off guard, which isn't very close when it comes to whitetails. The tracks lead off past a boulder, along the bank, and then up a narrow trail between some hazelnut bushes where the ground is still soft enough for you to follow the trail. You decide to give it a try.

Since you'd been hoping to do some stalking on this trip, you came well prepared. You have in your rucksack a small vial of aniseed oil, or extract, bought at the supermarket before you left. Also a pair of oversized wool socks you picked up at a rummage sale. To a deer you smell human. Anise, though it isn't a scent he's familiar with, smells more like fermenting apples than like people. So you put a drop behind each ear, one on each wrist, where it will volatilize the best, rub some on your boots, and put two drops on your fingertips which you then proceed to wipe off on your clothes. The socks you put on over your shoes so you can walk more silently. Then you set off.

But you don't follow the trail exactly. You try to keep to one side of it, or cross back and forth over it. A deer will watch its backtrack closely; you don't want to be seen on its trail when it turns around.

It's still early in the morning, and you know deer usually move up-hill in the morning from their nighttime browsing, so at midday they can catch forty winks in a cool spot halfway up the hill. There, scents of anyone or anything approaching will drift up to them, and they have a clear lookout for their half-open eye. Because of this habit of the deer, had you just set off stalking at dawn without finding any tracks to follow, you would have made your way up a hill quickly and gone down the other side slowly, hoping to take an ascending deer by surprise. But this time you have the tracks, and there's a likely looking hill in the direction in which the tracks seem to lead.

You've already started moving, remembering the old rule for silent walking—on hard ground, toes first; on soft ground, heels first—when you realize you didn't check the wind. A deer can hear your feet snapping a twig at three hundred yards, if it's downwind it could easily smell you twice as far away, and if you've been smoking it could probably catch a whiff of your activity in the next county. You try to test the wind by dropping a piece of dead grass. It just drops, not showing you a thing. A wet finger doesn't show you much either; it feels cool all around. Then you notice a few leaves stirring. The wind is blowing towards you—onwards. *Slowly.* The deer will not be going that far or that fast. You have several hours ahead of you to catch up.

Not only do you move slowly, you move arhythmically, taking one step forward, then three, then one, or two. The even noise pattern of a biped—and no matter how carefully you walk, you'll make some noise—has no resemblance to any of the forest's quadrupeds. In addition, any sounds you must make you try to coordinate with wind gusts rattling the leaves. You stop often to look around, to check the tracks when possible, to observe the distance.

What you're looking for is not a deer, but part of a deer. With cover all around, it's highly unlikely you'd see the whole animal— that only happens in clearings. You're looking for a likely colored solid slab that might be a deer's side, a white patch of its belly—if the white you see is the flag, it's gone. Something glistening in the

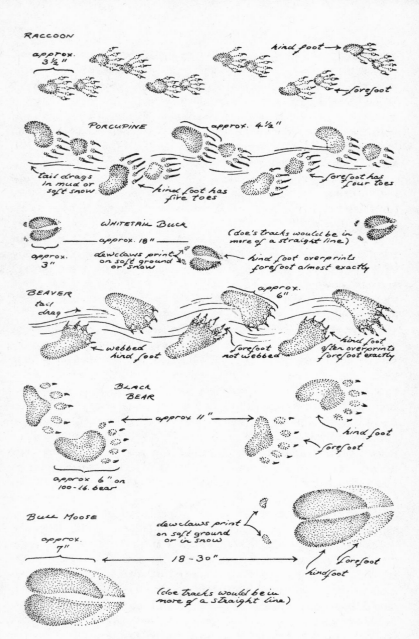

RACCOON

approx. 3½"

hind foot →

← foresoot

PORCUPINE

approx. 4½"

tail drags in mud or soft snow

hind foot has five toes

foresoot has four toes

WHITETAIL BUCK

approx. 18"

(doe's tracks would be in more of a straight line.)

approx. 3"

dewclaws print on soft ground or snow

hind foot overprints foresoot almost exactly

BEAVER

tail drag →

approx. 6"

webbed hind foot

foresoot not webbed

hind foot often overprints foresoot exactly

BLACK BEAR

approx 11"

hind foot

foresoot

approx 6" on 100-lb. bear

BULL MOOSE

approx. 7"

dewclaws print on soft ground or in snow

18-30"

foresoot

hindfoot

(doe tracks would be in more of a straight line.)

A SAMPLING OF ANIMAL TRACKS
(Walking Gait)

bushes could be an eye, a shining tree branch a buck's antlers.

Nothing ahead, but there are some clear tracks now veering off to your side. They aren't too deep, the feet are alternating, and the two halves of the split hoof are still close together. Good, the deer is moseying along. Had it bolted, the tracks would be deeper, the split hoof would have opened up from the extra weight of bounding, and the tracks would have alternated two on a side instead of singly as it ran.

You're still inching along when suddenly you realize you can't read the tracks any longer. Without quickening your pace, you move towards a small gap in the bush where the twigs have been freshly chewed on. Behind them you find the tracks again. The deer seems to have shifted back and forth. Does it suspect something? You can't tell. Since it's still heading up the hill, you follow.

After another half hour and a hundred yards, your sixth sense tells you to look behind yourself. Deer check their backtrack, maybe you should too. . . .

Here, dear reader, as they used to say in the old novels, we remove you from the picture to spare you the blunder. I turned around, a little too quickly at that, found the deer had somehow circled behind me and was brazenly looking at me as if I were a zoo specimen. Then he raised the flag and bounded off.

Come dinnertime, I decided, I would throw some incense on the fire the way the American Indians did with herbs. Deer can be extremely nosy, and such a strange odor, combined with its natural fascination with the flickering lights of a fire, would surely draw that impudent deer to within a half-dozen yards of camp for another look.

BEARS

Like most wild animals, bears are by human standards unpredictable. If you see one, keep your distance, preferably increasing it as rapidly as he probably will. Throwing stones at a bear to get some action out of him, although it has been done by some campers, is stupidity to such a degree I won't even admonish against it. Chances of a bear attacking you without provocation are slim, even though the chances increase markedly if it's a she-bear with cubs.

There are four major species of bears in North America: the Black (which is often brown in color), the Alaskan Brown, the Polar, and the Grizzly. The second most dangerous and unpredictable is the

Grizzly, the most dangerous being the semitame tourist-fed beggars that frequent national park sites. I can understand the bears not being able to read, but most of the people who come to the national parks have been able to read at least enough to get a driver's license. Why don't they understand the simple words "Please Don't Feed the Bears"?

MOOSE

For sheer size, nothing beats a bull moose. There was one in the Tetons feeding by the lake-shore rushes when we paddled our canoe past the spot. He was so blasé about it, I almost felt we could have paddled undisturbed right under his belly, between his legs. Needless to say, it would not have been advisable to try.

If you're in moose country, primarily Canada and Alaska, their favorite snacking grounds will be marshy ponds with a good selection of lily pads and aquatic grasses. Come wintertime, they go for tender willows.

Moose are best trailed from a distance if at all. Although it's possible to stalk up almost next to a deer, this would be more than a little foolish where moose are concerned. Normally they will just gallop off, but during rutting season, roughly September through November, there's only one word for a bull moose—mean. Let him sulk in peace. Should you stumble across him by accident, and he tilts his head a bit, giving you a dirty look, make like a squirrel with the nearest high tree.

ELK

Found primarily in the high mountain country of the Rockies and some northwestern states, the bull elk is a magnificent animal of from seven hundred to a thousand pounds, ranking second only to the moose in size. Its branched antlers sometimes rise a full five feet above the head. The cow elk is considerably smaller, sway-backed, and without antlers. Both the bull and the cow have a shawl of extra-heavy hair running down their necks.

Elk are particularly wary and shy of man. Your chances of getting close to them are slim. However, you may well see them in the distance browsing on twigs and leaves. Winter is the best time to spot them, since they go farther afield then in search of food. Even if you don't catch sight of them, you may one day be startled by their whistlelike bugling.

BEAVER

The largest North American rodent, famous for its hydraulic engineering skills, and Susan's favorite animal. Everywhere we go, if there's a chance of a beaver dam around, she's off and looking. Beavers are nocturnal animals, so the best time to catch them at work compulsively chomping down trees is around dusk, when they are just beginning their shift and there's still enough light for you to see them.

PORCUPINE

Probably the most approachable of the wild animals. I once came across a porcupine that played possum and carried him back to camp. After a while he reluctantly got up from beside the tent and shuffled off into the woods again. Although they don't throw their quills, and their locomotion is not much faster than molasses, porcupines can snap their tails like lightning when frightened. Ever been slapped with a full pincushion?

RACCOON

The Algonquins called him *arakun,* meaning "he scratches with his hands." The spelling has changed over the years, but he's still the same mischievous camp follower. A nocturnal raider of any food particles left around camp, but a lovable one. Yes, he really does wash his food before eating it, or at least makes the attempt.

That's just a small number of the animals you are likely to find around camp. But it will give you some idea of the diversity and fun you can expect. Get to know the animals, the birds, and don't forget the insects. You'll love every furry and feathered minute of it—well, almost every minute. There was the night a whippoorwill convention met in the trees surrounding the glade in which we were tenting. It was whippoorwill here and whippoorwill there all night. By morning we were so tired from alternately trying to sleep and giggling at the concert, we might as well have been back in the city with the trucks rumbling beneath our windows. No, come to think about it, I'll take the whippoorwills every time.

A FIRST-TIME FISHING GUIDE

Many a book on survival will tell you how to catch trout and catfish, and even pike, by hand. You just walk around the stream or pools until you see a fish, then stick yours hands in the water, sneaking them up slowly under his belly. After tickling him for a few minutes, he's half hypnotized, so you pick him out of the water and get him ready for lunch. Now don't get me wrong, I'm not saying this can't be done. I've even seen landlocked salmon picked from pools in this fashion. But if you're planning to stock your larder by tickling fish into the frypan—well, I hope you don't mind some skimpy menus.

Now frogs, they're something else. If you stumble across a two- or three-pound bullfrog and want the camp cook to give *grenouilles à la provençale* a try, just creep up slowly and stroke its underside from throat to belly a few times. Once the frog is hypnotized, you can pick it up and butcher it. Catching frogs by tickling is a good way to get in practice for catching fish by tickling. On the other hand, it's just as easy to grab the bullfrog right off—who knows? he may not be in the mood to be hypnotized.

Before we go further, let me say point-blank that I'm not a real fisherman. Although I probably get as much of a thrill from hooking a fish as the most ardent angler, spending the day trying to catch that big rainbow in the pool up by the stump, that's eluded me for years, on a one-pound leader is just not my game. Nor whiling away the winter hours tying flies. Although fly-fishing is a beautiful art that will yield more fish, and the fashioning of flies is fascinating, I lack the patience for either. No, for me fishing is an attempt, albeit not always a successful one, to get something tasty into my frying pan. Were gill netting allowed, I'd probably leave the hooks home altogether.

Whether you catch any fish or not—and something to reconcile yourself to is returning to camp empty-handed—you learn a lot about the outdoors by going fishing. You can't even make a show of fishing without getting some kind of feel for how the streams flow, how the shore pools and bays interact with the land to feed the lakes and give the fish a spawning ground, how the marsh life subsists, even the temperature levels of the water gradient—fish aren't fools, they'll go for the cool spots in the heat of the day. If all else fails to comfort you, you can always remind yourself that the money for your fishing license —even if you're just using a hand line—is helping to restock the country's lakes and rivers. One warning: If you've never been fishing before and catch one, chances are you'll be hooked.

A HAND LINE

The most primitive and least expensive form of fishing, next to catching them by hand, which I leave to mountain boys and Indians, is the hand line. As the name implies, this is merely a hand-held line with a hook on the end of it. One of those classic red and white floats or bobbers is usually attached at some point on the line to keep the bait from reaching bottom. The hand line works just as in those calendar photos you see of barefoot boys with cheek of tan and bamboo pole dipping out across a quiet lake, except you use your arm instead of a pole. A nine-foot bamboo pole is not the handiest thing to lug along on a camping trip.

Get small hooks with long shanks. They're easier to remove from the fish. A number 6, 8, or even 10 hook, although it might look awfully small to you, is fine for panfish—panfish being that general category of finned denizens whose fate it is to be put into the prefix of their name.

If you're going for bottom fish like the catfish and carp, which live in turbulent, muddy waters hardly any other fish frequent, you may

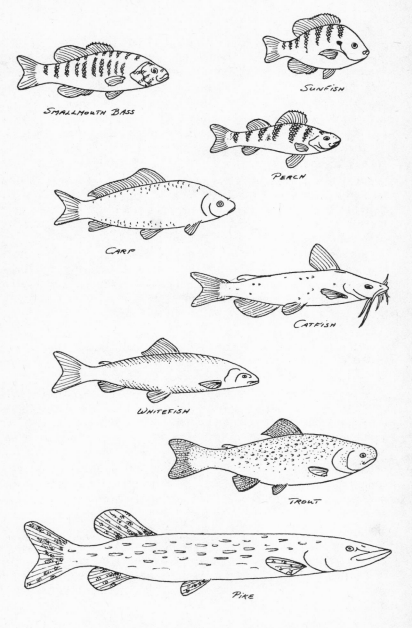

SMALLMOUTH BASS

SUNFISH

PERCH

CARP

CATFISH

WHITEFISH

TROUT

PIKE

COMMON VARIETIES OF PAN FISH

want to skip the float and use a lead sinker instead. Or you can use both in combination, the sinker assuring that the bait will bottom, the float giving you something to keep your eye on.

Use a strong line, say ten pounds or better. Your average fish will probably weigh less than a pound. But when he decides to go the other way, there'll be a lot more strain on the line than you think.

Bait your hook with the traditional worm, cricket, or other large insect in such a way that it can still move around. It's pretty hard to beat worms though. If you're too squeamish to thread a worm on the hook you probably shouldn't be fishing. Remember, if you catch a fish you've got to kill and clean it. Still, bread makes good bait for most of the smaller fish. Knead it in some bacon grease for extra flavor.

Now throw the baited hook, line, and sinker away from shore, or preferably, boat. The expression "hook, line, and sinker" comes from the guy who forgot to hold onto the end of his line when he threw it out and thus lost it. Hold onto yours. Tie it to a stick—on which you can also roll it up when done—and tuck it underfoot before you throw out the line.

So there it is, your line is out, the bobber is floating serenely on the water. What do you do next? You relax and look around, dream a bit, puff on your pipe, and pretend not to look at the float, all the while watching it out of the corner of your eye.

Suddenly the float begins to dimple the quiet water. The nibble is so light you can't feel it on the line. You yank it in? Wrong. Patience. The fish is nibbling. Give it time to make up its mind. Now the float bobs all the way underwater. You give the line a short quick tug to set the hook in the fish's mouth. But nothing happens. You reel the line in. The worm's gone. Outsmarted again.

Somewhere between these two tugs is the one that catches the fish. You'll rarely be able to set the hook on the first nibble. You have to anticipate when the fish is going to take a big enough bite to pull the bobber under—and tug the line just as he's halfway through. If you're bottom-fishing without a bobber, the same rule of patience applies, only you won't have the bob to gauge the bite by. However, you'll learn the feel of a nibble versus a real bite soon enough. Then you pull your fish in hand over hand.

Hand-line fishing will get you assorted sunfish such as bluegill and pumpkinseed, smallmouth bass, perch, whitefish, and catfish almost anywhere in North America. It's not going to get you trout, unless you're both lucky and experienced.

SPIN-FISHING

For most anglers the true art of freshwater fishing lies in fly-casting. However, fly-fishing is usually well beyond the range of the amateur. Fishing with a spinning rod, on the other hand, while esthetically not as pleasing, is much easier to learn and lends itself to a greater variety of fish and terrain. Casting with a spinning rod is easy even for the rank amateur. The fixed spool eliminates the backlash problem of the line tangling in itself, which is such an exasperation to many would-be fishermen. And a spinning set, like a fly rod, is light enough for the backpacker to lug around. Stow-A-Way has a telescoping tubular fiberglass rod weighing only four ounces, for instance. Its seventeen inches collapsed extend out to seven feet. The addition of the spinning reel brings the weight up to only thirteen ounces.

When buying a spinning rod, check that the handle grip, which should be made of good smooth cork, fits comfortably in your hand. The fine windings holding down the guides, through which your line passes up the rod, should be even and neat. If they are not, it's a poorly put together rod. The action of the rod ought to be crisp. That is, when you wave it back and forth, its return snap should be solid. If it acts limp, forget it. The reel seal must hold the reel snugly. All metal parts should be rustproof.

For spinning as for hand-line fishing, a ten-pound test line is about right. You don't need one that strong if you're really going to play the fish, letting it run with the line, exhausting itself, before reeling in your catch. But if you just want to get them in the frying pan, why fool around?

As to bait, it's with spinning that the myriad artificial lures and flies begin to multiply. For years I had my doubts about these. I knew they must work. After all, other people caught fish with them. But deep down, I felt they couldn't really. I mean, fish wouldn't honestly be dumb enough to strike at a piece of twinkling metal or a bunch of carefully cut up and tied together pieces of feathers. . . . One day, however, I caught a fair-sized perch, and while checking his belly to see what he'd had for lunch, I came across a snaptop from a can. Assuming this particular perch hadn't developed a taste for beer and the skills to open a can along with it, the evidence was too strong to question. So last summer, with great hesitation, I began using a few lures, primarily a Mepps. Even though I shook my head in disbelief every time I caught a fish with one, catch them I did. The best lures to use in a given region generally are the ones selling best in that area. Fishermen always keep an eye out for what the other guy caught the big one with.

The finer points of casting are really best taught by someone at your side. If you want to try it on your own, however, here's basically how it's done. Rig your gear according to the instructions that come with it. Put on a lure, say the Mepps. I usually put on some bait as well to improve my chances.

Now pick up the rod. Hold it loosely—casting is wrist action. Pull out enough line to leave six to twelve inches dangling from the tip of your pole. Then pick up the line just in front of the reel, pull it back, and press it lightly with your index finger against the rod handle. Open the bail (the instructions that come with your reel will show you what type of bail you have and how to open it).

Sight the spot where you want to place the lure by lining it up with the tip of your rod. The rod itself should be held at about 2:30. Now lift the rod tip towards noon, bending your elbow and using only your forearm and wrist action. As the tip of your rod reaches overhead, the lure will continue on backwards, pulling the rod tip with it. At the rod's maximum backward bend, you flick the rod forward with your wrist till it reaches 2:30 again, at which point you lift your index finger and release the line. As the line flies out, you bring the rod down to 3:00 o'clock.

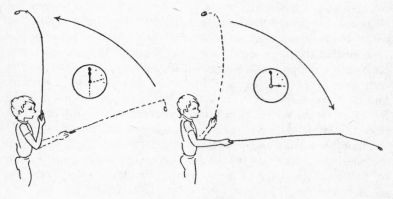

OVERHEAD CASTING IN SPIN FISHING

Let the lure sink a bit. Then start reeling in. Remember, however, that more fish are missed by reeling in too quickly than by winding in too slowly. When a fish strikes, snap the rod back to hook it.

WHERE THE FISH ARE

If you're going fishing, the first thing to do is think fish. The more you know about a fish's habits, the more likely you are to catch it. As the first mate of the cod-trawler S/T *Gargia* used to say when we pulled in a really full net of cod, "In ninety-nine percent of the ocean there's no fish, and look what we got." The same holds true for lakes and rivers—they're mostly empty. And with reason. There's no food around, it's too hot, the current's too swift, it's too muddy, the bottom's not comfortable—you name it and a fish can find the reason for not being where you are.

Most commonly, fish are found where there's a bit of variety and scenery in their underwater domain. It has nothing to do with esthetics; it has to do with where the insects and smaller freshwater life that make up dinner hang out and where the fish can find shelter from predators: weed beds; lily pads; on hot days, deep, cool holes to loll in waiting for a good meal to fall their way; places where streams enter lakes, washing oxygen and food in with them; coves; inlets; and other irregularities in the shoreline. When it comes to rivers, the preference is for downstream from boulders, where the swimming is easy, and around undercuts, waterfalls, and backwaters.

There are seasonal variations as well. The fish are in shallower water during spring and fall. Come summer heat or winter cold, they search out the more even temperature of deep water. In both hot and cold weather they are semidormant and sluggish. Water temperature plays such an important role that some fishermen take a thermometer with them to test for areas and depths of a lake that would be comfortable if they happened to be a fish. Mostly this means water in the 50–65°F. range. Which in turn usually means fishing around a foot or two from the surface if you're using a hand-held line.

The cycle of day and night also affects the fish. They will be in shallower shore water during the morning and evening, again because of the temperature, and in deeper water at midday. Then there's the moon. Some fishermen swear by it, others couldn't care less. Personally I find moonless nights, or even overcast ones, make for better fishing the next day, the logic being that the fish can't find food in the dark and thus are hungrier. This doesn't hold true for catfish, which depend almost solely on their sense of smell and on the feel of things according to their whiskers.

WHAT TO FEED THEM

Assuming you're going to start out with a hand line, the choice of bait is simple enough. You're limited to what you can dig up. There's the classic worm, of course, plus crickets, grasshoppers from the fields, any of the bugs you find under river rocks when you overturn them, hellgrammites, dragonfly nymphs, and other larvae found on land beneath rotting logs and the like. Pork rind, if you don't eat yours at breakfast, is tempting to smallmouth bass. Rarely will you go wrong with a juicy, wriggling worm, however.

If you use a spinning rod, on the other hand, the selection of lures available to you borders on the fantastic. In fact, one of your problems may be that you will become a lure collector.

Catfish are a bit choosier than most other fish—or less so, depending on how you look at it. They like their bait vintage: week-old chicken livers, limburger kneaded into a paste with flour. Judging from some of the odiferous baits used by catfish anglers, I wonder why no one's thought of the old sweatsock yet. Catfish make great eating, however, so it's worth catering to their tastes.

If you want to be really professional about baiting, when you catch a fish, you clean it on the spot, and check its belly for signs of what it's been eating. Then you go out and get the same stuff for your bait.

INTO THE FRYPAN

Before you clean the fish there's the problem of killing them. Usually this means just putting them in a creel or on the grass till they asphyxiate. Or if you prefer to keep them alive until the last minute, you can use a stringer, a line going through a fish's gills so he can swim around your feet while you continue catching his brethren. Personally I expect to eat my catch in rather short order, and so slit their throats at once from gill to gill, putting them out of their misery.

Some fish, such as trout, require little work to clean. Insert a sharp knife at the vent and make a slit from there to the base of the jaw with short, sharp strokes. Then cut across from gill to gill if you haven't already done so. Crook your index finger, stick it into the cavity by the vent, and run it up the backbone, removing all the viscera in one scoop. Stop when you get to the gills and give the whole mess a snap towards the top of the fish's head. The gills will come out along with everything else. If there are any small pieces left along the spine, run your thumbnail over it. Rinse, dry if possible, and panfry it, or them, as the case may be, in butter over a small fire. Fresh-caught fish needs no accouterments, a little salt and pepper at most.

Like trout, catfish do not need scaling. They don't have any scales. However, they do need to be skinned. Otherwise, you clean them more or less the same way you did the trout, although the gills won't pop out. I usually behead catfish before cooking.

Incidentally, the catfish's back fin will give you a sting every bit as nasty as that of a bee. Be careful when catching and cleaning them. If you do get stung, mix up a paste of meat tenderizer and water and spread it over the afflicted area. Works well for other stings too.

Most fish other than trout and catfish need to be scaled after cleaning. If your knife doesn't have a fish scaler, you can use a dull blade. Some people use the tines of a fork. It works fine. Just scrape from tail to head. The scales will fly off. Try not to get too many stuck on your clothes. Rinse off any scales that tend to cling to the fish even after being loosened. You can fillet the fish at this stage. But that's probably getting a bit optimistic about the size fish you'll get. Just pick the bones out from the tasty soft white morsels as you go. Don't overcook the tender meat, by the way. *Bon appétit.*

FOOD FOR THE PICKING

It's a bit hard to remember, in these days of frozen foods, plastic-wrapped fruit, and portion control, that man actually once lived only by what he could gather from the surrounding countryside. He did not always live well—or for that matter, in a severe winter, live at all. And I would be the last to suggest counting on the wilderness to feed you. Still, part of the joy of living in the great outdoors is giving a lift to your camp diet with some of the tasty foods found by chance in the wilds.

Don't worry either that gathering wild fruits will endanger the eco-system. I would hypothesize that campers leave more than enough food behind to feed the particular wildlife whose berries they've swiped. Besides, the wildlife usually gets there first. What you find is more likely than not—the pickings, as the saying goes.

No camping trip is really complete without some small savory taste of nature. Morels in the spring, then wild strawberries, later the blue-berries and rose hips, and in winter spruce needle tea—these luscious tidbits will long be remembered.

There is only one rule for eating wild, but it's a strict one. *Know what you eat.* Memorizing all the poisonous plants and mushrooms to avoid is, speaking practically, a waste of time unless your hobby is toxicology. There's simply too much variety and subvariety to keep straight. The way to begin your foray into foraging is to learn what you *can* eat. Later, mostly for the fun of getting to know nature better, you might want to delve into a deeper study of the flora and fungi you find along your way.

Weekend camping throughout the year in places you'd like to learn more about is the best way to get to know the edible plants. If you keep going back to the same area often enough, you'll be able to watch things change as the seasons progress. Soon you'll get a feel for what can be found when.

BERRIES

Probably the most familiar edibles you'll find in the wilds are the berries. The first difference you'll notice between wild berries and their civilized hybrid counterparts is that the wild ones look smaller and scrawnier. The next thing you'll find out is that they have infinitely more taste. Once you've had blueberries fresh from the bush—or barely warmed and sugared in trail-biscuit-crust tarts—you'll wonder what those insipid blobs are that you've been getting at the supermarket.

Blueberries are found where the soil is moist and usually acidic because of surrounding conifer forests. Where burned-over and logged areas have opened the ground to the sky, blueberries usually spring up in profusion. Grow over most of the United States and Canada. If you've got a canoe, head for the little islands in the lake where the birds may have, but the four-footed competition won't have, beaten you to the bushes.

Wild strawberries are another easy-to-recognize delight. You'll find them primarily in meadows or grassy strips bordering forest land. They range from the Arctic Circle to Florida and from coast to coast, except for the arid regions. Look for particularly choice clumps of them around large boulders and on well-drained, sunny hillsides. The leaves make fragrant tea, so while you're gathering, gather a few of those as well. Just toss them into a pot of water and brew as you would mint tea. Spruce tea can be made the same way. No need to dry the needles beforehand. Spruce tea, incidentally, is very high in vitamin C.

Gooseberries are one of my favorite wild berries. Currants are another. Both can be somewhat tart in the wilds. Usually found in conjunction with evergreen forests as a dense, prickly undergrowth, anywhere north of the North Carolina to southern California line.

Raspberries and blackberries are probably the most commonly picked of the wild berries, since they grow like weeds almost any place where the soil is reasonably sandy. A favorite location is along railroad tracks, abandoned or in use, where the land is open and sunny. But never pick them if trains still run the track, even if it's only a rarely used lumber spur in the wilds. Chances are the area around the tracks has been sprayed with assorted weed killers to keep the right of way clear.

Cranberries, considered the most important berry of the northern bog regions, are for tasty late-fall picking. It takes a light frost to bring the sugar out. If the animals don't get to them first, they can be picked and eaten when the snow's on the ground, for they will cling to the bushes through most of the winter.

Another winter berry is the by-now familiar rose hip. Overlooked for years by campers in this country, recently it's grown in popularity so much, because of its high vitamin C content, that I wouldn't be surprised to see it at the greengrocer's in a couple of years.

Rose hips are best eaten when firm, which means before winter really sets in. Once they've frozen a couple of times, they tend to soften and shrivel a bit. But as if to compensate the nibbler for the texture loss, they're sweeter after freezing. Make sure you remove the hairy seeds in the center. They won't harm you, but they're a nuisance in the throat, tickling and sometimes bringing on a prolonged coughing spell.

MUSHROOMS

If freshly picked wild berries are much tastier than their domesticated counterparts, the edible wild mushrooms are infinitely more so than their grocery-housed cousins. Unlike the berries, their nutritional value is next to nil. Mushrooms apparently have little to them besides water and flavor. But what flavor!

The problem with discovering it, however, is that mushroom picking has been given a dangerous reputation. It's well earned, of course. Probably everybody by now knows how deadly the poisonous amanita are. And there are other species almost equally deadly. Nevertheless, you can pick wild mushrooms—*if,* as with all wilderness goodies, you know not the multitude of possibly dangerous ones, but a few good edible ones, and know them well. That's the first rule. The second is, pick and eat only well-formed, mature specimens without internal blemishes.

An excellent way to learn about mushrooms—and they're colorful and fascinating fungi—is to join a mycological society, of which there are many in every part of the country where mushrooms are common. Such groups take frequent picking trips in season; and following in the footsteps of an expert is the best way to learn not only which mushrooms are which, but where they are as well—although probably no one will give away the best spots. Mushrooms will come up year after year in the same spot, and the better "mines" tend to be kept secret. One clue to where they'll be is the mushroom's high water content. You'll be apt to find them in meadows or forest regions, conifer and birch in particular, where there's plenty of soil moisture. Another clue is the mysterious mushroom ring. Where you find one mushroom you'll find more, all making a big circle in the forest.

If you do manage to ferret out an edible mushroom patch, you've got great eating in store for you. Take the Puffball, for instance, one of the most common mushrooms. Growing in clusters, the white gill-less balls on white stems will not be mistaken for anything else once you've seen and identified one. The overly mature ones turn brown, and when you stomp on them a cloud of dust, really the spores, is emitted. Hence the mushroom's name. Picked when they are still firm and white-fleshed, Puffballs are delicious sliced and sautéed in butter.

One of the most highly prized wild mushrooms, the Morel, is unmistakable because of its brown, spongy, deeply pitted, or convoluted and hollowed cap. Heavenly to eat. A spring-only mushroom that prefers the company of old, mature trees.

The Shaggy Mane, or as it's called in England, Lawyer's Cap, has a pronounced elongated hollow cap with yellowish hairy scales. Found in rich soil along deserted roads, trails, and pastures. Must be cooked very shortly after being picked, or it dissolves into a slimy blob of "ink."

Then there's King Boletus, which isn't called king for nothing. My childhood favorite back in Sweden, and I knew a spot where every fall I could consistently reap a couple of dozen Boletus, ranging in size up to half a foot across the cap. The Boletus cap is brown on top,

has a fine yellow spongecakelike bottom, the whole thing sitting on
top of a massive, thick stalk.

Of course there are also the Chanterelles, with their delicate apricot
aroma. But as soon as you leave the basic four—the Puffball, Morel,
Shaggy Mane, and Boletus—and start looking for other edible species,
it's best to do so with someone who's picked a lot of mushrooms, or at
least with a detailed field guide complete with color photographs.
When it comes to mushrooms, you have to be sure of what you're
eating.

VEGETABLES

Mushrooms and berries add a certain wilderness luxury to a camping diet. Cattails and skunk cabbage I find interesting, but I wouldn't
set off so readily in their pursuit. Also the field of edible plants is so
vast that to attempt to cover it in one book, much less one chapter,
would be a grave injustice. There are several good guides to edible
wild plants. I would certainly get hold of some of Euell Gibbons' such
as *Stalking the Wild Asparagus* and *Stalking the Healthful Herbs,* by
far the most enjoyable in the field, before I set off to forage the wilds.

BY THE WATER'S EDGE

There is just one more wilderness delicacy I can't resist mentioning.
Usually I see it used only as bait, and I cringe when I see it being fed
to the fish, because it's ever so much tastier than the fish one may or
may not catch. What I'm talking about is crayfish, those small lobster-
like crustaceans you'll see darting backwards in slow streams and by
the rocky edges of lakes. Boiled up whole with salt, a bit of onion,
preferably wild, and a pinch of sugar, their tails, although only shrimp-
sized, will shame the best Maine lobster.

The family camper who puts the kids on the job of catching the
crayfish by hand is almost guaranteed to get an afternoon's peace,
with dinner supplied to boot. The kids will have a great time wading
around in the water after the scurrying crayfish, a pastime that can
absorb and delight them for hours, while parents watch from shore
and make easygoing preparations for a mini Crayfish Festival.

TAKING HOME A BIT
OF THE WILDERNESS

Almost everyone likes to collect souvenirs, and campers are no different. The problem is, so much of the beauty that thrives in the
wilderness withers in civilization, or cannot be captured at all. How
does one bring home the fleet run of a deer, a diamond-dewed spider
web, the smell of wild honeysuckle in bloom, the rush of a summer
breeze rustling a whole forest of birch leaves? One doesn't, except in
memories.

Still, there are many things of substance we can gather—without
destroying nature's balance of things—to fulfill that collecting instinct
mankind developed sometime after the passing of his nomadic days.
Photographs, recorded sounds, animal tracks, leaves and seeds—such
things can be lifted from nature, leaving it intact, or enough so, and
brought back to help us rekindle the joy we felt on those occasions in
the wild. Too, they can help make each successive outing more enjoyable, if we use what we bring back to further our understanding of
nature. For to find what you're looking for—maybe a photograph of
a Purple-eyed Mariposa to complete your lily series, maybe a mink
track to round out your cast collection—you have to know where and
when and how to look.

CLOSE-UP PHOTOGRAPHY

Probably the most permanent, flexible, and perhaps best way of taking home the wilderness is with your camera. Not just those standard shots of majestic mountains or sun-dappled lakes, but detailed close-ups—very small but perfect fragments of nature.

Wildflower collecting is really better left to the professional botanist in this day and age; the rarer specimens would disappear if we all decided to pick them. Wildflower photography, well, that's something entirely different. Or how about a study of wood textures, or insects, or pine cones? The possibilities are almost as endless as the patterns of nature itself, so I'll let you put your own imagination to work, and mention only a few technical considerations to be taken into account.

If there ever was an equipment-oriented group, photographers are it, and one photographer's meat is another one's poison. Susan, the addicted shutterbug in our family, lugs around a battered old Yashica for her treasured two-and-a-quarter by two-and-a-quarter color shots. It weighs more than the standard thirty-five-millimeter cameras and is bulkier as well. No thirty-five-millimeter camera, however, and that includes the best of them, can turn out a color transparency to match the bigger two-and-a-quarter ones. That being said, let me hasten to add that if you, like most, are more comfortable with the thirty-five-millimeter size, by all means use it. You'll still get great close-ups.

Whatever their film size, most cameras in the medium or higher price bracket will take either close-up lenses or extension bellows. If you're taking close-ups for the first time, by all means use the close-up lenses. Not only are they less expensive than the bellows, they are considerably easier to use, and no conversion of exposure setting is necessary.

Speaking of conversion, if you're going in for close-ups, you're much better off with a single-lens reflex camera than with a viewfinder model or a twin-lens reflex unless you've had a great deal of experience with them. When you're not looking at your subject through the lens with which you take their picture, what you see and what the camera sees are slightly different. This is called parallax. What it means in effect is that you may end up with a picture of the upper half of a grasshopper when you thought you had the whole insect. Parallax can be compensated for. But the single-lens reflex is a far simpler solution for the beginner.

Close-up lenses are keyed by numbers correlated with how close you can get to your subject. The actual distance will vary from camera to camera, but the bigger the number, say 3 versus 2, the closer you can get. You can even use two close-up lenses together to get right inside a flower rather than photographing the whole blossom. Catch a bee tromping on the stamens of a lily, and when your photo is enlarged, you'll have a fantastic glimpse of nature beyond what the unaided eye alone can grasp.

To get good close-ups, you need a small lens opening; f/16 or less is the aperture usually recommended. Otherwise your pictures won't have enough depth. For instance, the front petals of a flower might be perfectly focused, while those towards the rear are a blur. The small lens opening in turn means you'll need a bright sunny day, a flash, or very fast film. A reflector will help concentrate the light, bringing up the shadows in your specimen. Crumple up some aluminum foil, then flatten it out again. The uneven surface will disperse the reflected light softly rather than in a bright beam. Prop the foil up against your pack or paddle next to the flower. Now the spotlights are lit and you're ready to take the picture.

But as you look through the camera lens, you notice that the daisy refuses to stay still, even with the camera mounted on a small tripod, as is recommended for close-up shots. What's happening is that the small wind movements are being amplified by your camera's narrow field of vision. Get out a jacket or poncho and block off the offending zephyr. Make sure you don't block off the light as well.

To get the best pictures, the trick is to really look at things through the camera. Forget about what the daisy looks like to the naked eye, which automatically takes in the surrounding area. Your eye may not really notice that twig which looks out of place when framed by the camera's viewer. Take your time and really scan what you're shooting through the camera lens—remember you get everything the camera's eye sees, and only what it sees.

PHOTOGRAPHING ANIMALS WHILE YOU SLEEP

No matter how much we may like a beautiful sunny day, a lot of animals in the wilds have a distinct preference for a nice moonlit night. Particularly the commoner ones in the medium-size range, such as beavers, badgers, skunks, and raccoons. Take advantage of their nocturnal habits by rigging your camera to snap pictures at night while you're asleep. It's one way of spreading out the enjoyment of your trip over the twenty-four hours of the day—and a surprise bonus is, you're often not quite sure which bait thief's mug shot you've got till you have the film developed. Even then. . . . I remember once getting a beautiful shot of a raccoon tail—but no raccoon. Never did figure out how he got in and out of the picture so fast.

The way you stay out of the picture and sleep while the action is going on is by means of a remote-control shutter release: the animal takes its own picture as it trips the release. You are capturing pictures of creatures which would probably stay away if you were around.

There are several releases that will activate your nighttime candid camera, ranging from inexpensive homemade pressure mats to the costlier photoelectric trips you can buy or put together from a kit. These devices should be used with a camera that has a fitting for a cable release, and for the photoelectric trip you'll need a mousetrap too. A tripod is advisable to steady the camera, since you won't be around to check on it.

Photoelectric trips work on cameras the same way as those that automatically open doors for you in many public buildings. Most supermarkets have now switched to pressure mats, those rubber ones you walk over at the entranceway. An electrical release uses a solenoid to convert the electrical impulse into physical movement. In the case of a camera, it depresses a plunger which works just the way a cable release does. To make it possible for an animal to activate the solenoid, a string is strung across a well-used path, or next to some food you've laid out, in such a manner that the animal has to step on or otherwise disturb the string in order to get at the goodies. See-through fishline, strong and relatively invisible, makes the best trip cord.

Now about the mousetrap: It should be modified by the addition of a couple of brass tacks along the line where the mouse's neck ordinarily would be snapped. Attach one wire from the solenoid to

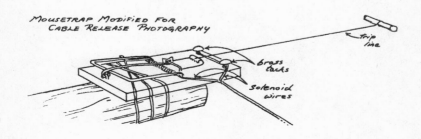

MOUSETRAP MODIFIED FOR CABLE RELEASE PHOTOGRAPHY

trip line

brass tacks

solenoid wires

the spring, the other to the brass tacks, and you have an open switch. Once the trap is sprung, the switch is closed, setting off your camera and flash attachment. Fasten your trip line to the trigger where the cheese would normally be placed. To keep the string taut, tie the trap to a log.

A pressure mat can be used as an electrical switch as well, but it's easier to set up a hydraulic one. You'll need a hydraulic plunger to fit your cable release (available from your camera store). Also get about ten feet or so of the special small-diameter plastic tubing that goes with it. A soft rubber bulb from a perfume atomizer or like device rounds off your equipment. Here's where the pressure mat has an advantage over the trip string. While a mouse could well set off your mousetrap, you can get a rubber bulb that requires at least the weight of a possum to set it off.

Again find or make a likely spot to lure an animal onto film. Dig a shallow hole, place a flat stone in it. On top of that lay your bulb, attaching one end of the hose to it. Fill the pit around the bulb loosely with leaves. Then lay over them something fairly large and flat and not too heavy. A piece of thin plywood a foot square works well. Cover the trap with some more leaves and other dry ground cover from the locale, leading your tubing away from it. Then press on the trap to see how much weight is needed to activate it, and also to make sure it works. Bait it, decide on the size of the area you want to photograph, set up and focus your camera, and attach the hose to the hydraulic plunger.

If there's any chance of rain during the night, or heavy dew, for that matter, make sure your camera is covered with a plastic tarp

tubing leading to
cable release
of camera

bait

plyboard

rubber
bulb

CROSS-SECTION OF PRESSURE MAT
FOR CABLE RELEASE PHOTOGRAPHY

(leaving the flash and lens free and clear, of course) before you hit the sack. And while we're on the subject of the night's sleep, you won't be taking more than one picture a night, unless you get up to advance the film and reset the trap. If you're base camping for a while, reset the trap each night in the same spot; the animals will get used to it, which means at least you're more likely to get the whole raccoon eventually rather than just its tail.

A last thought on animal photography: Pack the disposable part of instant self-developing film out with you. It is toxic to animals, and out of curiosity they will nibble on it and sometimes die.

STAR TRAILS, METEORS, AND PIGTAILS

If for close shots and for photographing wildlife at night a sturdy, though lightweight, tripod is recommended, for shooting star trails and meteors it's a necessity. You'll be using time exposures of up to an hour. Use a cable release as well to minimize camera movement. And to really see to it that you have no wriggling stars, or pigtails, as they're called, hold a piece of cardboard right over, but not touching, the lens when you open the shutter. Count to five before you take the cardboard away. Reverse the procedure when you close the shutter.

Capturing the image of star trails and tracing meteors are two simple things to do at night with your camera. The earth rotates fifteen degrees an hour. By aiming at the north star—your camera loaded with a sensitive black and white film such as Kodak Tri-X—and leaving the shutter, set at f/5.6 or so, open for an hour, you'll get a beautiful circular star trace pattern covering fifteen degrees of an arc. Besides the circumpolar trails, you can concentrate on individual constellations, trying for a complete collection.

Since the stars are so far away, you want to focus on infinity. The best time for photographing the stars is a clear moonless night, when they are at their brightest. An outline of bare branches at the edge of the picture heightens the effect. However, don't try for this on a windy night. Some branch movement will not blur the picture, but if it's continuous you'll have a problem with it. Remember this is a time exposure you're taking.

During periods of well-defined meteor showers, try a time exposure of the constellation from which they seem to emanate. You'll not only get the parallel curved traces of all the stars, but long bright meteor trails going off at all angles as well. If you get one long trail that goes

all the way across the picture from end to end and is equally bright
the whole way, you've captured the image of a man-made satellite. If
you get a parallel series of dots and dashes—well, watch for those
airplanes, they're all over the place. When you see one coming on the
horizon, close your shutter quickly. When it's gone, take another
picture.

COLLECTING SOUNDS

There you are in the wilderness, sharpening your senses more and
more, particularly your sense of hearing, which at home is used to
perceiving the alarm clock, the telephone, and traffic. In the wilds,
suddenly you hear the birds, insects, leaves, brooks, even occasionally
the squeak of bats, which for the most part is pitched in a range
inaudible to human beings. Wouldn't it be fun to take some of those
sounds back home with you? Bet no one would guess that terrifying
crunching is actually you walking on snowshoes in ten-degree weather.

With the compact tape recorders on the market today, making a
record of sounds is both easy and interesting. Most small battery-
operated recorders are of the cassette variety. If possible, avoid these.
They are excellent for most uses, but when it comes to sounds of the
wild, you want to be able to edit out that five minutes during which
the cuckoo refused to cuckoo, or the time Johnny stumbled over the
mike so you taped what sounded like an earthquake instead of the
crickets by your evening fire. With an open reel it's easy to cut out
sections you don't want. And it might be fun later to "compose" the
sounds on the cutting board, to give yourself a personal symphony of
a favorite locale, or a collection of insect sounds, or the contrasting
tones of streams and rivers and quiet eddies.

The use of an AVC (automatic volume control) microphone helps
to assure that everything making a noise is recorded. Of course, since
it automatically amplifies a cricket chirp and a bear's growl to more
or less the same level, you may prefer to use a regular microphone and
take your chances on missing some sounds entirely. Also an AVC is
more prone to pick up a lot of background noise. Whichever type you
use, when outdoors on a windy day, avoid the whistle the wind may
produce by wrapping a windscreen funnel around the mike. An oversized thin kitchen sponge works fine.

If you get really hooked on collecting sounds, you may well want
to take along a parabolic reflector, the big ear of recording. This is

a large metal disc varying in size from two feet in diameter on up. Through the center is a hollow tube which you use from the back as a "sight" to pick up your sound source. The microphone is attached to the front of this tube facing towards the disc and *away* from the source of sound. Say there's a warbler up in the tree by your camp. It's about twenty feet above you. Although you can hear it, the singing is not very loud; besides, you're getting a lot of background noise. So you aim the parabolic mirror at the bird. It then collects as much sound as you would if you had a two-foot ear. All this sound is then focused on one spot at the front center of the parabolic reflector, where the microphone is facing. The reflector's ability to pick up sounds verges on the phenomenal.

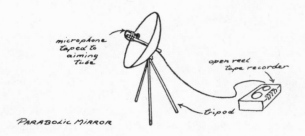

microphone taped to aiming tube

open reel tape recorder

tripod

PARABOLIC MIRROR

LEAFING THROUGH THE WILDS

You're walking through ankle-deep piles of fallen leaves in October. The kids are kicking them sky high with glee, and then they begin to ask you what kind of tree that leaf is from, and what about that odd round one. Well, why not start a leaf collection? It's easy, inexpensive, and a lot of fun. But collect your specimens, if in autumn, *before* they've fallen, when their color is at its peak. Or collect new ones in early summer, before the insects and the wind get to them.

There's a multitude of varieties of deciduous trees in North America. Many a camping trip spanning the entire continent would come and go before you completed the collection. You may want to start with just the varieties in one region.

The traditional way to collect leaves is to press them. The leaves from a weekend trip will last till you get home without pressing. For longer trips, keep them flat in the reflector oven or a notebook till you get a chance to press them.

You don't have to be fancy about the press. An old telephone book works fine. Slip the leaves in between the pages. Pile some more books on top, and you're all set. After they are dried and flat—it would be pretty hard to give a rule of thumb on the actual time it takes, because it depends on the type of leaf, the moisture in the air at the time you're pressing, the heat in your house, and so on—mount the leaves in a scrapbook, maybe jotting down when and where you picked them, and, of course, what they are.

You might want to mount the leaves right away, without pressing. This can be done on the trail if you take along some sheets of clear, self-adhesive plastic. Cut pieces to a size large enough to leave a two-inch border around the leaf. Or standardize the size of your mountings so they can handle any leaf. Lay the leaf on the sticky side of one piece of plastic, then cover it with a second one so the sticky sides bind. Start from the center and squeeze out the air bubbles.

TAKING HOME A TREE

Not only is digging out a small tree an awesome task, but its chances of survival at home are slim. And if everyone started digging out trees. . . . But seeds, well, trees scatter thousands of seeds about. Most of them never become new trees. They fall on fallow ground, the animals eat them—any number of calamities can befall a seed before it germinates. Taking home a few won't make any difference to nature. And with patience you'll grow a little tree.

Remember one thing, though, if you're in the northern part of the country: Seeds such as acorns and those from maples, lindens, birches, and the like won't sprout if you just plant them right off. The northern climes bring fierce winters during which bears and other animals hibernate. Seeds from these areas do much the same. After all, if they were to sprout as soon as they landed, the young shoots would burst through the snow and freeze. To avoid this, they have a built-in mechanism that prevents them from sprouting until they've lain on the moist ground through a winter cold snap. Usually they are buried among rotting leaves, twigs, and other debris. The process is called stratification, and you can supply it at home with equal ease. Just take a small plastic food container, punch some holes in it, fill it with leaves and your seeds. Sprinkle with a bit of water and put it away in the vegetable crisper of your refrigerator. Anytime from two to four months later, whenever you feel like planting your seeds, just fill some pots with good rich soil and do so. The seeds will be ready then.

TRACKING IN PLASTER

Children get excited about animal tracks. The next best thing to seeing them in the flesh is learning that a deer came down to drink not far from their tent during the night, or a raccoon washed his breakfast just there. Oh, if one could only take home the deer's cloven hoofprint, mud and all, to show friends! Well, it can be done, if you've brought some plaster of paris along. Make a plaster cast of the coveted track. We'll hope the kids don't get carried away with this particular hobby, however, for if you're going to try for several casts on a trip, you'll need three to five pounds of plaster. That fairly well excludes the activity from the backpacker's repertoire, unless you've got a family of teenagers who volunteer to lug the extra weight along.

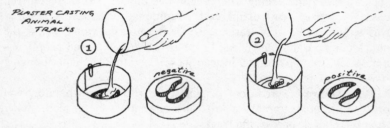

PLASTER CASTING ANIMAL TRACKS

First find a good print—usually this means by a watering hole, on soft moist ground, or a recently dried mudbank. Clear the print as well as you can, gently picking out any small twigs and huffing and puffing away the small debris. Then make a collar of a strip of cardboard, fastening the ends together with a paper clip. Press the collar firmly into the ground around the track. If the ground is moist, dust the track with plaster of paris. Then mix to a buttermilk consistency and pour in slowly enough plaster of paris to fill the print and cover the rest of the ground enclosed by the collar to a quarter-inch layer or so. Sprinkle some grass over the plaster of paris. Don't cover it completely. What you want is a webbing of binder to make the plaster stronger for transporting home. Then add about another inch of plaster.

After half an hour or so it should be dry enough to remove. Dig a small ditch around the collar, lift the cast gently. There will be a lot of dirt clinging to the cast. Leave it there, it's not completely dry yet. Wrap the whole thing in some extra clothes—I usually end up using my towel—and take it home. There you can brush the dry dirt off with an old toothbrush and tepid water. Don't try to fill and sand the small holes, a natural track is never perfect.

Winter is the easiest time to find tracks. And casting in snow is not much more difficult than casting in soil, as long as the temperature is below 30°F. The only extra items you need are a plastic squeeze bottle like the ones for catsup or mustard and a perfume atomizer. The atomizer is filled with water, the squeeze bottle with *dry* plaster of paris. Place a collar around the track as before. This time, however, dust the snow gently with plaster from the squeeze bottle, and when it's all covered with a thin layer, spray enough water over it so it can freeze. Wait till it does. Then dust and spray again. Follow this sequence four or five times, until you have a crust. Then pour in mixed plaster of paris gently as before.

The cast you take home will be a negative. That is, the imprint will stick up rather than being a depression like the original. To get a true cast, you make a cast of the cast. Traditionally the cast is smeared with a thin, even coat of Vaseline, so the fresh plaster won't stick to the old. Melted paraffin and linseed oil also work well. Some people use a nonstick frying pan spray instead these days, I understand, though I haven't tried it.

Once you've covered your original cast with some separator, you proceed as before to make a cast. This one should be an inch thicker than the highest part of the track.

Scratch the date found, location, and identification of the specimen in the plaster while it's still soft—kids like to add their name as finder, too. Let set for an hour before separating the casts. You may want to paint the finished product a matte brown to make it look more like the original ground. If you do, paint the actual imprint darker.

All these souvenirs of the wilds will trigger your memory, bringing back visions of the hills of pine and birch, shielding fieldmouse and bear alike, the cascading streams alive with fish, the tapestry of meadows in bloom, the howl of a coyote on a crystal desert night, the freezing rain as you huddled warm and content with a cup of cocoa in your shelter, the early moon rising over a still lake as you savored fresh blueberries in a pine-scented glen while the lonely loon called through the evening mist. But most of all it will bring back that flash of eternity, when you sat by a quiet pool in the company of a strangely quiet squirrel, the summer stars glittering overhead, a warm evening breeze sweeping down beside you, and the feeling you had for the universe—realizing you truly were a part of it, that all of it belonged within you, as you belonged within it.

CATALOG

EQUIPMENT AND WHERE TO GET IT

The following list includes most camping equipment suppliers that have a catalog and deal by mail. Those carrying a good line of basic equipment are listed under "General Lightweight Camping Equipment." Those categorized by a main product often also deal in other equipment to some extent.

Boots

Fabiano Shoe Co., Inc., South Station, Boston, Massachusetts 02210.
Limmer, Peter, & Sons, Intervale, New Hampshire 03845.
Mountain Traders, 1711 Grove Street, Berkeley, California 94709.

Canoes, Kayaks, and Equipment

Bemidji Boat Co., Inc., Highway 2 West, Bemidji, Minnesota 56601.
Canoe Imports, Inc., 74 South Willard Street, Burlington, Vermont 05401.
Canots Cadorette Canoes, Inc., 320 Twelfth Street, Grand'Mère, Quebec, Canada.
The Chestnut Canoe Co., Ltd., Fredericton, New Brunswick, Canada.
Grumman Boats, Marathon, New York 13803.
High Performance Products, Inc., Hingham Industrial Center B 56 Q, Hingham, Massachusetts 02043.
Klepper, Hans, Corp., 35 Union Square West, New York, New York 10003.

Old Town Canoe Co., Box 548, Old Town, Maine 04468.

Sports Equipment, Inc., Box T., Mantua, Ohio 44255.

Trailcraft, Box 606, Concordia, Kansas 66901.

Vega Integral Plastic Co., 5235 Winthrop Avenue, Indianapolis, Indiana 46220.

Voyageur Enterprises, P.O. Box 512, Shawnee Mission, Kansas 66201.

Freeze-Dried Food

Chuck Wagon Foods, Micro Drive, Woburn, Massachusetts 01801.

Dri-Lite Foods, 11333 Atlantic Avenue, Lynwood, California 90262.

Food Storage Supplies, P.O. Box 6128, Albany, California 94706.

Stow-A-Way Products, 103 Ripley Road, Cohasset, Massachusetts 02025.

General Lightweight Camping Equipment

* Indicates large selection

† Indicates co-op/discount pricing

ABC Sport Shop, 185 Norris Drive, Rochester, New York 14610.

Alpine Designs, P.O. Box 3561, Boulder, Colorado 80303.

Alpine Hut, 4725-30th Avenue N.E., Seattle, Washington 98105.

Bauer, Eddie, P.O. Box 3700, Seattle, Washington 98124.

Black, Thomas, & Sons, 930 Ford Street, Ogdensburg, New York 13669.

The Camp & Hike Shop, 4674 Knight Arnold, Memphis, Tennessee 38118.

Camp Trails, P.O. Box 14500, Phoenix, Arizona 85031.

*†Co-op Wilderness Shop, Oakland Cooperative, 3601 Allies Boulevard, Pittsburgh, Pennsylvania 15213.

*†Co-op Wilderness Supply, 47 Tamal Vista Boulevard, Corte Madera, California 94925.

*Eastern Mountain Sports, Inc., 1041 Commonwealth Avenue, Boston, Massachusetts 02215.

*Eiger Mountain Sports Corp., P.O. Box 150, San Fernando, California 91341.

Gerry, 5450 North Valley Highway, Denver, Colorado 80216.

*Highland Outfitters, P.O. Box 121, Riverside, California 92502.

Himalayan Industries, Box 950, Monterey, California 93940.

*Holubar Mountaineering, P.O. Box 7, Boulder, Colorado 80302.

Kelty, 1801 Victory Boulevard, Glendale, California 91201.

*Montico (Alpine Recreation Warehouse), 4-B Henshaw Street, Woburn, Massachusetts 01801.

*Moor & Mountain, Concord, Massachusetts 01742.

The North Face, P.O. Box 2399, Station A, Berkeley, California 94702.

Northwest Recreational Supply, P.O. Box 70105, Seattle, Washington 98107.

*†Recreational Equipment, Inc., 1525 Eleventh Avenue, Seattle, Washington 98122.

Sierra Designs, Fourth & Addison Streets, Berkeley, California 94710.

*The Ski Hut, 1615 University Avenue, Berkeley, California 94703.

Skimeister, Main Street, North Woodstock, New Hampshire 03262.

*The Smilie Co., 575 Howard Street, San Francisco, California 94105.

*Sports Chalet, P.O. Box 626, La Canada, California 91011.

Wilderness Shack, 515 South La Grange Road, La Grange, Illinois 60525.

Kits for Do-It-Yourself Equipment

Carikit, P.O. Box 1153, Boulder, Colorado 80302.

Eastern Mountain Sports, 1041 Commonwealth Avenue, Boston, Massachusetts 02215.

Frostline, Inc., P.O. Box 2190, Boulder, Colorado 80302.

Packs

Class 5, 2010 Seventh Street, Berkeley, California 94710.

Denali Company, Inc., 2402 Ventura, Fresno, California 93721.

Universal Field Equipment, Building 811-A, Mira Loma Space Center, California 91752.

Sleeping Bags

Alaska Sleeping Bag Co., 334 N.W. Eleventh Avenue, Portland, Oregon 97209.

Appalachian Designs, P.O. Box 11252, Chattanooga, Tennessee 37401.

Bugaboo Mountaineering, 689 Lighthouse Avenue, Monterey, California 93940.

Camp 7, 3235 Prairie Avenue, Boulder, Colorado 80301.

Pinnacle, Box 4214, Mountain View, California 94040.

Snowshoes

Snowcraft, P.O. Box 71, Saco, Maine 04072.

Tubbs Products, Wallingford, Vermont 05113.

Sportsman-Oriented Clothes and Heavier Camping Equipment

Bean, L. L., Freeport, Maine 04032.

Corcoran, Inc., Stoughton, Massachusetts 02072.

Gleason's, Don, Pearl Street, Northampton, Massachusetts 01060.

Gokey Co., 21 West Fifth Street, Saint Paul, Minnesota 55102.

Goldberg Army & Navy Store, 902 Chestnut Street, Philadelphia, Pennsylvania 19107.

Hudsons, 105 Third Avenue, New York, New York 10003.
Herter's, Inc., Waseca, Minnesota 56093.
Morsan, 810 Route 17, Paramus, New Jersey 07652.

Technical Mountain-Climbing Equipment

Forrest Mountaineering, Box 7083, Denver, Colorado 80207.
SMC, 1425 130th Avenue N.E., Bellevue, Washington 98005.

Tents

Bishop's Ultimate Outdoor Equipment, 6804 Millwood Road, Bethesda, Maryland 20034.
Eureka Tent & Awning Co., Inc., 625 Conklin Road, Binghamton, New York 13902.
Pacific Tent, P.O. Box 2028, Fresno, California 93718.
Stephenson's, 23206 Hatteras Street, Woodland Hills, California 91364.

FURTHER READING

Activities

Cruickshank, Allan D. *Hunting with the Camera*. New York: Harper & Row, 1957.
Hillcourt, William. *The New Field Book of Nature Activities and Hobbies,* rev. ed. New York: G. P. Putnam's Sons, 1970.
Keene, George T. *Star Gazing with Telescope and Camera*. New York: AMPHOTO, 1967.
Mayall, Newton R. and Margaret W. *Skyshooting—Photography for Amateur Astronomers*. New York: Dover, 1968.
Neely, Henry M. *A Primer for Star-Gazers,* rev. ed. New York: Harper & Row, 1970.
Reichert, Robert J. and Elsa. *Binoculars and Scopes and Their Uses in Photography*. New York: AMPHOTO, 1961.

Backpacking

Fletcher, Colin. *The Complete Walker*. New York: Alfred A. Knopf, 1968.
Manning, Harvey. *Backpacking One Step at a Time*. Seattle: The REI Press, 1972.
Manning, Harvey, ed. *Mountaineering: The Freedom of the Hills*. Seattle: The Mountaineers, 1960.
Wood, Robert S. *Pleasure Packing*. San Francisco: Condor Books, 1972.

Canoe and Kayak

Handel, Carle W. *Canoe Camping*. New York: Ronald Press, 1953.

Malo, John W. *Wilderness Canoeing.* New York: Collier Books, 1971.

Riviere, Bill. *Pole, Paddle & Portage.* New York: Van Nostrand Reinhold, 1969.

Rutstrum, Calvin. *North American Canoe Country.* New York: The Macmillan Co., 1964.

Urban, John T. *A White Water Handbook for Canoe and Kayak.* Boston: Appalachian Mountain Club, 1971.

Whitney, Peter Dwight. *White Water Sport.* New York: Ronald Press, 1960.

Cooking

Angier, Bradford. *Wilderness Cookery.* Harrisburg, Pa.: Stackpole Books, 1970.

Bates, Joseph D. *Outdoor Cook's Bible.* New York: Doubleday, 1964.

Bunnelle, Hasse. *Food for Knapsackers.* New York: Sierra Club, 1971.

Riviere, Bill. *Family Campers' Cookbook.* New York: Tower, 1965.

First Aid

American Red Cross. *First Aid Textbook,* rev. ed. 4th. Garden City, N.Y.: Doubleday & Co., Inc., 1957.

Wilkerson, James A. *Medicine for Mountaineering.* Seattle: The Mountaineers, 1967.

General Camping

Brower, David, ed. *The Sierra Club Wilderness Handbook,* rev. ed. 2d. New York: Ballantine, 1971.

Cardwell, Paul. *America's Camping Book.* New York: Charles Scribner's Sons, 1969.

Colby, C. B., and Bradford Angier. *The Art and Science of Taking to the Woods.* New York: Collier Books, 1970.

Henderson, Luis M. *Campers' Guide to Woodcraft and Outdoor Life.* New York: Dover, 1950.

Herter, George Leonard. *Professional Guide's Manual,* rev. ed. 10th. Waseca, Minn.: Herter's, Inc., 1971.

Jaeger, Ellsworth. *Wildwood Wisdom.* New York: Macmillan, 1945.

Kephart, Horace. *Camping and Woodcraft.* New York: The Macmillan Co., 1921.

Miracle, Leonard, and Maurice Decker. *The Complete Book of Camping.* New York: Harper & Row, 1961.

"Nessmuk." *Woodcraft and Camping.* New York: Dover, 1920.

Riviere, Bill. *Backcountry Camping.* New York: Doubleday Dolphin Books, 1971.

Map and Compass

Kjellström, Bjorn. *Be Expert with Map and Compass,* rev. ed. La Porte, Ind.: American Orienteering Service, 1967.

Lobeck, Armin K. *Things Maps Don't Tell Us.* New York: The Macmillan Co., 1956.

Rutstrum, Calvin. *Wilderness Route Finder.* New York: The Macmillan Co., 1967.

Nature

Bentley, W. A., and W. J. Humphreys. *Snow Crystals.* New York: Dover, 1962.

Borland, Hal. *Beyond Your Doorstep.* New York: Ballantine Books, 1962.

Brown, Vinson. *Knowing the Outdoors in the Dark.* Harrisburg, Pa.: Stackpole Books, 1972.

Brown, Vinson. *Reading the Woods.* Harrisburg, Pa.: Stackpole Books, 1969.

Burt, W. H., and R. P. Grossenheider. *A Field Guide to Mammals.* Boston: Houghton Mifflin Co., 1952.

Cobb, Houghton. *Field Guide to Ferns.* Boston: Houghton Mifflin Co., 1956.

Collins, Henry Hill. *Complete Field Guide to American Wildlife.* New York: Harper & Row, 1958.

Conant, Roger. *Field Guide to Reptiles and Amphibians.* Boston: Houghton Mifflin Co., 1958.

Craighead, John J., Frank C. Craighead, Jr., and Ray J. Davis. *A Field Guide to Rocky Mountain Wildflowers.* Boston: Houghton Mifflin Co., 1963.

Davids, Richard C. *How to Talk to Birds.* New York: Alfred A. Knopf, 1972.

Gibbons, Euell. *Stalking the Healthful Herbs.* New York: David McKay Co., 1966.

Gibbons, Euell. *Stalking the Wild Asparagus.* New York: David McKay Co., 1968.

Hale, Mason E. *Lichen Handbook.* Washington, D.C.: Smithsonian Institute, 1961.

Klots, Alexander B. *A Field Guide to the Butterflies.* Boston: Houghton Mifflin Co., 1951.

LaChapelle, Edward R. *Field Guide to Snow Crystals.* Seattle: University of Washington Press, 1969.

McKenney, Margaret. *Savory Wild Mushrooms.* Seattle: University of Washington Press, 1971.

McKenney, Margaret, and Roger Tory Peterson. *A Field Guide to the Wildflowers of the Northeastern and Central States.* Boston: Houghton Mifflin Co., 1954.

Murie, Olaus J. *A Field Guide to Animal Tracks.* Boston: Houghton Mifflin Co., 1954.

Olson, Sigurd F. *Runes of the North*. New York: Alfred A. Knopf, 1971.

Palmer, Ralph S. *The Mammal Guide*. Garden City, N.Y.: Doubleday, 1954.

Peterson, Roger Tory. *Field Guide to the Birds*. Boston: Houghton Mifflin Co., 1947.

Peterson, Roger Tory. *Field Guide to the Western Birds*. Boston: Houghton Mifflin Co., 1941.

Pough, Frederick H. *A Field Guide to Rocks and Minerals*. Boston: Houghton Mifflin Co., 1960.

Preston, Richard J. *North American Trees*. Ames, Iowa: Iowa State University Press, 1962.

Rey, H. A., *The Stars, a New Way to See Them*. Boston: Houghton Mifflin Co., 1962.

Schrenkeisen, Ray. *Field Book of Fresh Water Fishes*. New York: Putnam, 1963.

Smith, Alexander H. *The Mushroom Hunter's Guide*. Ann Arbor, Mich.: University of Michigan Press, 1958.

Wherry, Edgar T. *The Southern Fern Guide*. Garden City, N.Y.: Doubleday, 1964.

Survival

Angier, Bradford. *How to Stay Alive in the Woods*. New York: Collier Books, 1956.

Dalrymple, Byron. *Survival in the Outdoors*. New York: Outdoor Life/E. P. Dutton & Co., 1972.

Graves, Richard. *Bushcraft*. New York: Schocken Books, 1972.

Olsen, Larry Dean. *Outdoor Survival Skills*. Provo, Utah: Brigham Young University Press, 1967.

Troebst, Cord-Christian. *The Art of Survival*. New York: Doubleday, 1962.

Winter Camping

Brower, David, ed. *Manual of Ski Mountaineering*. San Francisco: Sierra Club, 1962.

Caldwell, John. *The New Cross-Country Ski Book*. Brattleboro, Vt.: The Stephen Greene Press, 1971.

Lederer, William J., and Joe Pete Wilson. *Complete Cross-Country Skiing and Ski Touring*. New York: Norton, 1970.

Osgood, William, and Leslie Hurley. *The Snowshoe Book*. Brattleboro, Vt.: The Stephen Greene Press, 1971.

Rutstrum, Calvin. *Paradise Below Zero*. New York: The Macmillan Co., 1968.

MAP SOURCES

Depending on the time of year and the area in question, it can take up
to two or three months to get your topographical maps, so plan ahead.
First send for an index map for the state, or in the case of Canada, a
regional index map of the area you're interested in. From this you can
then select the specific maps you need.

Maps of Areas East of the Mississippi

United States Geological Survey, Washington, D.C. 20240.

Maps of Areas West of the Mississippi

United States Geological Survey, Federal Center, Denver, Colorado
80225.

Maps of Canada

Map Distribution Office, Survey and Mapping Branch, Department
of Energy, Mines and Resources, Ottawa, Ontario, Canada KIA
OE9.

PARK, FOREST, AND CAMPGROUND
INFORMATION SOURCES

United States

Division of State Parks, Montgomery, Alabama 36104.

Travel Division, Pouch E, Juneau, Alaska 99801.

Department of Economic Planning & Development, Suite 1704, 3003
North Central Avenue, Phoenix, Arizona 85012.

Department of Parks and Tourism, 149 State Capitol, Little Rock,
Arkansas 72201.

Department of Parks and Recreation, P.O. Box 2390, Sacramento,
California 95811.

Colorado Department of Natural Resources, 6060 Broadway, Denver, Colorado 80216.

Department of Environmental Protection, State Office Building, Hart-
ford, Connecticut 06115.

Division of Economic Development, 45 The Green, Dover, Delaware
19901.

Division of Recreation & Parks, Gaines Street at Monroe, Tallahassee,
Florida 32304.

Georgia State Parks, 270 Washington Street S.W., Atlanta, Georgia
30334.

Department of Land & Natural Resources, 465 South King Street,
Honolulu, Hawaii 96813

Department of Commerce & Development, Room 108 Capitol Building, Boise, Idaho 83707.

Department of Conservation, Division of Parks, Springfield, Illinois.

Department of Natural Resources, Division of State Parks, Indianapolis, Indiana 46204.

Iowa Conservation Commission, 300 Fourth Street, Des Moines, Iowa 50309.

State Park and Resources Authority, 801 Harrison, Topeka, Kansas 66612.

Department of Public Information, Capitol Annex, Frankfort, Kentucky 40601.

State Park & Recreation Commission, Old State Capitol, Baton Rouge, Louisiana 70801.

Department of Economic Development, Gateway Circle, Portland, Maine 04102.

Department of Forests & Parks, State Office Building, Annapolis, Maryland 21404.

Department of Natural Resources, Box 1775, Boston, Massachusetts 02105.

Michigan Tourist Council, Stevens T. Mason Building, Lansing, Michigan 48926.

Department of Natural Resources, Centennial Office Building, Saint Paul, Minnesota 55155.

Mississippi Park System, Woolfolk Building, Jackson, Mississippi 39201.

State Park Board, P.O. Box 176, Jefferson City, Missouri 65101.

State Highway Commission, Helena, Montana 59601.

Department of Economic Development, Box 94666 State Capitol, Lincoln, Nebraska 68509.

Department of Economic Development, Carson City, Nevada 89701.

Department of Resources & Economic Development, P.O. Box 856, Concord, New Hampshire 03301.

State Promotion Office, P.O. Box 400, Trenton, New Jersey 08625.

State Park and Recreation Commission, P.O. Box 1147, Santa Fe, New Mexico 87501.

Parks and Recreation, State Campus Building 2, Albany, New York 12226.

Travel and Promotion Division, State Department of Conservation & Development, Raleigh, North Carolina 27611.

Travel Division, North Dakota Highway Department, Bismarck, North Dakota 58501.

Department of Natural Resources, Room 913 Ohio Departments Building, Columbus, Ohio 43215.

Tourism and Information Division, 500 Will Rogers Building, Oklahoma City, Oklahoma 73105.

Travel Information Division, State Highway Department, Salem, Oregon 97310.

Department of Environmental Resources, P.O. Box 1467, Harrisburg, Pennsylvania 17105.

Parks & Recreation, 83 Park Street, Providence, Rhode Island 02903.

Department of Parks, Recreation and Tourism, P.O. Box 1358, Columbia, South Carolina 29202.

Department of Game, Fish & Parks, State Office Building, Pierre, South Dakota 57501.

Division of Tourist Information, 2611 West End Avenue, Nashville, Tennessee 37203.

State Parks Board, Capitol Station, Austin, Texas 76011.

Tourist & Publicity Council, State Capitol, Salt Lake City, Utah.

Department of Forests & Parks, Montpelier, Vermont 05602.

Division of Parks, Conservation Division, Richmond, Virginia 23219.

Tourist Promotion Division, Department of Commerce & Economic Development, General Administration Building, Olympia, Washington 98501.

Division of Parks & Recreation, Department of Natural Resources, State Office Building, Charleston, West Virginia 25305.

Department of Natural Resources, Madison, Wisconsin 53701.

Travel Commission, 2320 Capitol Avenue, Cheyenne, Wyoming 82001.

Canada

Alberta Government Travel Bureau, 1629 Centennial Building, Edmonton, Alberta, Canada.

Department of Travel Industry, Victoria, British Columbia, Canada.

Manitoba Government Travel, 408 Norquay Building, 401 York Avenue, Winnipeg, Manitoba, Canada R3C OP8

Travel Bureau, Box 1030, Fredericton, New Brunswick, Canada.

Tourist Development Office, St. John's, Newfoundland, Canada.

Northwest Territories Tourist Office, 400 Laurier Avenue West, Ottawa, Ontario, Canada.

Nova Scotia Travel Bureau, Box 130, Halifax, Nova Scotia, Canada.

Department of Tourism and Information, Parliament Buildings, Toronto, Ontario, Canada.

Travel Bureau, P.O. Box 940, Charlottetown, Prince Edward Island, Canada.

Tourist Bureau, Quebec City, Quebec, Canada.

Tourist Branch, SPC Building, Regina, Saskatchewan, Canada.

Department of Travel & Publicity, Whitehorse, Yukon Territory, Canada.

INDEX